revised and updated

Layout Workbook

a real-world guide to building pages in graphic design

revised and updated

Layout Workbook

a real-world guide to building pages in graphic design

KRISTIN CULLEN

with contributions by Dennis M. Puhalla, Ph.D., in this edition

Second edition published in 2018

First published in 2005 by Rockport Publishers, an imprint of The Quarto Group, 100 Cummings Center, Suite 265-D, Beverly, MA 01915, USA.

T 978.282.9590 F 978.283.2742
QuartoKnows.com

Rockport Publishers titles are also available at discount for retail, wholesale, promotional, and bulk purchase. For details, contact the Special Sales Manager by email at specialsales@quarto.com or by mail at The Quarto Group, Attn: Special Sales Manager, 401 Second Avenue North, Suite 310, Minneapolis, MN 55401, USA.

10 9 8 7 6 5 4 3 2 1

ISBN: 978-1-63159-497-7

Digital edition published in 2018
eISBN: 978-1-63159-498-4

Library of Congress Cataloging-in-Publication Data found under *Layout Workbook: A Real-World Guide to Building Pages in Graphic Design*.

Design: Kristin Cullen
Printed in China

To design is to transform prose into poetry.

PAUL RAND

author, graphic designer, teacher

8 INTRODUCTION

chapter one
10 *the function of design*
COMMUNICATING MESSAGES
establishing function 12
the role of the designer 14

chapter two
16 *inspiration*
CULTIVATING CREATIVITY
discovering inspiration 18

chapter three
24 *the design process*
UNDERSTANDING METHODOLOGY
the value of process 26
developing a project brief 26
research and information gathering 30
brainstorming 32
conceptualization 34
experimentation and development 36
execution 40

chapter four
42 *intuition*
TRUSTING THE INNER VOICE
intuition defined 44
the benefits of intuition 46

chapter five
52 *structure and organization*
BUILDING FOUNDATIONS
grid systems in graphic design 54
the anatomy of grids 56
working with basic grids 60
visual balance 68

234 BASIC GLOSSARY

236 INDEX OF CONTRIBUTORS

238 BIBLIOGRAPHY

239 ABOUT THE AUTHOR
ACKNOWLEDGMENTS

chapter six
74 *the interaction of visual elements*
ESTABLISHING HIERARCHY
hierarchical development 76
the principles of spatial organization 78

chapter seven
94 *typography*
SHAPING LANGUAGE
the function of type 96
typographic characteristics 96
typeface selection 100
designing with type 104

chapter eight
122 *design analysis*
SEEING THE WHOLE AND ITS PARTS
the importance of analysis 124
evaluation considerations 126

chapter nine
130 *profiles*
LOOKING CLOSER
aufuldish & warinner 132
capsule 136
cheng design 138
ci studio 142
concrete [the office of jilly simons] 146
cook design 150
evelock design 154
renate gokl 158
hammerpress studio 162
hat-trick design 164
helicopter 168
hendersonbromsteadartco. 170
hoet & hoet 174
the jones group 176
kangaroo press 178
kearneyrocholl 180
kinetic singapore 184
kolégram 186
kontour design 190
lichtwitz 194
mitre agency 196
nb: studio 198
no.parking 202
noon 206
petrick design 208
rick rawlins/work and visual dialogue 210
rmac 212
samatamason 214
shinnoske design 218
studio najbrt 220
superbüro 224
visocky o'grady 228
wilsonharvey/loewy 232

INTRODUCTION

Design is the visual synthesis of ideas. It captures thought and language, transforming them anew. Design commands the imagination and intellect, creates connections, fosters understanding, and provides meaning. Compelling examples of visual communication solutions range from simple to complex, trivial to significant. Design shapes the visible environment and delivers information to everyone within it; it is functional, conveying messages with purpose. Design is always present, taking on myriad formats, including print, digital, and environmental. Engrained into the fabric of cultural experience, design affects daily life in mundane and extraordinary ways.

For the designer, design is a creative journey—a process of discovery—that is fueled by inspiration and creative passion, as well as the desire to enrich and ignite communication. Designers are engineers and craftsman of visual messages. They contribute their learned and innate knowledge, critical thinking and analysis abilities, and acute aesthetic and visual skills to the process. Design is an intriguing, evolutionary field, and the designer must constantly adapt to satisfy and challenge the ever-changing needs of communication.

Although design and designers continue to advance and diversify, the basic foundation of design practice lies in the understanding and application of the fundamentals of layout. The following pages are dedicated to these fundamentals and examine the function and value of visual communication. This book illuminates the broad category of layout—from function, inspiration, process, and intuition to structure, hierarchy, and typography. The objective is to educate and inspire as well as promote creativity, while encouraging the design of strong, thoughtful, and informative layouts. Featuring primarily print communications, each chapter aims to engage the viewer emotionally, intellectually, and visually—sharing the wonder of design.

THE FUNCTION

To design is much more
than simply to assemble, to order, or even to edit;
it is to add value and meaning,
to illuminate, to simplify, to clarify,
to modify, to dignify, to dramatize, to persuade,
and perhaps even to amuse.

PAUL RAND
author, graphic designer, teacher

OF DESIGN

COMMUNICATING MESSAGES

The function of graphic design is the communication of messages through the juxtaposition of words and pictures. It is the visual synthesis of thought and ideas in the form of publications, exhibitions, and posters, as well as signage, and digital interfaces. Graphic design is tactile, interactive, and environmental. Responding to public needs, it is a powerful visual medium that is present in all aspects of daily life. Graphic design extends itself into our cultural experiences and speaks to society on practical, emotional, and intuitive levels. It affects human experience from the most mundane to the most extraordinary ways.

establishing function

Design delivers information to intended recipients who receive and use (or ignore and abandon) its content in innumerable ways. The function of design goes beyond its myth as simply decoration; it is far more meaningful and essential to our daily lives. Though sophisticated aesthetics and excellent visual execution are essential to design, communicative function is imperative—it is the foremost purpose of design, which is amazingly rich and multifunctional. Design educates, inspires, and entertains. It informs, warns, and encourages. It engages, creates awareness, and nurtures dialogue, while also directing, guiding, promoting, persuading, and influencing. Design conveys attitudes, expresses thoughts, and triggers emotions. The depth of design is so broad in scope with its abundant applications across media and platforms.

design objectives

communication
education
information
guidance
encouragement
promotion
inspiration
awareness
dialogue
persuasion
entertainment
direction
motivation

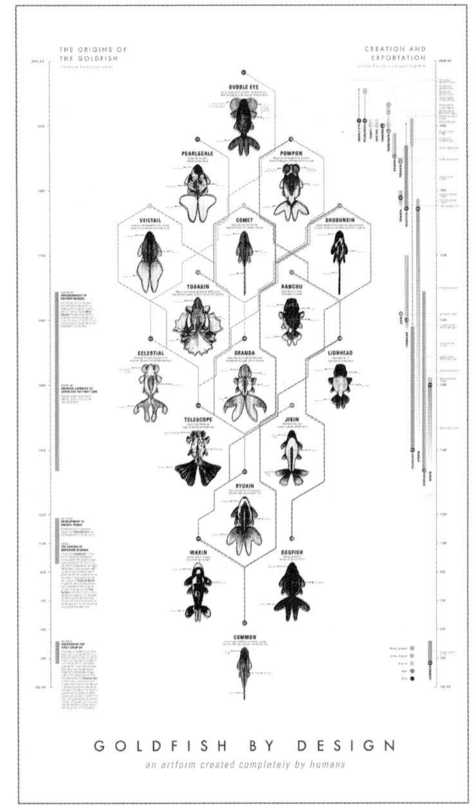

| **erin kennedy** | Information graphics and data visualization inform and explain a specific story for a specific audience. They may display quantifiable or unquantifiable elements.

| **wilsonharvey/loewy** | Business cards are one part of identity systems and represent people, businesses, and organizations. They serve as reminders or symbols of an exchange, dialogue, or meeting, while also having the function of conveying contact information clearly.

The function of the design must be established before the design process can begin. Is the design an invitation, annual report, poster, or book? What is its primary objective? Who is it trying to reach? What is the desired reaction of the viewer? Determining the function of the piece is critical and provokes numerous questions that inform the designer and help focus the development of the design.

| **lichtwitz** | Packaging establishes the mood of the product that lies inside. It is the first impression of the piece and dramatically influences its marketability.

determining the function of the design

Will the design…

announce or invite and request participation?

inform and create awareness?

educate or instruct?

identify or symbolize and represent people, places, and things?

illustrate and explain?

spark imagination and ignite creativity?

interpret and clarify?

influence and motivate action?

solicit trust or faith?

package, promote, sell, or advertise?

protect and store?

guide and provide navigation?

display and exhibit?

commemorate and mark history?

feature and showcase?

anger and incite?

entertain and amuse?

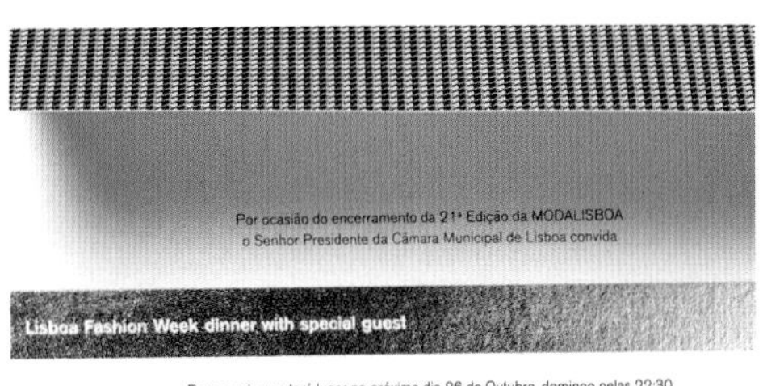

| **rmac** | Invitations promote and request participation. They are timely; once the event ends, the design no longer serves its primary task.

| **visual dialogue** | Design creates awareness and motivates action. It can inspire individuals to open their minds and actively participate in events that bring positive change to local, national, and global communities.

the role of the designer

The designer adopts multiple personalities throughout the design process. They are analysts, strategists, decision makers, and managers, as well as articulate problem solvers and conceptual and symbolic thinkers. Designers often play the roles of writer and editor, as well as cultural anthropologist and sociologist. They must possess a broad range of skills to effectively solve visual-communication problems with impact. The designer must understand the relationship between color, form, and space, as well as structure, hierarchy, and typography. Through education and practice, the designer builds skills while enhancing intellect and visual acuity. It is the designer's primary responsibility to create strong communicative experiences that support the function of the design on behalf of the client and for the viewer.

skills of the designer

problem solving

communication

analysis

visualization

management

composition

organization

information gathering

systemization

critical thinking

aesthetics

representation

research

perception

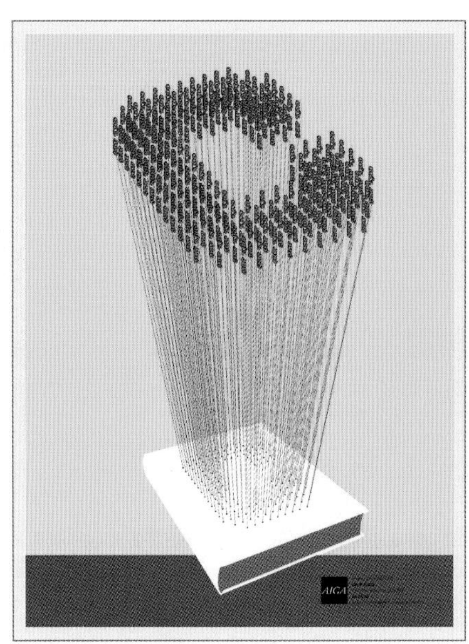

| **344 design, llc** | Posters create impact with a strong focal point that directs the eye into the composition and leads the viewer to content that is accessible on closer examination.

| **no.parking** | Books entertain and educate for extended periods of time. They require in-depth engagement, so the layout must be consistent, dynamic, and readable to maintain attention.

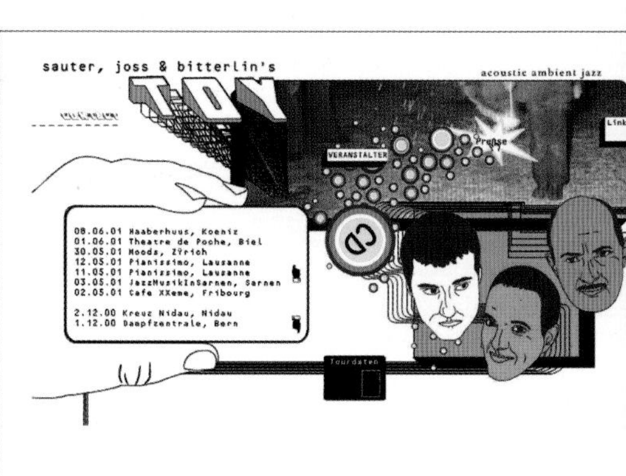

| **superbüro** | Websites impact the viewer immediately to capture their interest. There is no time to wait for complicated designs to be revealed and deciphered.

The designer simplifies, translates, and shares ideas through the thoughtfully and carefully executed manipulation of visual elements. The appropriate relationship of form to content, as well as the utility and function of the design, is managed by the designer. He or she develops and controls the visual presentation of information to enable comprehension and relate form to function with aesthetic grace, creating meaning and sending messages through visualization. The designer must communicate information in an accessible and effective visual format that serves the function of the design, not the designer.

FINAL THOUGHTS The primary function of design is the communication of messages. Ideas are shared from person to person through compelling visualization. It is a challenge to effectively deliver messages that are dynamic, engaging, and informative, while satisfying the objectives of everyone participating and affected by the design process and final visual solution. The designer plays a pivotal role, shaping communication to create connections between the client and viewer.

| **mitre agency** | Design may commemorate history. It captures the essence of the past, brings it into the present, and carries its memory into the future.

| **ci studio** | Branding creates a unified identity and visual image that can be applied to multiple pieces. Well-planned and clearly articulated guidelines help others understand and follow the strategic system.

I begin with an idea,
and then it becomes something else.

PABLO PICASSO
artist, ceramist, painter, printmaker, sculptor

INSPIRATION

CULTIVATING CREATIVITY

Inspiration is boundless. From places and books to culture and art, as well as nature and science, inspiration comes from everywhere, and the opportunities for seeking it are without end. Inspiration is the spirit or energy that motivates the creative process and provides the impetus to solve visual-communication problems. It engages the senses of the designer and fosters originality. Inspiration signals the beginning of an idea. It guides and informs the designer, giving shape to visual solutions and bringing design to life. It defines the navigable pathway that leads to clear and dynamic designs.

discovering inspiration

Inspiration is found, or discovered, and transformed into thoughts and ideas. Inspiration cannot be defined easily as one specific thing or another because inspirational factors are different for everyone. Two designers may share the same experience, yet only one may find something special that sparks creative insights and furthers the passion for design. Inspiration arrives as a result of the unique way the designer looks at, and reacts to, his or her environment. Everyone's senses are piqued in unique ways, yet everyone has the potential to visually interpret his or her findings and make the ordinary extraordinary. From city lights to architecture to materials and textures, anything can spark ideas that will develop into concrete solutions. No matter what inspires, the influence of inspiration keeps the designer moving forward and encourages continued development toward advanced, thoughtful, and dynamic work.

Attentiveness, observation, and open mindedness are critical to recognizing inspiration, which can arrive at any time without notice. The designer must be fully aware of his or her environment, always looking for anything that commands attention or stirs emotions in positive and negative ways. Inspiration is captivating, originating from both good and bad situations. Learning to see, listen, and feel with acuteness is critical to gleaning inspiration. The designer must willingly, actively, and carefully examine everything and pay close attention to details.

| rick johnson & company |
This letterhead system for Belize Saltwater Outfitters, a company specializing in fishing tours in Belize, reflects the themes of adventure and travel. Design director Tim McGrath found design inspiration in books, such as *Carouschka's Tickets* (pictured), *Hong Kong Apothecary: A Visual History of Chinese Medicine Packaging*, and *Maya Designs*.

| **crush** | This catalog for Simultané—a boutique and fashion label—was inspired by their collection as well as a designer's sketchbook. Photographs of the Simultané studio, fabric, sketches, and notes are incorporated into the design. The inspirational findings, which are layered throughout the piece, reflect the creative process that sparks the design of the clothing.

Seeking inspiration is not a chore that requires extra effort. Rather, it is a natural reaction that stems from the desire to create and communicate. The designer must experience life and vigorously explore the inspirational forces of daily environments, taking as much from them as possible. In addition to outside influences, the designer must also look inward and tap into the subconscious, which is another useful source of creative inspiration. Recalling past experiences is equally powerful as inspirational and motivational factors that influence the design process.

THE DESIGNER MUST **WILLINGLY**, **ACTIVELY**, AND **CAREFULLY** EXAMINE EVERYTHING AND PAY CLOSE ATTENTION TO DETAILS.

| **d-fuse** | *D-Tonate_00* is a collection of multi-angle films and multi-audio tracks. From the cover design and interior packaging to the digital interface and films, a primary source of inspiration was Japan, which is where the piece was launched.

Amassing a collection of inspirational notes, drawings, photographs, quotations, and sounds—the elements of the collection are limitless—is a valuable resource for every designer. It is important to capture inspiration in any form when it strikes, even if it cannot be used immediately. In time, the inspiration will find its place and reveal its value as the beginning seed of the design process. The collection can take on any format that best suits the individual designer. It can be a notebook or sketchbook, as well as a storage box or pin-up board, which the designer adds to on a daily basis. Use the collection to create new and inventive solutions, which could become inspiration for other designers.

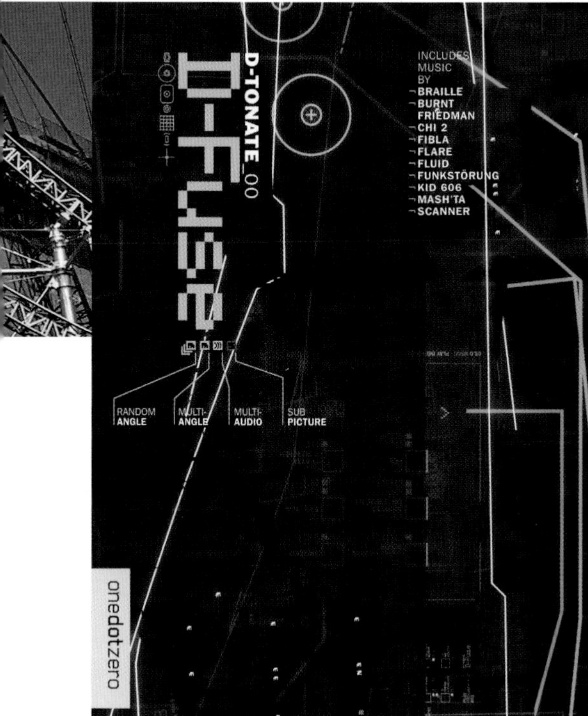

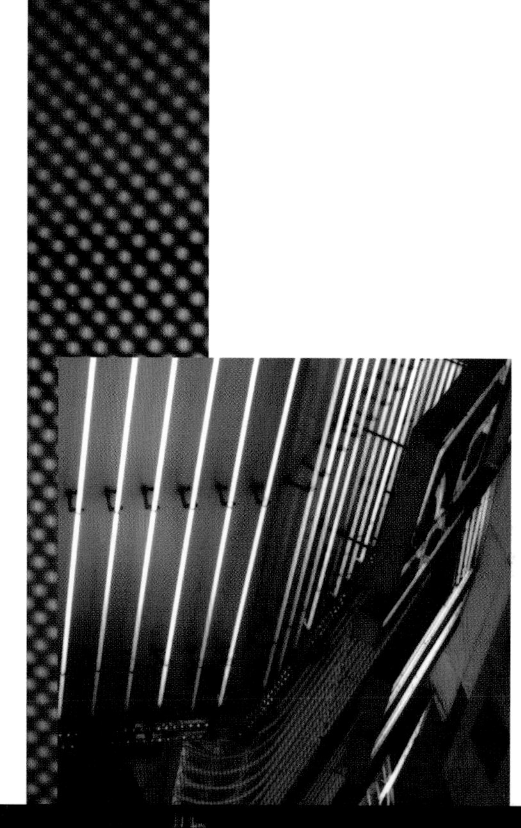

| **d-fuse** | Urban architecture and lights, as well as maps, graphic shapes, and textures, contribute to the visual language system used throughout the design.

nurturing inspiration

Carry a notebook or camera everywhere to record findings.

Become immersed in design.

Be committed to discovering and collecting inspirational factors.

Take a walk.

Take breaks throughout the day.

Listen to music.

Spend the day outdoors.

Communicate regularly with other designers.

Explore areas of interest beyond design.

Go to a movie, play, opera, concert, museum, or gallery opening.

Visit family and friends.

Read a diverse selection of books, magazines, and journals.

Go for a drive.

Attend conferences, lectures, and events.

Take a different route home after work.

Explore.

Create diversions from everyday routines.

Go on vacation or spend a weekend away from home.

Try something new.

FINAL THOUGHTS Learning to develop the ability to perceive, gather, and use inspiration is the responsibility of the designer. It is vital to react to the everyday environment with heightened senses, making the most of experiences. Inspiration provides insight into creativity and design. A wellspring of inspirational factors (and knowledge gained from them) shapes and influences the designer and the design process in countless ways.

| **mitre agency** | This poster for the Downtown Farmers Market combines a range of inspirational factors, including folk art, old advertisements, and packaging labels. The sources of inspiration are weathered, typographically bold, and richly colored; these same qualities are reflected in the contemporary design.

THE DESIGN

The recognition of
the value of the journey,
as opposed to the imagined value points of ending,
informs the idea of process.

TOMATO
london-based art collective

PROCESS

UNDERSTANDING METHODOLOGY

Design is a process of discovery. It is a journey that reveals visual communication through very distinct stages, which include research and information gathering, brainstorming, conceptualization, experimentation and development, and execution. When approaching any design problem, the focus of the designer must not be on the final product. Although the end result is important, the path that leads to it is equally significant. Valuable discoveries and insights, which foster growth and understanding, are gained through each stage of the design process. No matter how large or small the project, every step demands attention. Though the design process is exhausting at times, especially if the designer is working under time restrictions, it will ultimately benefit the outcome of the design, as well as the designer.

the value of process
developing a project brief

Design is an analytical field that demands a range of skills, including management, problem solving, and visual acuity. At the beginning of the process, a great deal of planning is required before sketching and designing can begin. An intellectual methodology will guide the designer, as well as the design—from initiation to completion. A solid design process is the foundation on which layouts are systematically built. The process is the supporting guide that allows the designer to control the progression of the project from one stage to the next.

The design process encourages the designer to carefully analyze the communication problem and craft an effective solution. It enables the designer to understand the project and its intended function before visual explorations begin. Whereas the stages of the design process most often remain the same with every project, the passage through the stages is uncharted. The designer must be willing to alter its course to produce diverse, original, and effective solutions. Additionally, to avoid derivation or imitation, the designer must be mindful not to jump into the conceptualization, development, and execution stages too quickly or without enough background information. The design must be comprehensively considered from beginning to end to avoid naïve ideas that do not effectively solve the problem.

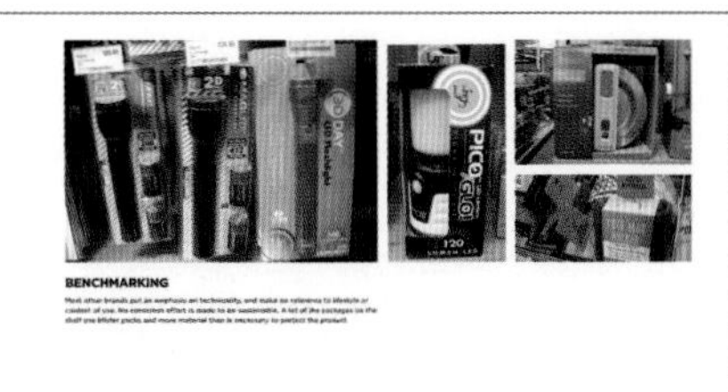

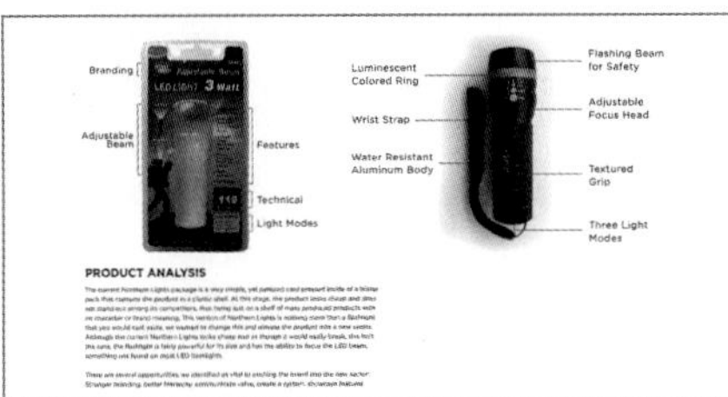

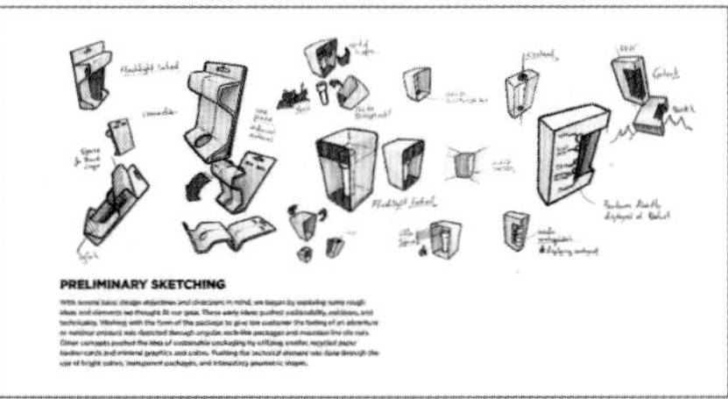

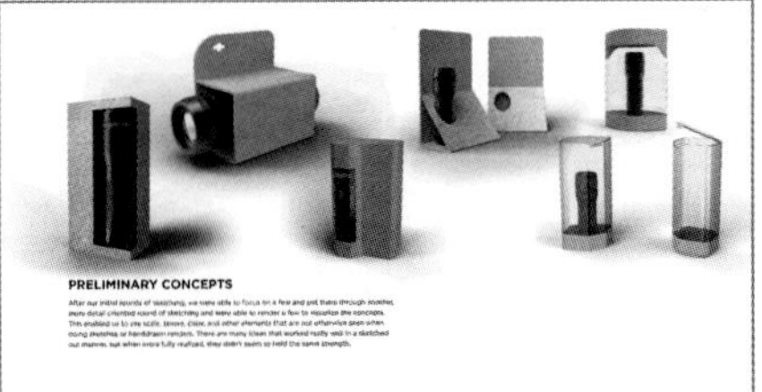

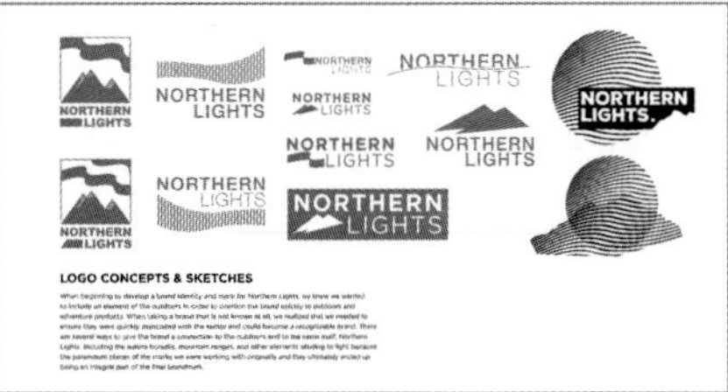

A process-development group collaborative from the University of Cincinnati—Tommo Brickner, Brad Clary, Christopher Lefke, and Rebekah Leiva—presents a strategy for a product and package design. It progresses through several stages: identifying the problem, targeting the audience, benchmarking, product analysis, ideation, preliminary concepts, and refinement.

Preparing the project brief is an essential step that initiates the design process. At the beginning stage, the project brief provides a meticulous overview of the project, while informing all parties involved in the development and production of the design. The project brief addresses the design in detail and includes every aspect of the problem, as well as the roles of the client, designer, and other project contributors. It is used throughout the process as a reference tool to ensure that the design reflects the project objectives, moves in the proper direction, and relates to the needs of the client and viewer. Design is calculated and meaningful and should reflect function with a high degree of communicative and aesthetic proficiency.

defining the essential details The project brief begins with a detailed review of the research and information provided by the client, which the designer needs to clarify and simplify for efficient use. Throughout the development of the project brief, questions address initial and long-term concerns, as well as responsibilities and expectations. The designer is not expected to know everything, but he or she is responsible for asking the client to fill in any missing pieces. Additionally, the designer should never make decisions based on assumptions; collaboration with the client is absolutely critical. There is no excuse for confusion or misunderstandings at any stage of the process. Details should be clarified during initial meetings so that everyone is clear on the plan of action. Although questions are essential at the onset of the project, the designer must continue to ask questions throughout the design process, including inquiries to the client and additional project participants, such as printers and proofreaders.

The primary goals and messages of the client need to be clearly defined in the project brief before moving to the next stage of development—research and information gathering. Restrictions, such as the budget, must also be noted and assessed to determine their impact on the design. Working with the client, the designer must establish the project schedule, which includes imperative dates, such as concept and design presentations, as well as deadlines and delivery. It is important to share the project brief with all participants to ensure that everyone understands the scope of work and the plan for executing it.

In the development of the project brief, it is important to take into consideration the role of the viewer. The client and designer must determine toward whom the project is directed. Understanding the target audience shapes the direction of the design and dramatically influences the end result. It is helpful to define the general characteristics of the viewer, including age, geographic location, and general likes and dislikes. The designer must also consider how the viewer will interact with the design so he or she can choose a format that will allow the design to meet the communication needs of the viewer. The viewer, although not an active participant of the design process, will define most of the designer's decision making.

establishing responsibilities While preparing the project brief, the designer must begin to document and gather the textual and visual elements used in the layout. A clear assessment of all of the elements will determine what exists and what is needed to move forward with design development. What the client and designer each contribute to the content of the design also needs to be established and noted. If anything is missing, the designer must ask the client to provide it. A running list of tasks to be completed in a timely manner, such as contracting an illustrator, developer, or photographer, must be added to the project brief. It is important for the designer to see the visual elements that will be incorporated into the design in the early stages of the process—this essential part of the project must be defined as soon as possible.

The project brief outlines and establishes the relationship and level of involvement between the client and designer by specifying each of their roles. It is important to learn how to interact with the client to avoid future pitfalls. Everyone involved with the project will adopt a certain amount of responsibility; it is wise to establish what is required early in the process to avoid confusion when anything is needed. When the project brief is completed, reviewed, discussed, and approved by all necessary parties, the designer can comfortably move to the next stage of the process.

THE PROJECT BRIEF

ADDRESSES THE DESIGN IN DETAIL AND INCLUDES EVERY ASPECT OF THE PROBLEM, AS WELL AS THE ROLES OF THE CLIENT, DESIGNER, AND VIEWER.

project brief functions

States the primary goals and messages of the design.

Provides a meticulous overview of the project.

Determines project restrictions, as well as the schedule and budget.

Outlines the client–designer relationship.

Establishes the responsibilities of everyone involved with the project.

Is used as a reference tool throughout the process.

Defines the characteristics of the viewer.

the actions of the client

Initiates the design project.

Determines the primary design objective.

Seeks returns from the design.

Respects the expertise of the designer.

Articulates anticipated outcomes and reactions.

Suggests the desired attitude of the design.

Prepares budgetary information.

Establishes deadlines for delivery.

Actively participates throughout the process.

Approves the design.

Provides feedback.

A series of questions, which can be tailored to address individual projects, provides a starting point to begin the project brief.

the design problem

What type of project is needed (annual report, brochure, poster)?

What is the function and purpose of the design?

What are the client's objectives/goals for the design?

What is the primary message the client wants to communicate?

What considerations must be made to meet the needs of the client and viewer?

Are there any limitations or restrictions?

What is the budget?

What is the schedule?

the client–designer relationship

What are the responsibilities of the client?

What are the responsibilities of the designer?

What is the level of client involvement?

In what stages of the design process will the client be directly involved?

What are the important dates, such as presentations and delivery?

How often will the client and designer interact?

What is the best method of communication (email, meetings, phone)?

Who are the primary contacts?

essentials of the client–designer relationship

respect

open communication

shared vision

trust

creative interaction

collaboration

the viewer

Toward whom is the project directed?

What are the characteristics of the viewer?

What makes the viewer unique?

How will the viewer interact with the design?

What are the needs of the end user?

research and information gathering

Following the preparation of the project brief, research and information gathering is the second stage of the design process. It begins with a thorough review of all materials provided by the client. The designer must read, evaluate, and understand all the information presented in its entirety before he or she can intelligently work with it. Analyzing the content will increase the designer's knowledge of the topic and affect how the piece is designed. In addition, as the designer is educated about the topic, ideas will spark, and the visualization process will begin. The more information the designer accumulates and digests, the greater the chance for the success of the project.

The designer should not rely solely on materials provided by the client. Additional research and information-gathering is often needed to expand the designer's familiarity with the topic beyond the initial client presentation. Independent research also broadens understanding and influences what the designer can bring to the design. The designer must acquire as much information as possible and, like the project brief, share the findings with relevant project participants. Without thorough research and information gathering, the design may be incomplete and lack a solid foundation.

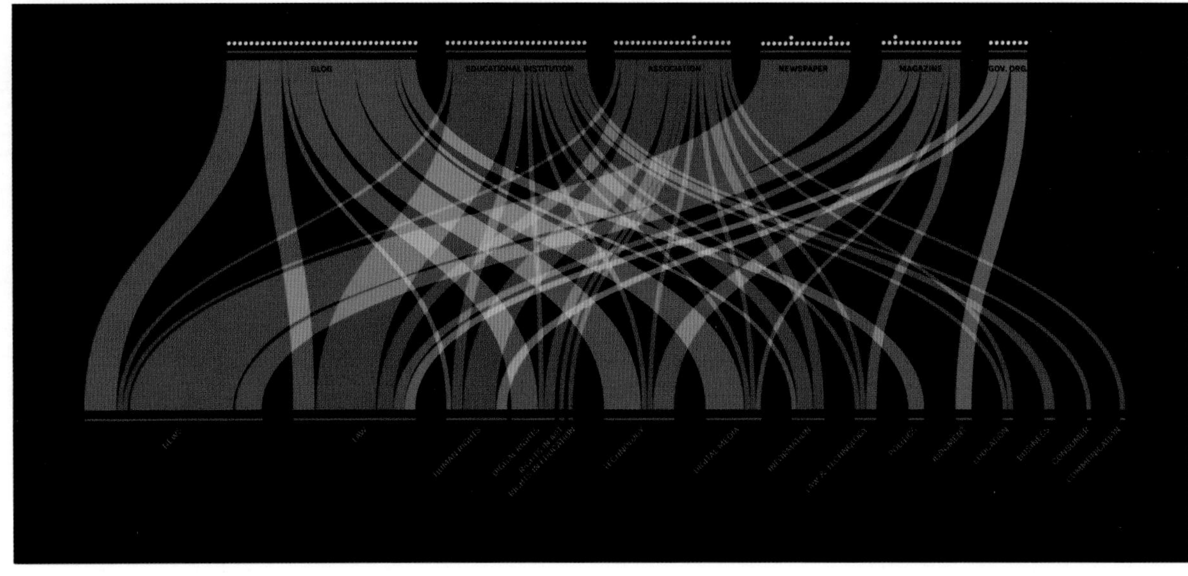

| **densitydesign** | Giulia DeRossi's data visualization focuses on information gathering. The subject matter is related to communication on the Internet.

the client Another important step of the research and information-gathering stage is to review the client's current communication materials and strategies. This process leads to an awareness of how the client approaches his or her public image and visual position in the past. It is helpful to discuss what the client likes and dislikes about the current communication materials and how he or she envisions future evolution. Ask the client for examples of any prior materials, as well as compelling and successful competitive pieces. This does not mean the client should request that the designer tailor the design based on other examples; rather, it provides the designer with a more complete understanding of the client's perspectives on design. Bringing the client into the research and information-gathering stage is a valuable way to foster a positive client–designer relationship. The client will feel part of the solution, while the designer may be able to use this opportunity to help educate the client further about design.

the competition Investigating the communication materials of competitive markets is another key component of the research and information-gathering stage. Gaining insight into the existing market is critical to designing work that appropriately and effectively functions within it—and advances it. Research can often prevent inadvertently designing a piece similar to a project already in existence. The designer must determine how the design will fit into the market and attend to the needs of the client while appealing to, and reaching, the viewer. Depending on the complexity of the project, professional researchers can be brought into the research and information gathering stage to broaden the understanding of the target business environment, as well as the requirements of the viewer.

Regardless of the broad or narrow scope of the project, the research and information-gathering stage will enrich the designer and help achieve strong, well-informed visual solutions. It should occur before brainstorming, conceptualization, or experimentation and development begins. Research and information gathering provides a critical knowledge base that will propel the design in the right direction.

research and information-gathering tips

Gain an understanding of the topic.

Read, evaluate, and understand all provided materials.

Independently research additional information.

Review the client's current communication materials.

Investigate competitive markets.

brainstorming

Brainstorming is an expressive, problem-solving activity that promotes idea generation, helps the designer think about and work through complicated design problems, and encourages creative expression. Every thought and idea is valuable and worth recording. There are no right or wrong answers, no limitations to the process. Be inventive. Brainstorming ignites the mind of the designer who must think freely and openly—without restraint—to gain useful results.

Brainstorming can be performed individually or with a team of designers. Working in collaboration offers multiple points of view to the design problem, which can be more beneficial than a singular approach. While one designer may brainstorm prolifically and conceive amazing solutions, one perspective may sometimes be limiting. Engaging several thinkers in the process is a great way to obtain a broad perspective and initiate the development of thoroughly considered, innovative solutions. Occasionally, it is helpful to invite the client into brainstorming sessions. This educates the client and actively involves him or her in the design process; it also provides the designer with an external, non-design point of view.

| **richard bloom (formerly apt5a design group)** | A list of ideas outlines the brainstorming process for the Chronophonic CD. Inspired by the title, *Footwork*, the list (at right) reflects the kinetic images used in the final design to connote the energy of the music.

breakdancers, the Charleston, Flappers, '40s dancing, soccer players (jumping, kicking), athletes jumping, jump shot, passing a player, long jump, dribbling up the court, hurdling, martial arts, wall-eye angle, jump kick, punching, flailing, celebrating, perspective of foot kicking close to camera, arms up, other dynamic perspectives

Inspiration boards are collections of imagery that inspire and motivate the designer into action. They are useful tools that capture the mood or essence of the design direction and influence its development.

The brainstorming process might include free writing, mind maps, lists of ideas or keywords, and inspiration boards. (Words and pictures contribute to brainstorming.) Stream-of-consciousness writing, or freewriting, helps the designer get thoughts immediately onto paper, whereas running lists record keywords and emotions associated with the design. Mind maps begin with one main idea placed in the center of a page with branches of subthemes extending out from the central theme. Each branch, or string of word associations, represents a new thought sequence. Inspiration boards combine selections of imagery that influence the direction of the design. After initial brainstorming exercises, the broad scope of ideas will be reviewed, filtered, and developed into specific, workable ideas so the designer can move into the conceptualization stage.

brainstorming techniques

Practice freewriting.

Create mind maps.

Build visual inspiration boards.

Write down lists of ideas.

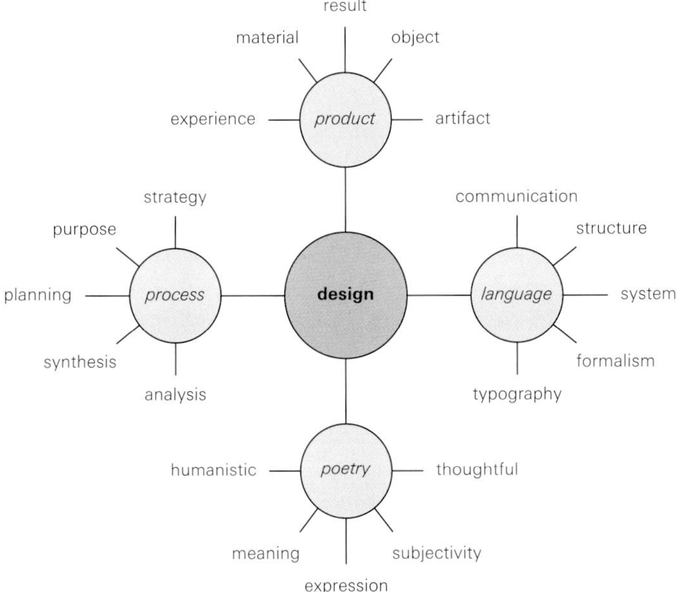

Mind mapping begins by placing a topic or theme in the center and creating branches of thoughts that stem from one main idea.

| **344 design, llc** | A collection of notes, brief writings, and sketches mark the idea-generation process that led to the design of the Solar Twins CD. Extensive preliminary thoughts and studies are critical to the success of all designs; they ignite creativity and inspire intelligent, unique solutions.

conceptualization

During the conceptualization stage of the design process, the designer must formulate the visual scheme, or plan, of the project. The concept is the thematic link between the design, its function, and the delivery of the message to the viewer; it is imperative to the success of the design. A strong concept will add depth to the project, while creating and maintaining viewer interest, providing focus, and promoting a cohesive visual solution. The designer always considers the function of the design, as well as its end user, and must be careful not to complicate the design with a concept that is inappropriate, unapproachable, or too abstract to deliver the message to the viewer. The design aims to be accessible, interesting, informative, and communicative.

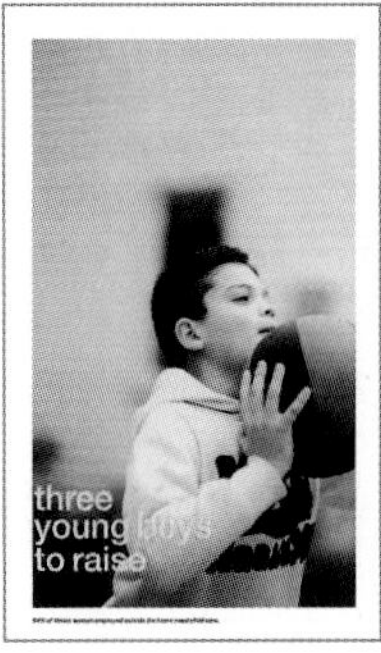
three
young boys
to raise

and
support

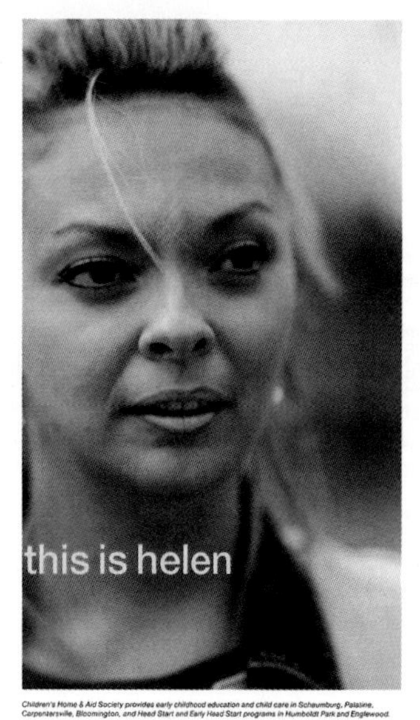
this is helen

Children's Home & Aid Society provides early childhood education and child care in Schaumburg, Palatine, Carpentersville, Bloomington, and Head Start and Early Head Start programs in Humboldt Park and Englewood.

Helen had her job cut out for her. It was going to be pretty tough. She had no family close by to watch her boys. She had never left them with anyone else before, and didn't feel comfortable leaving them at any of the child care centers she had already visited. Coping with the aftermath of a divorce, finding someone to care for her boys who were 1, 2, and 9 years old, and finding a job so she could make ends meet created an overwhelming and frightening situation.

It became less so when she was able to enroll her two younger boys at Children's Home & Aid Society's child care center in Palatine. The staff was very helpful and gave her hope that things would work out. She found a job as a hostess in a restaurant and goes to work without worrying about her children. She feels that the children are receiving good meals at the center, and that they are loved and well cared for.

For Helen, the subsidized child care has helped her financial situation. But she feels that the staff at the center have been the biggest help of all. She feels that the children could not be at a better place. The staff noticed a speech delay in her youngest child, and arranged for the child to receive therapy at the center while Helen was at work. The convenient arrangement was an enormous help to Helen. Although it's a 50 minute drive to the center from her home, Helen feels the service is worth it.

divorced after
ten years of marriage

Children's Home & Aid Society of Illinois 2003 Annual Report

| **samatamason** | Concepts may be straightforward and objective. The annual report for the Children's Home & Aid Society of Illinois relies on the directness of the content to deliver the message; in this case, symbolism is unneeded. Three true, personal stories are shared through the simple typography and candid photography. The purpose of the concept was to present the narratives as clearly and efficiently as possible.

Any design project can adopt a number of directions when developing its concept. If the content is clear and direct, the concept may result in a more objective and straightforward solution. However, if the content is layered with multiple types of information and a rich narrative, the designer may develop a deeper conceptual direction to represent content. The use of analogies and metaphors is another effective way to deliver messages that are engaging and relatable. Designers often use symbolism to help the viewer understand what the client is trying to communicate.

Regardless of the type of project, a singular, focused idea that drives the design must be determined at the end of the conceptualization stage. A solid design scheme will allow the designer to visualize the outcome of the piece, shift into the experimentation and development stage, and begin composing the visual elements with clarity.

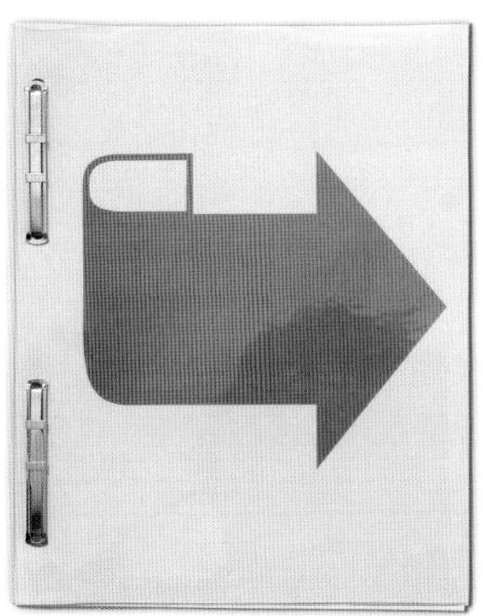

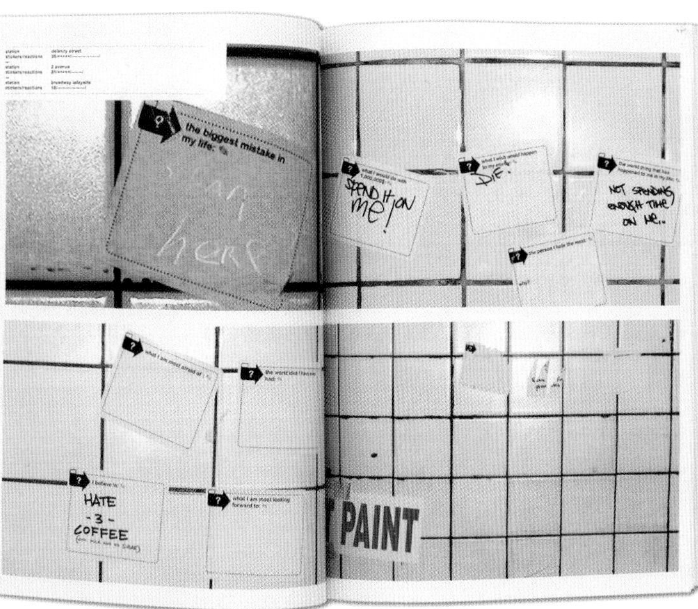

| **superbüro** | Progressive projects often rely on strong concepts. The book design is based on collecting and archiving the results of an experiment in which 300 stickers were placed in New York City subway tunnels asking people to react to questions. The format of the design is dictated by the idea of experiments. The metal binding connotes a notebook or chart in which to record results. Sheets of stickers are bound and displayed on their actual stock, whereas the results are shown as snapshots that display the evidence.

experimentation and development

After the conceptualization stage, it is time to transform the visual elements into cohesive solutions. The experimentation and development stage follows a path from visual studies to refined variations. This stage begins with experimentation, which is important because it opens the mind of the designer and pushes his or her visual skills. Experimentation is a free, expressive process that is insightful, playful, and challenging. Like brainstorming, the designer must not be limited during the experimentation stage, because, in most cases, the client will not see any of these initial studies. Experimentation does not need to generate definitive results. It may simply confirm that a new or more refined visual direction is the best solution.

During the experimentation stage, the designer may do a range of visual studies. For example, explore typefaces or develop a range of interchangeable color palettes. Consider diverse ways of handling illustration or photography. Examine the textual and visual content, and determine multiple ways of sequencing information. Test different grids and systems of proportion that structure the page. Introduce graphic shapes and linear elements. Additional options may include stepping away from the computer, working by hand, or passing the visual studies onto another designer for a fresh perspective and additional experimentation. Try anything different or new. Take the opportunity to be innovative. It can be comfortable, easy, and time efficient for the designer to revert to previously used solutions for design problems—especially under the stress of looming deadlines—but doing so will only create an inferior design. Experimentation is critical; it enhances the design process and encourages original solutions that may not otherwise be considered.

Thumbnail sketches are small, loose studies that quickly address basic compositional variations. Considering all visual elements of the design, rough lines mark textual content, while boxes might be used to indicate the position of graphic shapes, illustration, or photography.

Through experimentation, the designer can test the strength of the concept as well as the visual investigations that do or do not work. The designer should evaluate preliminary studies based on comparative factors. By making and then assessing a range of visual directions, the designer will be able to confidently select directions that have the greatest potential and develop them into refined solutions. One key value of experimentation is that it challenges the designer to think beyond the initial concept.

After evaluating experimental studies, the designer selects the strongest directions for development. Thumbnail sketches that address the entire compositional space of the page, as well as the use of all visual elements, will help the designer quickly produce several variations. The thumbnails should be loose, created with rough lines that mark typographic content—such as paragraph and text alignments—and boxes designating graphic shapes and imagery. Thumbnails indicate relationships between elements on the page. Thumbnail sketching is a time-saving exercise. In some cases, nothing is more efficient than rough thumbnails that can be quickly drawn, reviewed, eliminated, and developed.

During the experimentation stage, the thought process was open and free. Visual studies were general and not reflective of the entire composition. In the development stage, multiple design solutions will come together and incorporate all the visual elements. The designer must now determine the primary grid or system of proportion that will structure and organize the design. Final typefaces must also be selected and implemented into a consistent, decisive typographic system to be applied throughout the design. The hierarchy of the design should be coordinated to logically lead the eye through dominant and subordinate levels of information. Compositionally, the space of the page must be controlled and exhibit dynamic, harmonious, and orchestrated form.

Producing variations is essential during the development stage. Variations can be vastly different or merely subtle, with just slight changes in the proportions of the primary grid, typefaces and settings, diversified color palettes, or compositional factors, such as orientation and position. Each variation allows the designer to compare the different directions and evaluate those that are strong or weak. In addition, the client often will want to see several variations before deciding on the final direction. Variations are the last component of the experimentation and development stage. At this point, the client and designer will select the direction that is most appropriate and interesting for refinement and completion during the execution stage.

experimentation ideas

Do multiple studies exploring color, composition, and typography.

Step away from the computer.

Develop several treatments for illustration or photography.

Sequence the textual and visual content in numerous ways.

Try anything different or new.

Introduce graphic shapes and linear elements.

Work by hand.

Share the studies with another designer for additional insight.

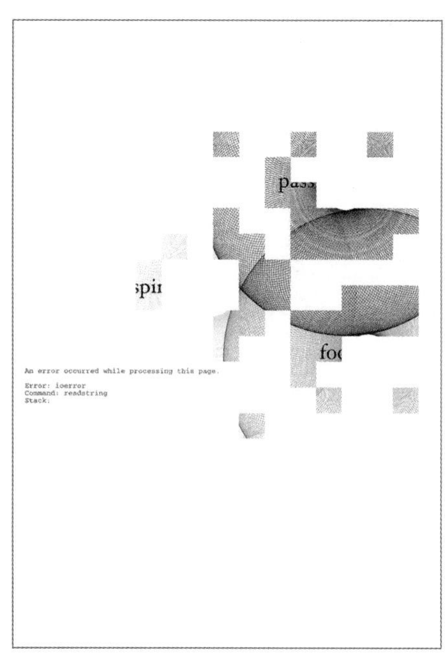

| **vrontikis design office** | Select experimental studies provide a look into the development of this poster. The studies are rough at this stage but successfully provide a range of options that includes typographic and photographic solutions, as well as an interesting use of graphic shapes. Because an infinite number of solutions are available for all design problems, diverse exploration is essential.

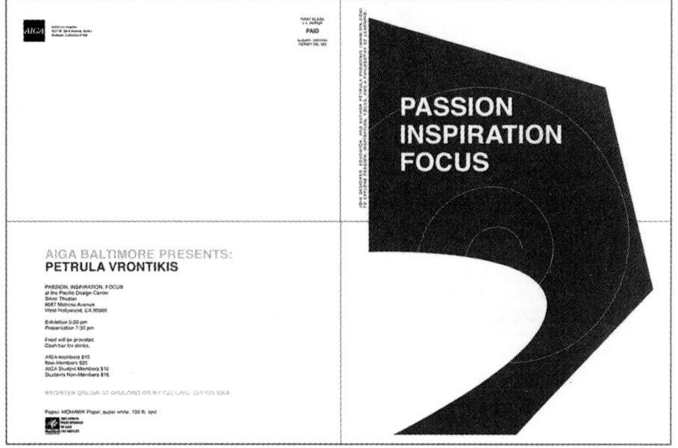

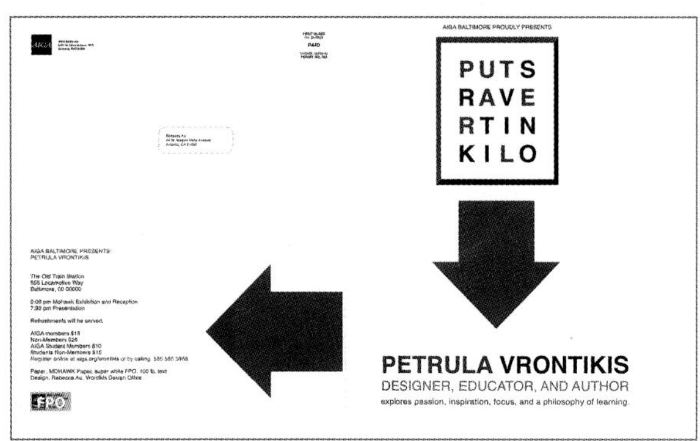

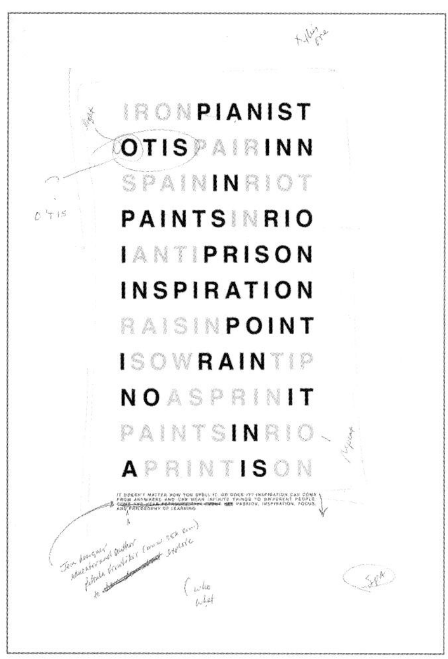

petrula_A

IRONPIANIST
SPAININRIOT
PAINTSINRIO
NOASPIRINIT
RAISINPOINT
IANTIPRISON
ISOWRAINTIP
IPRINTISONA
INSPIRATION

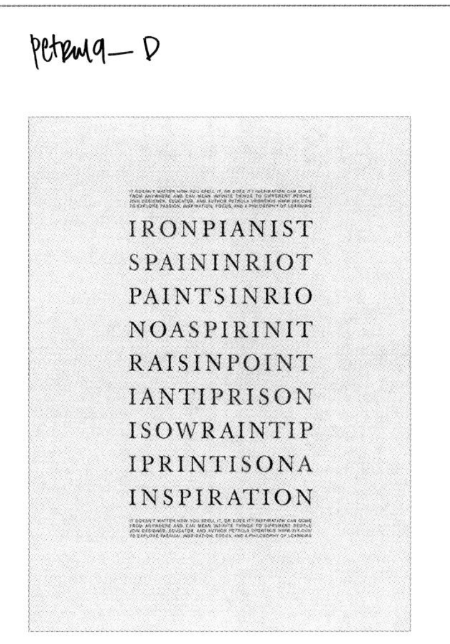

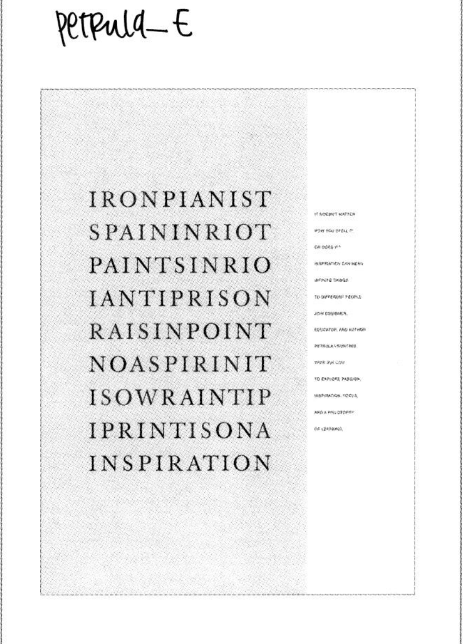

| vrontikis design office |

The next step of the development stage is creating variations based on the most effective solution chosen from the experimental studies. Variations can be vastly different (or subtle) with changes to the compositional factors, such as color, orientation, position, and typography. In this example, the variations demonstrate the infinite range of options available when working in one focused direction. Comparing variations is an essential step in choosing the strongest solution.

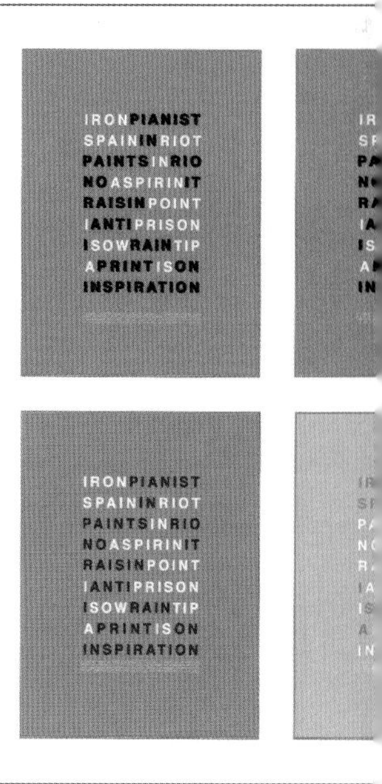

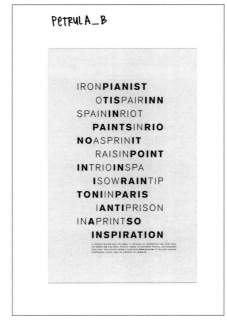

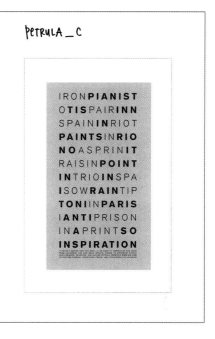

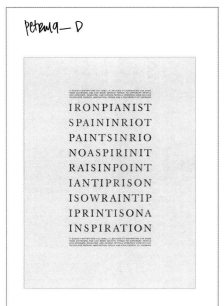

execution

At this point in the design process, the concept has been finalized and experimentation has resulted in a diverse set of exploratory studies. Additional development of the studies brought all the visual elements together into several variations, which were narrowed down to select the final direction. During the execution stage, the designer must examine every detail of the piece with a keen eye. He or she must preview the compositional space and organize the content logically and with sequential flow. Alignment, orientation, and position of the visual elements must be methodically coordinated to create appropriate relationships. The hierarchical system must ensure an ordered arrangement of textual and visual content with content designated into distinct levels of importance.

After working on a project, the designer often may become attached to it (even without intending to), which sometimes makes it difficult to analyze the design with objectivity. As a result, it is helpful to present the design to others for an objective evaluation of its visual presentation and utility. Does the design demonstrate a consistent, unified system that applies to all the visual elements? Is the message of the piece clearly communicated? Will the viewer be able to use it effectively? Is the design aesthetically strong?

A good starting point is to review the project brief and use it as a checklist to determine if the final design successfully reflects the goals and function originally outlined. Be objective during this stage, and peruse the design carefully. In addition, ask the client to review the final design to ensure satisfaction and approval of the visual solution before sending it to production. It is not too late to make changes that may improve the quality of the piece. In most cases, subtle refinements are often critical.

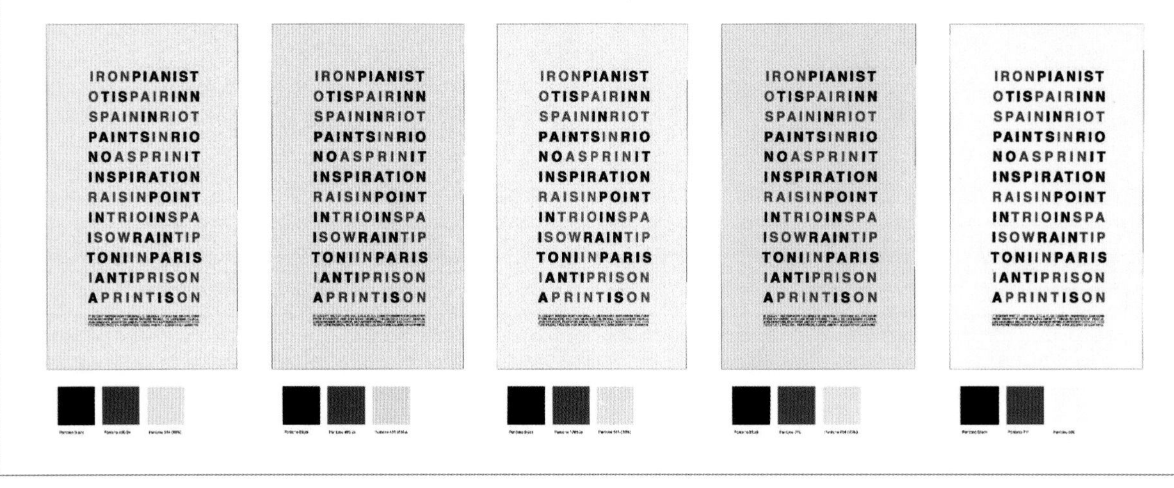

| vrontikis design office |

At the end of the execution stage, the design is reviewed carefully and objectively to ensure that all details are refined. In this example, subtle variations in color are assessed.

IRONPIANIST
SPAININRIOT
PAINTSINRIO
NOASPIRINIT
RAISINPOINT
IANTIPRISON
ISOWRAINTIP
IPRINTISONA
INSPIRATION

IT DOESN'T MATTER HOW YOU SPELL IT, OR DOES IT? INSPIRATION CAN COME FROM ANYWHERE AND CAN MEAN INFINITE THINGS TO DIFFERENT PEOPLE. JOIN DESIGNER, EDUCATOR, AND AUTHOR PETRULA VRONTIKIS WWW.35K.COM TO EXPLORE PASSION, INSPIRATION, FOCUS, AND A PHILOSOPHY OF LEARNING.

FINAL THOUGHTS It is important to value and become engaged with each stage of the design process. A comprehensive methodology will provide a logical progression from the beginning to the end of a project. The designer will grow, learn, and improve with each design, whereas the design process—which is unique to every design and designer—will become more acute through each new experience. Always remember to trust the process.

| **vrontikis design office** |
The final design is the natural evolution of a thoroughly developed design process. All stages are critical to ensuring appropriate and effective visual solutions.

for in-depth analysis information, refer to *chapter 8: design analysis*

There is a vitality, a life force,

a quickening that is translated through you into action,

and because there is only one of you in all time,

this expression is unique.

And if you block it,

it will never exist through any other medium,

and will be lost.

MARTHA GRAHAM

choreographer, dancer

INTUITION

TRUSTING THE INNER VOICE

Designers are creative thinkers and visual problem solvers. Every project demands a different aesthetic and intellectual approach to communicate appropriately, effectively, and distinctively. Although basic design rules and techniques must be learned, applied, and practiced, visual solutions are not formulaic. Each designer contributes his or her individual knowledge, skills, experiences, and intuitive abilities to the design process, which shape and distinguish projects. Unique to every designer, intuition enhances acuity and dramatically influences the outcome of the final design.

intuition defined

The fundamentals of design are universal. Color, form, and space, as well as structure, hierarchy, and typography, can be taught and learned. They are the foundation of design practice; their informed use must be inherent to the strength (and success) of the design and the designer. There is no question that design education, whether formal or informal, is essential. However, understanding the fundamentals is only as effective as their application. Comprehension alone does not guarantee good design.

The basics of visual communication include visual language systems, structure and organization of compositional space, and hierarchy, as well as designing with color and type. However, these basics do not specify methods for composing visual elements in all situations (there are too many variables with each project). Certainly, there are a number of factors such as symmetry, figure-ground, position, and spatial relationships that influence compositional decision making. There is also a rich history of strong design examples to review and analyze. Yet, interestingly, no two designers will produce the same design, even when using identical content. In addition to experience and practice, intuition is often the defining force that individualizes and distinguishes one designer from the next. An innate sense for working with design fundamentals and composing the page is a critical component of the design process.

| **katherine varrati** |

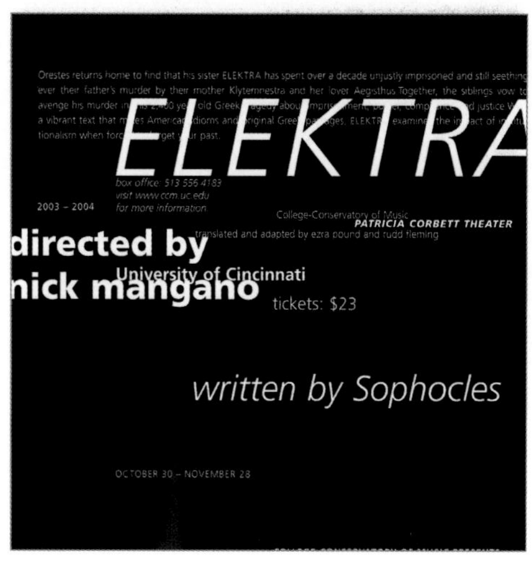

| **heather mcfadden** |

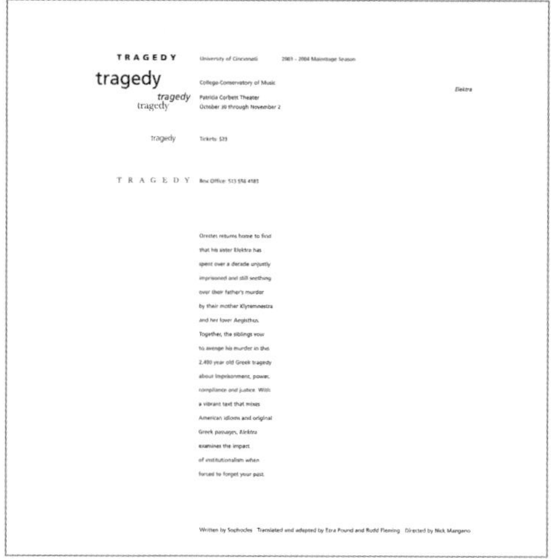

| **paige strohmaier** |

Intuition is a different level of thinking, or cognition, that complements rational thought. It presents itself naturally and without hesitation. It is an immediate, involuntary insight that arrives unexpectedly without the influence or interference of rational thought. The inner voice, and the knowledge that it brings, is independent and unexplainable, yet is always accessible if one is open to it. In a very general sense, intuition has the ability to lead and protect, enlighten and inspire. It synthesizes brain impulses, whether innate or learned, and brings forth new and unexpected thoughts that may not otherwise emerge through logical reasoning.

connecting the conscious and subconscious

Intuition is the unpredictable connection that bridges the gap between the conscious and subconscious mind, which provokes the arrival of wisdom into consciousness. Intuition strikes at any time—even if it arrives unnoticed—and is informed by past experiences, those both remembered and forgotten, which are stored in memory. It is also influenced by the present and anticipation of future events. It stems from dreams, imagination, and inspiration. It can be sparked by the everyday environment, which constantly influences and stimulates the brain. Although it is not fully understood and is difficult to verbalize, intuition works for the benefit of the designer with meaning and purpose.

the influence of rational thinking Rational thinking analyzes and questions thoughts. Though essential to the design process, logical reasoning can sometimes inadvertently suppress intuition and prevent the designer from exploring new creative opportunities. For example, the need to justify every action (and the fear attached with not being able to do so) often discourages the designer from responding to and trusting his or her gut. The designer may believe that reacting to intuition invalidates the design and makes it careless, flighty, or too abstract. The inexperienced designer may doubt personal instincts and rely only on learned knowledge that he or she believes is absolute—or, the designer may find it difficult to trust the effectiveness of the design unless the intellect behind it is thoroughly explained. The designer is worried that a methodology that includes intuition is unrelated to the practical concerns of the client and viewer. These concerns are reasonable and need to be kept in check, yet none negate the positive influence of intuition on the design process. It works in conjunction with learned knowledge and rational thinking to achieve effective design solutions, taking them a step further.

for in-depth grid, hierarchy, and typographic information, refer to *chapter 5: structure and organization*, *chapter 6: the interaction of visual elements*, and *chapter 7: typography*

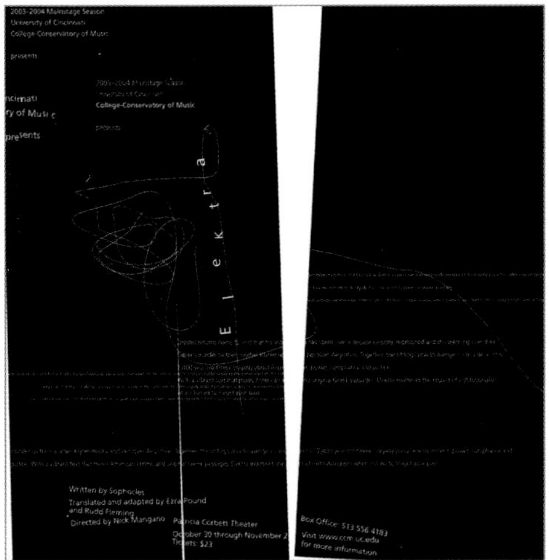

| **hans schellhas** |

This collection of typographic studies shows the range of solutions to one design problem. Each student designer was given the same specifications, such as page format, grid, text, and typeface. With an exploration of hierarchy, compositional factors, and objective and subjective representation, as well as the individual influence of intuition, the designers developed unique and varied solutions.

intuitive functions

guidance

protection

inspiration

enlightenment

synthesis

the benefits of intuition

Designers are naturally inclined to creativity. Intuition is beneficial because it cultivates imagination and allows the designer to move beyond his or her comfort zone, thereby increasing the potential of the designer (and the design). It can lead to fresh and innovative solutions or strengthen the aesthetic, concept, and visual presentation of the design. Intuition increases the number of ideas generated and provides the impetus to push the design beyond expectations. In addition, intuition eases decision making for the designer and influences the composition of the visual elements. The inner voice, or gut reaction, informs the designer about what works in the development of compelling and effective layouts. The designer must also know that intuition alone does not dictate solutions—intuition is a supporting factor and helps the designer through a logical process.

| hendersonbromsteadartco. |

Intuition enhances the creative potential of design and leads to fresh, innovative solutions that exceed expectation. In the poster for Triad Health Project, an AIDS service-and-support organization, intuition helped define a "campy and tongue-in-cheek" attitude. Art director Hayes Henderson adds, "You see a problem and you say, 'This is what you need to do!' It's just built in. Everybody's got one."

nurturing intuition Intuition requires nurturing to become a productive component of the design process. The designer must respond to his or her immediate feelings and bursts of insight without worrying about the final outcome. It takes experience and practice to believe that instincts are valuable. Whereas rational thinking is powerful and reliable, intuitiveness is equally commanding. Relying solely on rational thinking sometimes results in repetitive solutions and stale, boring design. Trusting intuition encourages the designer to take chances—risk taking adds vitality to the design and a certain sense of the unexpected. The designer must react to intuitive sense and test it out through experimentation to see how it fits into and relates to the design problem, if at all.

Intuitiveness is cultivated in numerous ways. The designer must be careful not to analyze the suggestions of the inner voice before testing them out. It is useful to go through the process of experimentation, even if the insights seem impractical. Do not abandon or prejudge their worth. Reason will counter many gut reactions and stifle intuition. The designer must also continue fostering intuition through active involvement during the design process, as well as in activities and environments outside of design. Take periodic breaks to take your mind off the project. Try collecting thoughts verbally and visually. Actively seek out inspiration, which stimulates idea generation. Expect the unexpected and be open to anything. Ask questions and be informed. Always feed the subconscious to enhance its effectiveness. With experience, the designer learns to decipher the helpful insights from insignificant ones.

THE INNER VOICE, OR GUT REACTION, **INFORMS THE DESIGNER ABOUT WHAT WORKS** IN THE DEVELOPMENT OF COMPELLING AND EFFECTIVE LAYOUTS.

breaking the myths of intuition

Learned knowledge is enhanced by intuition.

Intuition need not be feared, doubted, or mistrusted.

Useful intuitive insights do not invalidate the design.

Intuition can positively inform the design process.

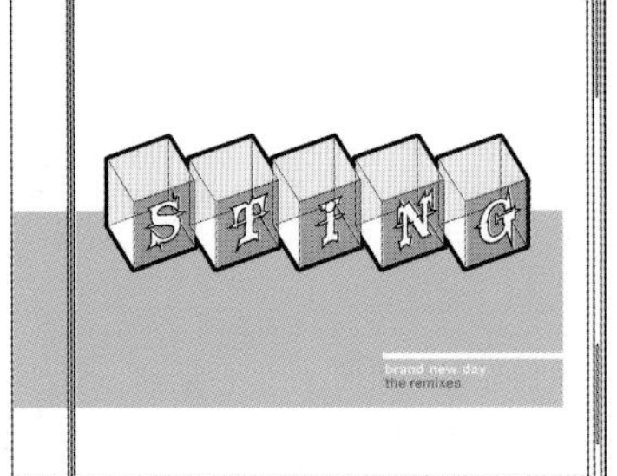

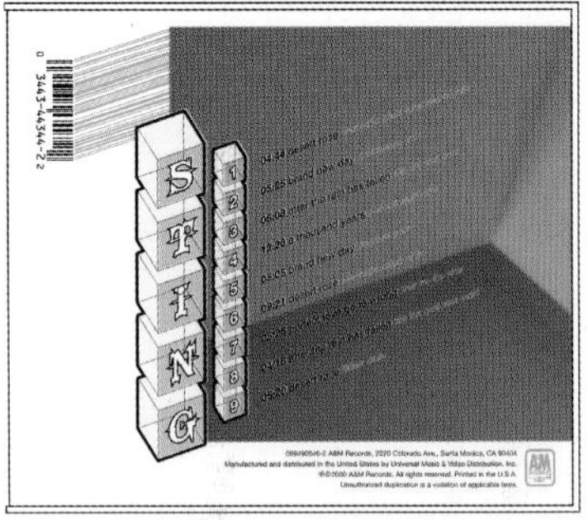

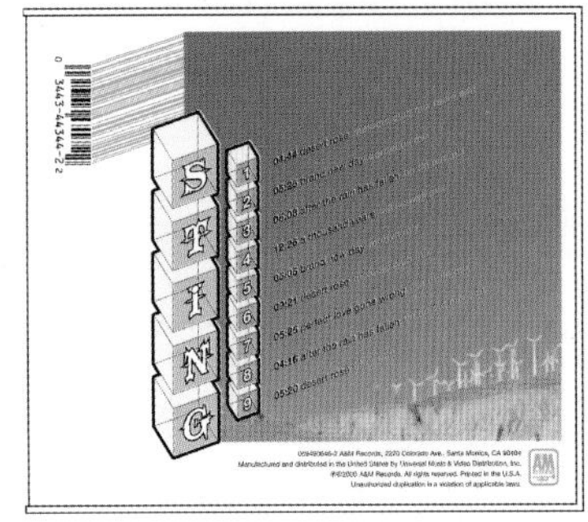

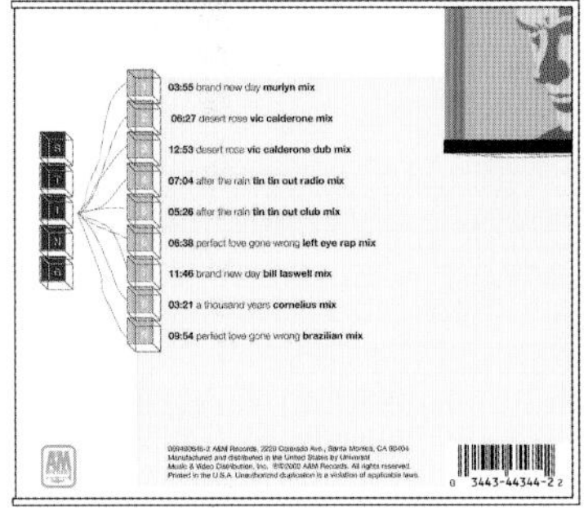

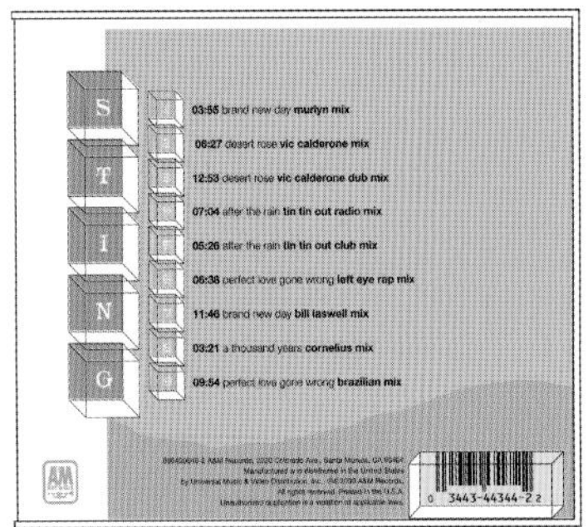

| **344 design, llc** | This set of variations and the final version (on the facing page), for Sting's *Brand New Day: The Remixes* demonstrate how intuition can ignite creativity and lead to an increase in the number of ideas generated. "Intuition is my design process," says designer Stefan Bucher.

nurturing intuition

Actively listen and react to the inner voice.

Do not be afraid to take risks.

Learn to trust feelings and insights.

Test intuitive thoughts to understand their value.

Expect the unexpected.

Do not overanalyze intuition.

Do not abandon or prejudge instinctive ideas.

Experiment.

Take periodic breaks when working on a project.

Be open minded.

Ask questions and be informed.

Record thoughts and collect visuals.

Seek out inspiration.

understanding the limits Although its advantages are great, intuition is not always useful or appropriate. The reliance on intuition does not negate a thorough design methodology of the project from inception to completion. Some insights are completely impractical and useless, with no effect on design development. Remember: Intuitiveness contributes to the design, but it does not determine its success or failure. The designer still needs to be fully aware of, and meet, the project objectives. He or she cannot refute constructive criticism because the design claims to be inspired by intuition. If the pragmatic focus is lost because of the influence of intuition, the design is purposeless and insights are ineffective.

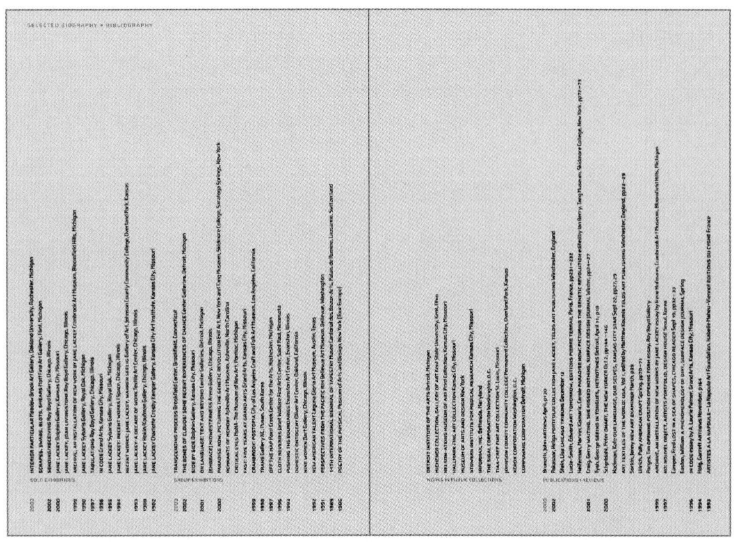

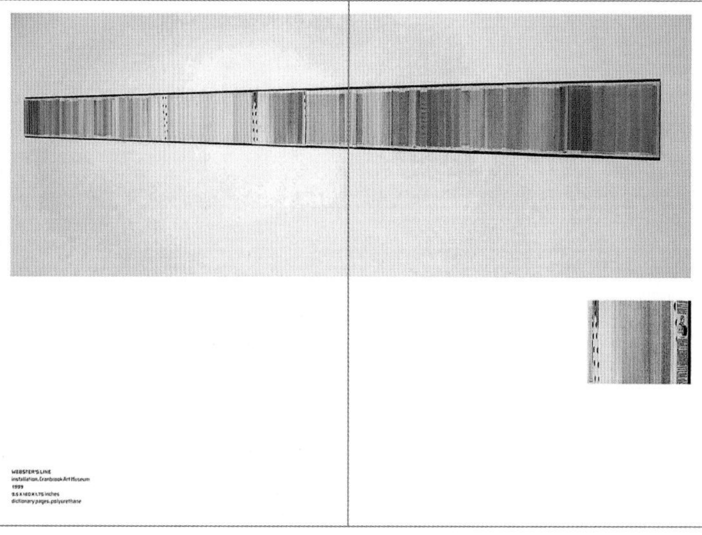

| **concrete [the office of jilly simons]** | Contemplating the design of *Interior Particular* [*Jane Lackey*], an exhibition catalog featuring Lackey's work, designer Jilly Simons explains, "Intuition usually plays a large role in many of my solutions. You may research and study, but, ultimately, the faculty of sensing beyond the use of rational processes often provides that which may not be evident."

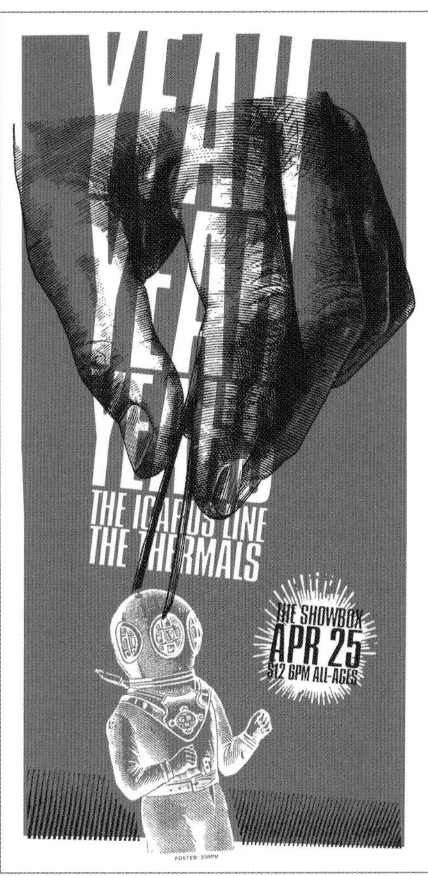

| **andrio abero** | Discussing the Yeah Yeah Yeahs poster, designer Andrio Abero states, "I thought about the concept more than I usually do with other posters, but my choices of imagery were intuitive, especially the hand and tweezers. Intuition is what makes my designs stand out. If it looks right and I feel it's strong enough, that's when I output the film to be printed. Intuition means being experimental. How else will your skills as a designer grow?"

FINAL THOUGHTS Intuition is the creative force that leads the designer by helping him or her make choices that affect the design process from conceptualization to execution. In combination with learned knowledge, intuition encourages solutions that can range from the ordinary to the unconventional. Incorporating intuition into the process allows the designer to tap into and investigate unknown depths of his or her abilities. Its value grows as the designer accepts, trusts, and follows his or her instincts time and again.

| **cavarpayar** | "In the design process, there are things that you think about rationally, those you learn about, and those you are looking for," says designer Lana Cavar. "And then, there is the most interesting part [of the process] you cannot be rational about. You just feel it for some strange reason. If you feel right, it will fit into the concept perfectly and make it more interesting and unique."

STRUCTURE AND

...human activity itself has
since the earliest times,
been distinguished by the quest for order.

JOSEF MÜLLER-BROCKMANN
author, graphic designer, teacher, typographer

ORGANIZATION

BUILDING FOUNDATIONS

The word *grid* is used to define the structural force behind the design. Grids are organizational tools that establish the active space of the page and help the designer make thoughtful decisions about composition and order. Grids enable the designer to maintain control, create visual connections, and unify the design.

grid systems in graphic design

Simply stated, grids are a series of intersecting axes that create horizontal and vertical divisions of space on the page. These intervals accommodate the placement of the visual elements, which, if positioned effectively, create movement across, down, within, and outside the surface of the page. The designer arranges the visual elements to interact, rather than conflict, establishing a pathway through the design that reveals dominant and subordinate levels of information. The designer is in complete control—visual elements are composed on gridded surfaces with assigned voices that, in combination with others (from whispers to shouts), are visually melodic.

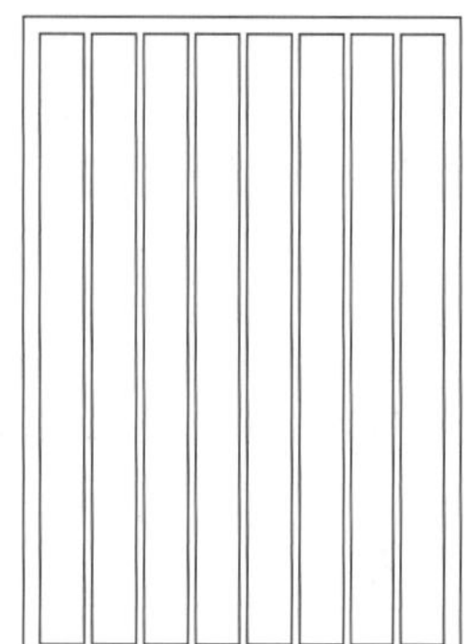

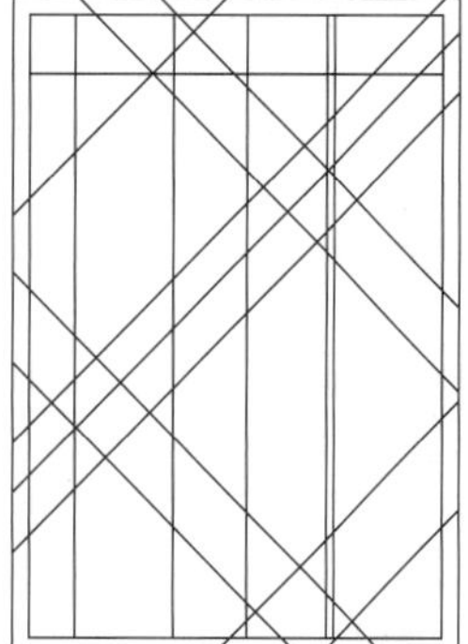

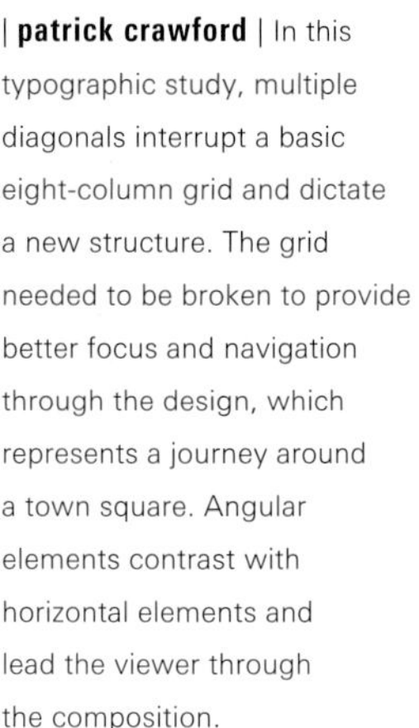

| **patrick crawford** | In this typographic study, multiple diagonals interrupt a basic eight-column grid and dictate a new structure. The grid needed to be broken to provide better focus and navigation through the design, which represents a journey around a town square. Angular elements contrast with horizontal elements and lead the viewer through the composition.

| **sumo** | The cover of the *Northern Film & Media Location Guide* combines beautiful imagery with an elegant type treatment. The physical shape of the booklet connotes environments, vistas, and landscapes, which is conceptually appropriate to the content that lies inside.

Grids vary in size and shape from simple to complex, depending on the range and amount of information that must be incorporated into the design. Always developed with the content in mind, grids are reinvented with every project. They are modeled after structures and systems of proportion found in architecture, fine art, mathematics, music, and nature; grids are also informed by the instinct of the designer. Theorized throughout history by the likes of Pythagoras, Vitruvius, Michelangelo, Leonardo da Vinci, and Le Corbusier, common systems of proportion include the Fibonacci sequence, the golden section, and modular scales. Whether mathematical or intuitive, grids are devoted to cohesion and harmony.

Falsely seen as restrictive, grids allow diverse visual elements to coexist. Visual elements are mutually dependent on their relationship to each other to communicate comprehensive messages. Flexibility is inherent in grids, providing unlimited creative opportunities for the designer. Remember, grids do not dictate the design or its outcome. They work with, rather than against, the intentions of the designer. The designer uses, adapts, breaks, and abandons grids for the benefit of the design. The skilled and experienced designer composes the visual elements gracefully or clumsily and determines if the design is active or static, compelling or boring, communicative or uninformative.

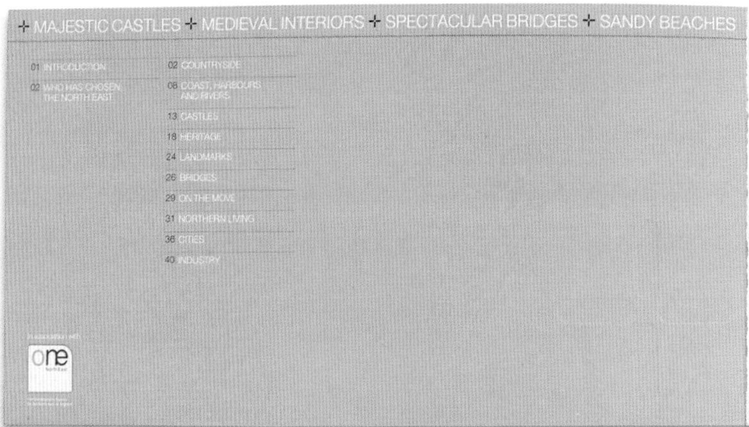

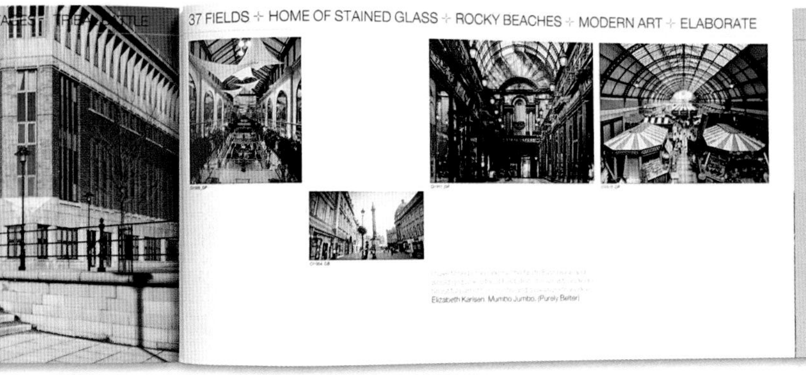

| **sumo** | An interior spread demonstrates the flexibility of multiple-column grids. Imagery changes in scale and position along the vertical alignment points to provide contrast, rhythm, and variation in the design.

| **sumo** | The structure of the design is introduced on the first spread. Dividing the page into multiple columns enables a systematic arrangement of the visual elements. Although the horizontal flow of the spread is flexible to accommodate text and imagery of variable widths, the starting point of all elements consistently begins from the top margin.

the anatomy of grids

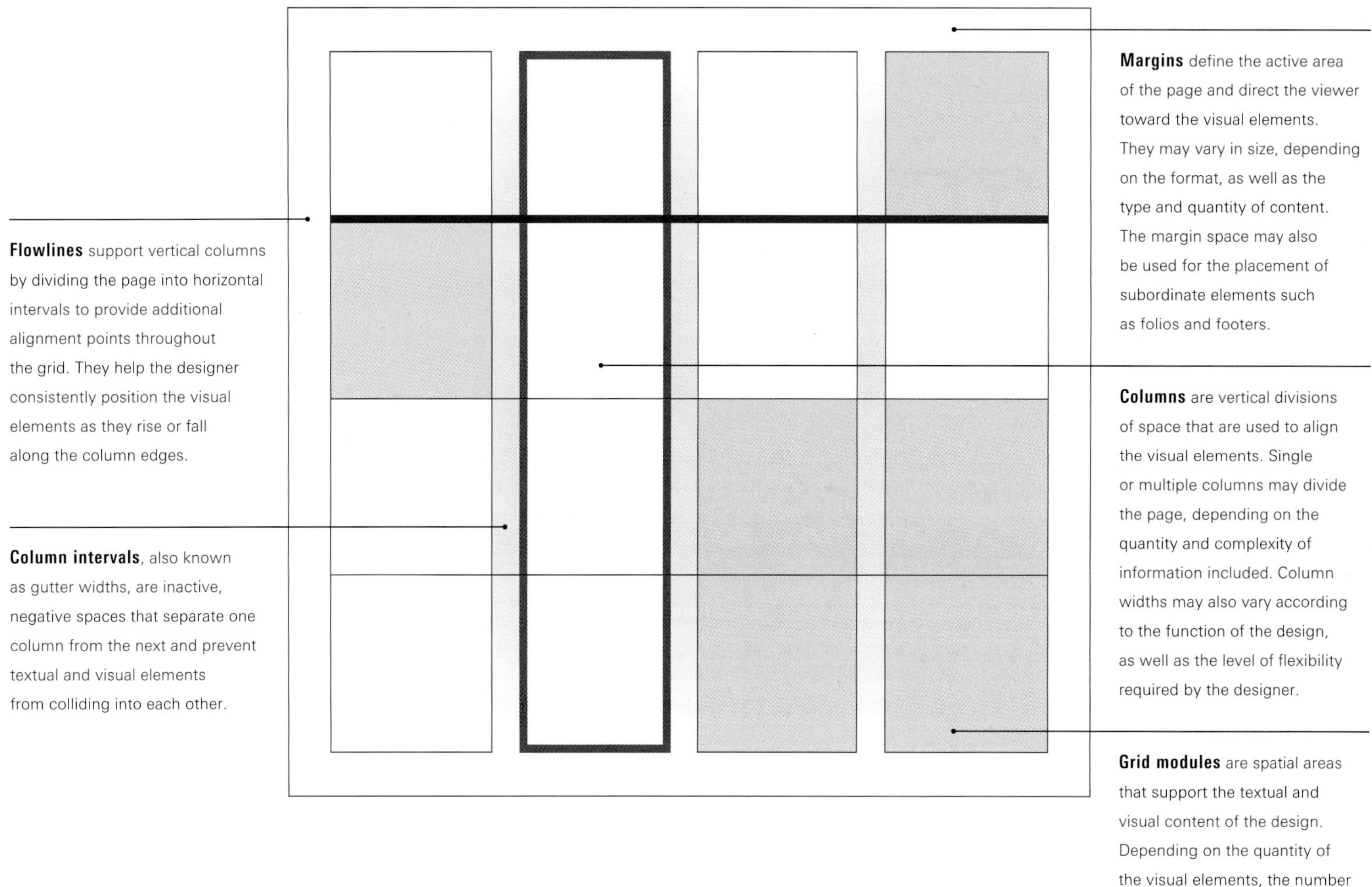

Margins define the active area of the page and direct the viewer toward the visual elements. They may vary in size, depending on the format, as well as the type and quantity of content. The margin space may also be used for the placement of subordinate elements such as folios and footers.

Flowlines support vertical columns by dividing the page into horizontal intervals to provide additional alignment points throughout the grid. They help the designer consistently position the visual elements as they rise or fall along the column edges.

Columns are vertical divisions of space that are used to align the visual elements. Single or multiple columns may divide the page, depending on the quantity and complexity of information included. Column widths may also vary according to the function of the design, as well as the level of flexibility required by the designer.

Column intervals, also known as gutter widths, are inactive, negative spaces that separate one column from the next and prevent textual and visual elements from colliding into each other.

Grid modules are spatial areas that support the textual and visual content of the design. Depending on the quantity of the visual elements, the number of active modules may vary from one design to the next.

Smaller margins increase the active area of the composition. They are useful when working with multiple-column or modular grids, which accommodate complex designs with a variety of visual elements.

Larger margins decrease the active space of the page but increase the amount of negative space. Ample margins provide a stable composition and direct the viewer toward the positive areas of the design, while also leaving finger room to hold the piece.

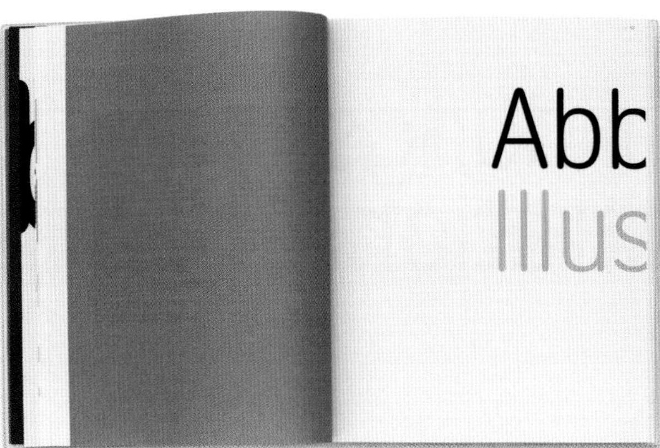

| **lichtwitz** | In this catalog design, margins are broken to allow typography to move off the page. The implied movement expands the visual environment outside the surface of the page and provides sequential flow from one page to the next.

margins define the active area of the compositional space and direct the viewer toward the visual elements. Margins can vary in size, depending on the format of the page, as well as the textual and visual content of the design. Left and right, as well as top and bottom, margins can be equal all around or larger and smaller, depending on the proportions of the page. On double-page spreads, the inside margins must be large enough so that nothing is lost in the gutter. In addition, the margin space can be used for the placement of subordinate elements, including folios and footers.

Smaller margins increase the usable surface area of the composition, which accommodates complex designs with various visual elements. For example, in this book, small left- and right-side margins extend the active space of the page to support considerable amounts of textual and visual content on each spread. (Multiple columns divide the compositional space.) Larger margins decrease the active space of the page but increase the amount of white space, creating an open visual environment that is approachable, inviting, and soothing. For example, books of continuous text without extensive visuals benefit from large margins. Ample margins provide a stable compositional space that directs the viewer toward the positive areas of the design, while also leaving finger room to hold the piece.

Margins are not intended to trap the visual elements within the compositional space; they are used to activate the positive areas of the design. In many cases, the outer margins can be broken to allow the visual elements to move off the page. The implied movement expands the visual environment outside of the composition.

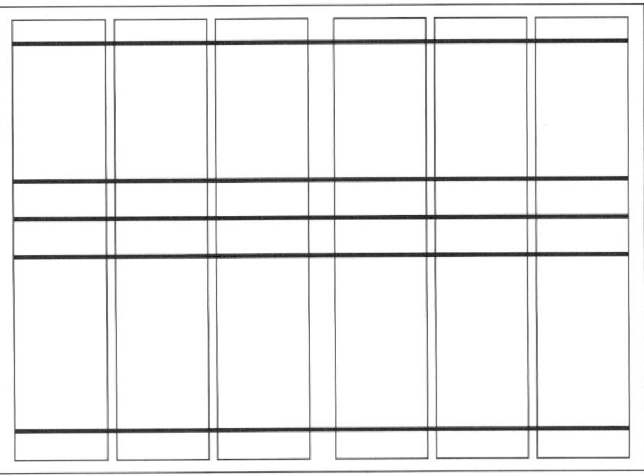

columns are vertical divisions of space used to align the visual elements. Single or multiple columns can divide the page, depending on the quantity of textual and visual information. Columns can also be distributed evenly across the page. In other cases, column widths can vary according to the specific content and function of the design, as well as the amount of desired compositional flexibility. It is a general rule that more columns, or spatial divisions, foster additional flexibility for the arrangement of the visual elements.

column intervals are the spatial divisions that reside between columns. They are much smaller in width than columns and prevent collisions of textual and visual information by providing an inactive negative space that separates one column from the next. Column intervals are critical when the visual elements juxtapose in the same position from column to column. For example, if continuous text is broken into side-by-side columns, the column interval prevents the viewer from moving from the line of one paragraph into the line of the paragraph next to it.

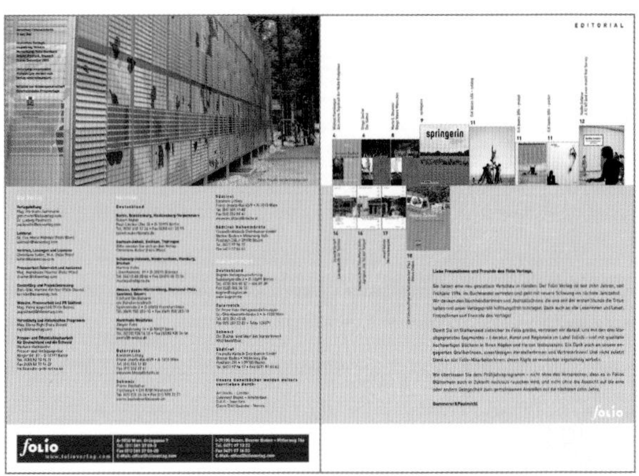

| **no.parking** | A three-column grid accommodates a range of text. The simple structure also includes three central flowlines, as well as one at the top and bottom, which provide alignment points for the composition of text, graphic shapes, and imagery. Column intervals provide breathing room between juxtaposed columns of continuous text.

flowlines divide the page into horizontal spatial divisions and create additional alignment points for the placement of the visual elements. They are guides that help the designer establish consistent alignment across and down the page. Flowlines dictate the horizontal positions of visual elements and how they rise or fall along the column edges.

grid modules are spatial fields that accommodate the placement of the visual elements. The designer can assign specific modules for textual content and imagery and apply this system throughout the design. Doing so creates consistency because the viewer can expect to see similar information positioned in the same grid modules. When assigning grid modules, be careful to prevent monotony. Although repeating the position of visual elements helps maintain consistency, it can also diminish the rhythmic, active sequence of the design. The designer can also choose to work more loosely and vary the position of the textual and visual content that appears in the grid modules intentionally. This increases the harmony, rhythm, and tension of the design and eliminates ineffective repetition and predictability.

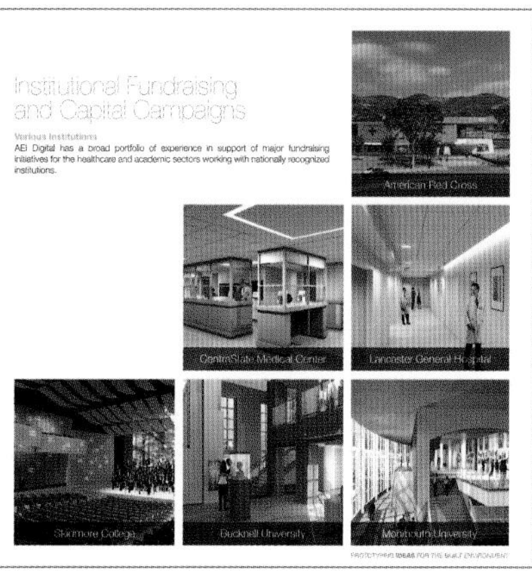

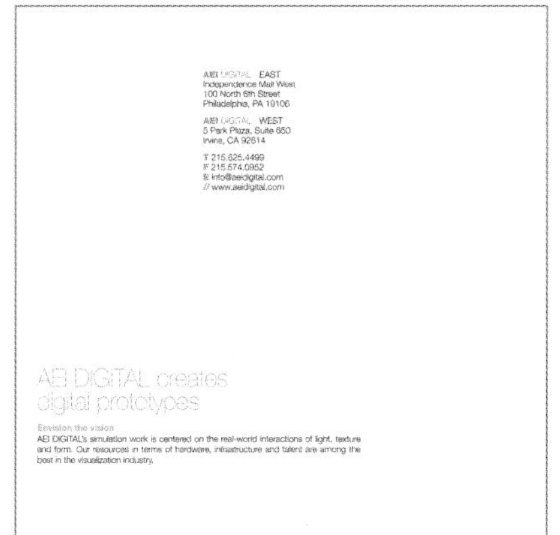

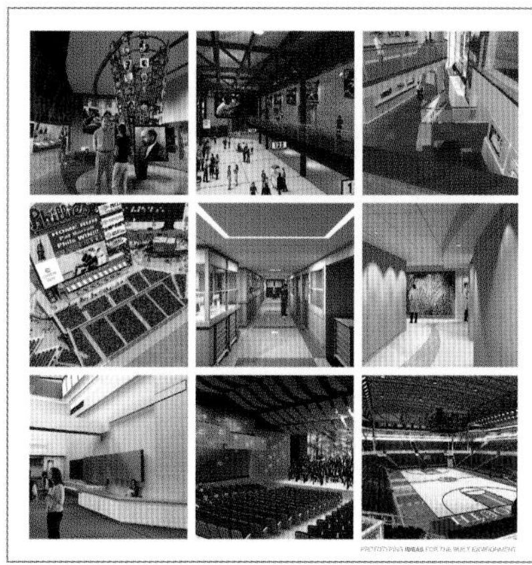

| gravica design/talisman interactive |

Modular grids can accommodate a range of visual elements. In this example, the grid, which is divided into nine square modules, is evident. The designer has chosen to crop imagery based on the module proportion, and the text spans the length of two units. The type size has been adjusted appropriately to fit the measure without sacrificing readability.

working with basic grids

development and application A well-planned foundation is an imperative starting point in the development of the design. A number of grid options are available to the designer, but they all serve the same primary function. Grids allow the designer to intelligently control and organize the compositional space and orchestrate the visual elements dynamically, rhythmically, and harmoniously in relationship to each other. Spatial connections are established that direct the eye toward positive space and effectively lead the viewer through the composition.

The goal of working with grids is to order and unify the compositional space; the underlying structure should be apparent without actually being seen. The designer must compose the visual elements to balance and contrast the shape of the page, while also providing the viewer with a clear sense of direction and movement through the design. The designer encourages viewer interaction and readability through dynamic visual compositions. It is important to experiment with grids with a playful sensibility, but use them wisely.

| wilsonharvey/loewy |

This pocket-size travel guide demonstrates the use of a four-column grid. Small margins increase the active area for the composition of the visual elements. Elements can fit comfortably into one column measure or run across the entire page.

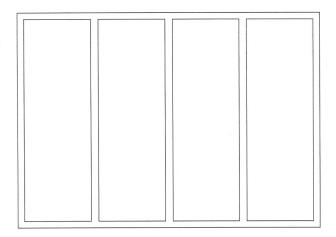

Grid proportions and spatial relationships are determined by the page format, as well as the complexity of the visual elements. Grids should be tailored to accommodate specific visual elements. If grids are arbitrarily developed without consideration of the textual and visual content, the designer will encounter difficulties. Arbitrary grids can become too dictatorial or loose, force thoughtless decisions, or provide too few or too many spatial divisions to accommodate all the necessary content. Without clear focus and development, grids will limit the designer, instead of providing the foundation to construct an effective, meaningful design.

the functions of grids

control

organization

rhythm

harmony

unity

dynamism

readability

movement

balance

direction

contrast

interaction

order

We coined the curious word "Retrospectacle" to describe an exhibition that celebrates the Denver Art Museum's decision, twenty-five years ago, to build a department and collection of modern and contemporary art. That collection now numbers more than 5,000 works of art–photographs, paintings, sculptures, installations, and media works by artists from all over the world–that range in date from the late 1900s to this year. Of special note are the 213 works recently given as a promised and fractional gift from Vicki and Kent Logan.

The richness of the collection is almost entirely due to the many artists, donors, and supporters who over the years have shared their special interests with us, either by providing us with funds to acquire what we needed, or more often, by giving us works directly from their studios or collections. A perpetual lack of funds has made it difficult for us to pursue specific goals, but in retrospect, our ability to respond to serendipitous opportunities has added more range to the collection than any of the numerous acquisition plans we conceived.

I initially set out to collect examples of each major movement in art since 1945, the year historically used to mark the beginning of contemporary art–a goal that now seems incredibly naive in a world where technology, international borders, and ideas about art and life change with equal speed. Here's a bit of history to put it all in context. When I arrived in 1978, Denver–in fact all of Colorado–was headed for one of the worst recessions in its boom-and-bust history. Jimmy Carter was President, the Shah of Iran still reigned, and Menachem Begin and Anwar el-Sadat shared the Nobel Peace Prize. AIDS had not been identified, and there was no indication that communism would collapse in a mere eleven years. Computers were still clunky, unaffordable novelties few individuals had ever used, and digitized photography was decades away.

| aufuldish & warinner |

Yellow fields are used to reinforce the structure and call attention to the text within, which is composed throughout the design in columns of varying width. The graphic shapes define the margins, as well as the columns and column intervals, which are easily detected. The flexible grid adds variety and rhythm from page to page.

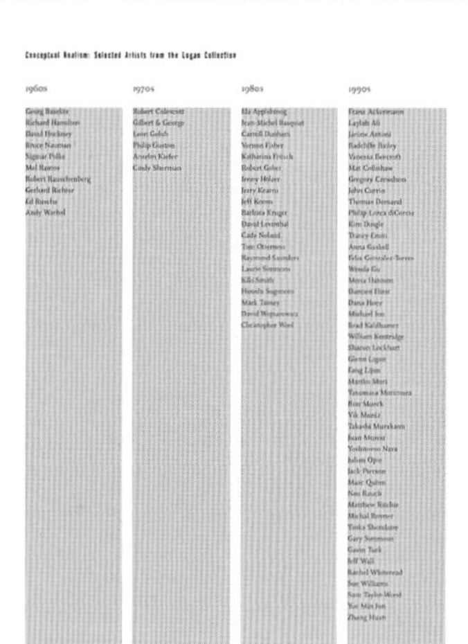

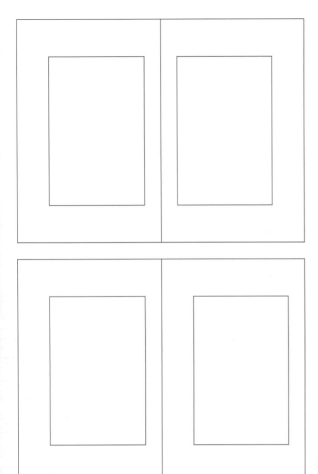

A 2:3 classical page proportion for a single-column grid is appropriate for large amounts of continuous text. When working with one column, determining the ideal typeface, size, line length, and leading is imperative. Traditionally, the columns mirror each other to create a balanced, symmetrical presentation. An alternative is to repeat the column position on the facing page to create asymmetry and provide a contemporary feel.

single-column grids are basic structural systems. They provide a simple compositional framework suitable for presenting large amounts of body text, also called continuous text. The space of the page is defined by the margins, which divide the active area into one column. For example, a classical approach is common. Classical margins are large on the sides and bottom and smaller at the top. The inner margin is typically half the size of the outer margin. In addition, the positions of the columns on the spread are mirrored. The column can also be repeated on the facing page in the same position to create an asymmetric composition.

Margins are a key consideration of single-column grids and need adjustment to improve the appearance of the visual elements, especially the text. The single column should not be too wide or narrow and must accommodate an ideal line length for readability. The combination of typeface selection, size, and leading must be carefully considered and tested to achieve optimal results.

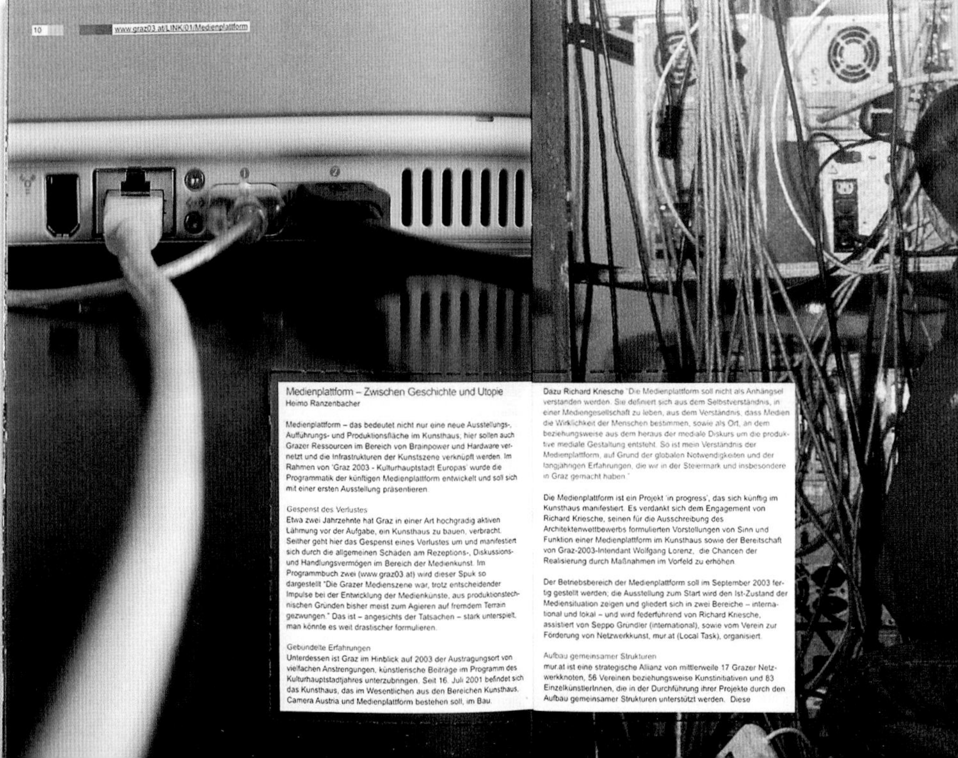

Medienplattform – Zwischen Geschichte und Utopie
Heimo Ranzenbacher

Medienplattform – das bedeutet nicht nur eine neue Ausstellungs-, Aufführungs- und Produktionsfläche im Kunsthaus; hier sollen auch Grazer Ressourcen im Bereich von Brainpower und Hardware vernetzt und die Infrastrukturen der Kunstszene verknüpft werden. Im Rahmen von 'Graz 2003 - Kulturhauptstadt Europas' wurde die Programmatik der künftigen Medienplattform entwickelt und soll sich mit einer ersten Ausstellung präsentieren.

Gespenst des Verlustes
Etwa zwei Jahrzehnte hat Graz in einer Art hochgradig aktiven Lähmung vor der Aufgabe, ein Kunsthaus zu bauen, verbracht. Seither geht hier das Gespenst eines Verlustes um und manifestiert sich durch die allgemeinen Schäden am Rezeptions-, Diskussions- und Handlungsvermögen im Bereich der Medienkunst. Im Programmbuch zwei (www.graz03.at) wird dieser Spuk so dargestellt "Die Grazer Medienszene war, trotz entscheidender Impulse bei der Entwicklung der Medienkünste, aus produktionstechnischen Gründen bisher meist zum Agieren auf fremdem Terrain gezwungen." Das ist – angesichts der Tatsachen – stark unterspielt, man könnte es weit drastischer formulieren.

Gebundelte Erfahrungen
Unterdessen ist Graz im Hinblick auf 2003 der Austragungsort von vielfachen Anstrengungen, künstlerische Beiträge im Programm des Kulturhauptstadtjahres unterzubringen. Seit 16. Juli 2001 befindet sich das Kunsthaus, das im Wesentlichen aus den Bereichen Kunsthaus, Camera Austria und Medienplattform bestehen soll, im Bau.

Dazu Richard Kriesche "Die Medienplattform soll nicht als Anhängsel verstanden werden. Sie definiert sich aus dem Selbstverständnis, in einer Mediengesellschaft zu leben, aus dem Verständnis, dass Medien die Wirklichkeit der Menschen bestimmen, sowie als Ort, an dem beziehungsweise aus dem heraus der mediale Diskurs um die produktive mediale Gestaltung entsteht. So ist mein Verständnis der Medienplattform, auf Grund der globalen Notwendigkeiten und der langjährigen Erfahrungen, die wir in der Steiermark und insbesondere in Graz gemacht haben."

Die Medienplattform ist ein Projekt 'in progress', das sich künftig im Kunsthaus manifestiert. Es verdankt sich dem Engagement von Richard Kriesche, seinen für die Ausschreibung des Architektenwettbewerbs formulierten Vorstellungen von Sinn und Funktion einer Medienplattform im Kunsthaus sowie der Bereitschaft von Graz-2003-Intendant Wolfgang Lorenz, die Chancen der Realisierung durch Maßnahmen im Vorfeld zu erhöhen.

Der Betriebsbereich der Medienplattform soll im September 2003 fertig gestellt werden; die Ausstellung zum Start wird den Ist-Zustand der Mediensituation zeigen und gliedert sich in zwei Bereiche – international und lokal – und wird federführend von Richard Kriesche, assistiert von Seppo Gründler (international), sowie vom Verein zur Förderung von Netzwerkkunst, mur.at (Local Task), organisiert.

Aufbau gemeinsamer Strukturen
mur.at ist eine strategische Allianz von mittlerweile 17 Grazer Netzwerkknoten, 56 Vereinen beziehungsweise Kunstinitiativen und 83 EinzelkünstlerInnen, die in der Durchführung ihrer Projekte durch den Aufbau gemeinsamer Strukturen unterstützt werden. Diese

Das geheime Tagebuch der Anaïs Nin
Monika Wogrolly

1. August 1933
Mein Mann Hugo denkt, ich halte mich in Paris auf. Doch ich habe beschlossen, mir eine Zeit abseits dessen zu gönnen, was mich am Leben erhält, abseits meiner Lieben. Ich verdinge mich in einer Bar in Graz als Tänzerin. Niemand weiß, dass ich hier bin, nicht einmal Vater. Auch Henry Miller ahnt nichts. Ich schreibe keine Briefe, nur parallel zueinander zwei Tagebücher. Ein offizielles, in dem ich in Paris bin, das ich für Hugo und Henry bestimmt habe, und ein intimes Tagebuch über Graz. Als ich zuletzt in New York und Paris war, wurde ich gleichermaßen von Eduardo, Hugo, Henry, meinem Analytiker Allendy und Otto Rank belagert. Manchmal besuchten sie mich unmittelbar nacheinander.

Die Lügengeschichten, die ich jedem von ihnen auftischte, kosteten mich immer mehr Mühe. Oft widersprach ich mir und blickte in vergrämte und entsetzte Gesichter. Oder ich brachte keine Lust, kein Feuer mehr zustande, und das Hotelzimmer, in dem ich Allendy mit der Peitsche traf, wurde zum Schauplatz meines Spotts über die Männer. Ich fühlte, dass es an der Zeit zum Rückzug war. Ich wollte wieder zu mir kommen und durchsuchte den Weltatlas nach einem Ort, an dem mich niemand vermutete.

Ich schloss die Augen, machte ein Spiel daraus und tippte mit dem Finger irgendwohin. Als ich die Augen aufschlug, hätte ich nach Tahiti reisen müssen. Beim zweiten Versuch traf mein Finger auf eine Stadt in Österreich. Ich überlegte nicht lang. Und da ich ein Stadtmensch bin, beschloss ich, mich nach Graz zu begeben. Ich liebe es, über den Hauptplatz zu promenieren und die Menschen zu beobachten. Die Stadt erinnert mich an Italien und hat Aspekte vieler Orte, an denen ich war. Die Leute beobachten mich, ich gefalle ihnen. Fast alle hier malen, schreiben oder sind einer anderen Kunstrichtung hingegeben. Alle hier träumen von Ruhm und davon, eines Tages eine Büste im Stadtpark zu sein.

2. August
Mir begegnete vor einiger Zeit ein Pärchen, das mich an Henry und June erinnert. Vor allem die Frau nimmt mich für sich ein. Einmal baten sie mich, ihnen beim Sex zuzusehen, und ich erfüllte diesen Wunsch. Sie lieben ausgefallene Plätze. Ich fantasiere oft – und es erregt mich –, dass in fünfzig oder hundert Jahren arglose Einwohner der Stadt auf diesen Parkbänken und an den Stellen in Graz sitzen werden, wo unser Glück stattfindet. Heute waren wir bei prächtigem Wetter auf dem Schloßberg. Ich lag mit M. im Gras, während S. uns zusah. Die Stadtparkwiese ist auch ein beliebtes Ziel.

Mein Schamgefühl dem Tagebuch gegenüber wächst ins Groteske. Ich weiß nicht, warum, aber gewisse Intimsphären möchte ich mir erhalten. Das hat mich diese Stadt gelehrt. Denn einesteils erscheint sie mir wie ein offenes Buch, erscheint einladend und will alles von sich preisgeben. Andernteils bleibt Graz ein Geheimnis. Es ist die Alltagsstimmung, die mich trägt und entführt. Es sind die trüben Tage, die sich abwechseln mit heiteren. Ich werde mir einen Verlag suchen und eine Möglichkeit, von hier aus Briefe zu versenden, ohne erkennen zu geben, wo ich bin. Niemand soll wissen, dass ich hier war.

[mehr unter dem Link]

28 www.graz03.at/LINK/03/Reportage/GrenzenImNeuenEuropa

Grenzlandwanderung
Mit anderen Mitteln hat die weltbekannte Fotografin Inge Morath die südsteirische Grenze überwunden. "Grenz Räume" heißt das Projekt, das sie gemeinsam mit Christine Frisinghelli und Regina Strassegger entwickelt hat, dessen Fertigstellung sie aber nicht mehr erleben durfte. Inge Moraths Heimat war das südsteirisch-slowenische Grenzland und gerade im Jahr 2003 wäre die Fotokünstlerin 80 Jahre alt geworden. Nun ist sie im Jänner dieses Jahres 78-jährig in New York gestorben.

So wird das Projekt zum Nachruf auf eine Österreicherin von Weltrang, die – wie so viele ihrer Generation – erst jenseits des Atlantiks werden konnte, was sie war. Regina Strassegger hat eine Grenzland-Wanderung als Zeitreise aufgezeichnet, in der Inge Morath das Bindeglied ist. Damit haben die Vorarbeiten für das Kulturhauptstadtjahr 2003 immerhin eine Heimholung noch bei Lebzeiten zustande gebracht. Wesentliche Stationen waren Slovenje-Gradec/Windisch-Graz – Herkunft der Morath'schen Ur- und Großeltern in der ehemaligen Untersteiermark; dann die Jahre traumatischer Grenzerfahrungen der beiden Weltkriege, Vertreibung, Faschismus, Kommunismus; schließlich die Gegenwart – eine Region wächst wieder zusammen, feiert ab und zu wieder gemeinsame Feste, treibt Handel. Uralt-Ängste der Nachbarn werden langsam Vergangenheit. Im Mittelpunkt des Projekts steht ein 60-Minuten-Film, der zum Glück bereits abgedreht ist. Parallel dazu wird eine umfassende Ausstellung der Morath-Grenzland-Fotografie vorbereitet. Sie geht nach ihrer Premiere in Graz (Camera Austria im Kunsthaus) auf eine internationale Tournee, u. a. nach New York, Budapest und Slovenje-Gradec. Geplant sind zudem ein Buch und ein Kalender.

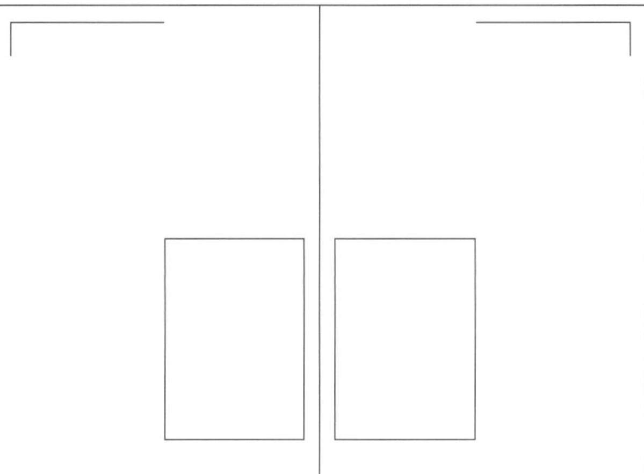

| **lichtwitz** | Open margins are spacious and direct the eye to the text, which is pushed toward the center and bottom of the page. The margins foster dramatic tension used effectively in the symmetrical composition.

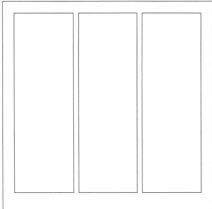

Multiple-column grids are divided into several intervals. Columns increase flexibility and provide unlimited compositional options. Complex projects, which require the interaction of diverse visual elements, are perfect candidates for multiple-column grids.

multiple-column grids contain several spatial intervals that provide endless compositional options. They are flexible and accommodate a range of visual elements. Multiple-column grids are suitable for complex projects, including books, magazines, and publications that contain diverse content. The quantity of textual and visual content, as well as the page format, will help determine the ideal number of intervals.

Multiple-column grids provide opportunities to create rhythm, drama, movement, and tension through the interaction of visual elements. For example, textual and visual elements can reside in several columns, span the page, overlap other elements, rest on fields of color or texture, or run off the page. Scale, orientation, and position variations promote hierarchy and contrast in multiple-column grids. However, be cautious—too many divisions of space and activity can lead to confusion and disorder.

PART OF A LARGER WHOLE

Students Document Historic Buildings in Illinois Communities

there is a better stock of historic buildings in our smaller communities than in our bigger cities"

Prior Case Study Helps Community Preserve Landmark

| **renate gokl** | In this newsletter, a multiple-column grid is used effectively and dynamically. The structure is evident and reinforced through linear elements and graphic shapes that align along column edges and connect the visual elements. The use of white space is also proficient, whereas changes in the scale of imagery, typography, and line length provide depth and rhythm.

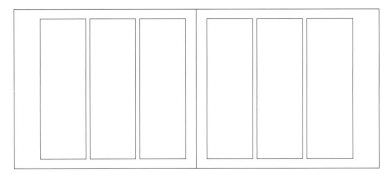

| visocky o'grady | A three-column grid defines the structure of this annual report. The simple system is accessible and provides a clear presentation of information. Body text fits into the one-column measures, whereas larger headline text spans the width of two columns. Generous left and right margins provide ample finger room to hold the piece.

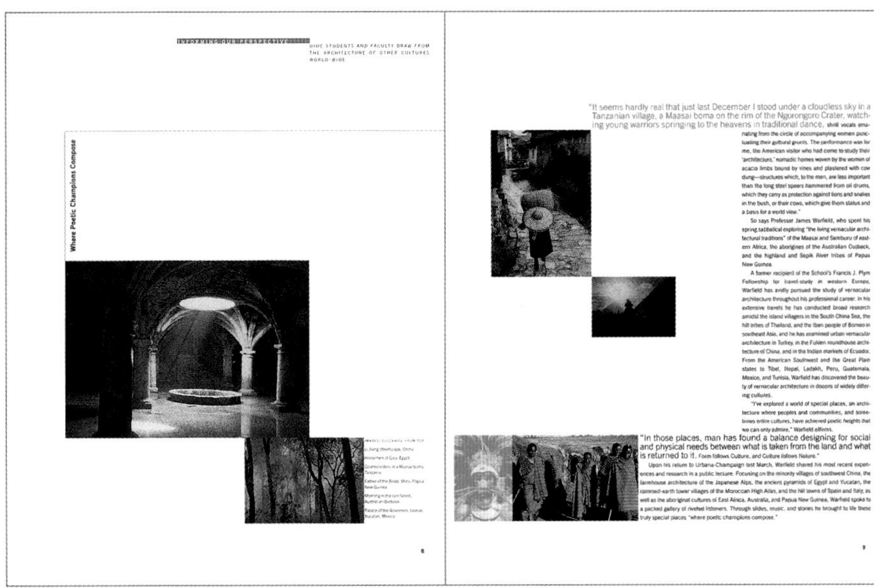

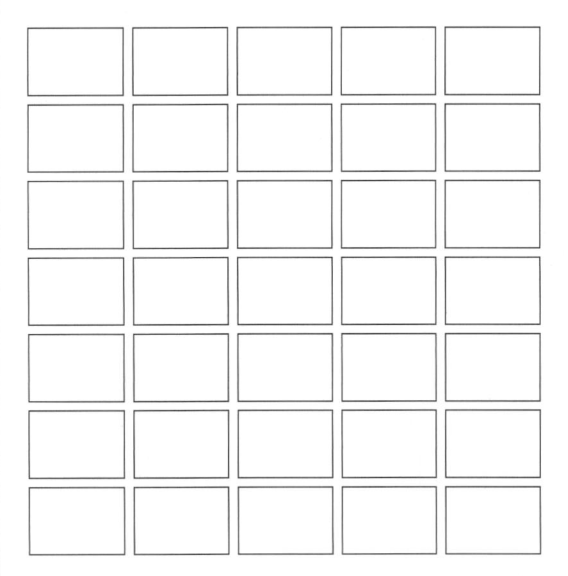

Modular grids divide the page into horizontal and vertical spatial units called modules, which are active areas of the composition that accommodate the visual elements. The designer gains flexibility as the number of modules increases.

modular grids are an extension of multiple-column grids with the addition of horizontal flowlines that divide the page into spatial units or modules. Modules are the active areas of the page that accommodate the visual elements. Because the number and size of the spatial units is dictated by the content, the designer must assess the amount of text and imagery to determine the appropriate module shape. For example, the size of a module could be determined by the ideal width, or line length, of the body copy (it can span multiple modules), as well as the smallest size of a photograph or illustration.

Like multiple-column grids, modular grids increase compositional flexibility and are also suitable for publications, including magazines and newspapers. It is often the case that modular grids are components of extensive visual language systems, which means that the grid is applied to multiple pieces over time. The grid must be flexible enough to accommodate changing content while maintaining the ability to be understood and easily adapted by several designers.

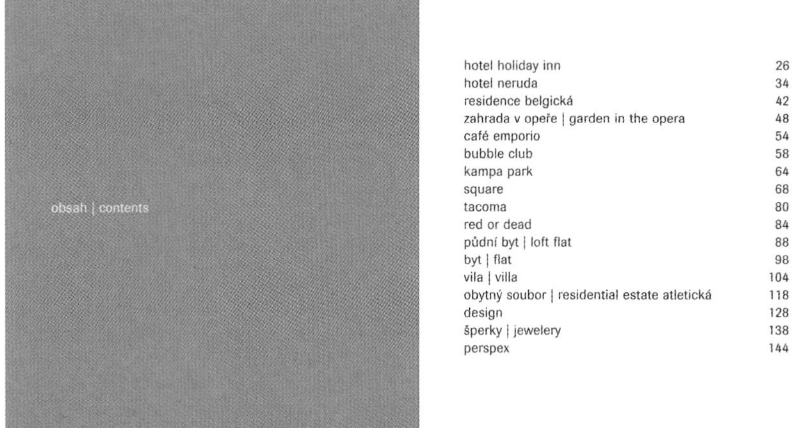

obsah | contents

hotel holiday inn 26
hotel neruda 34
residence belgická 42
zahrada v opeře | garden in the opera 48
café emporio 54
bubble club 58
kampa park 64
square 68
tacoma 80
red or dead 84
půdní byt | loft flat 88
byt | flat 98
vila | villa 104
obytný soubor | residential estate atletická 118
design 128
šperky | jewelery 138
perspex 144

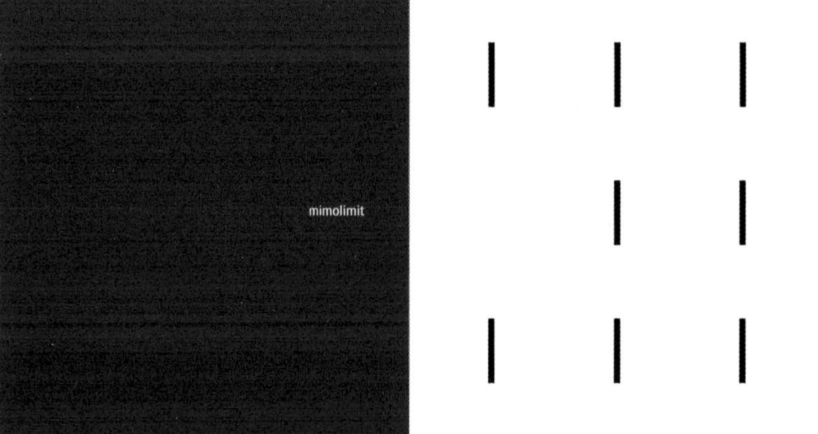

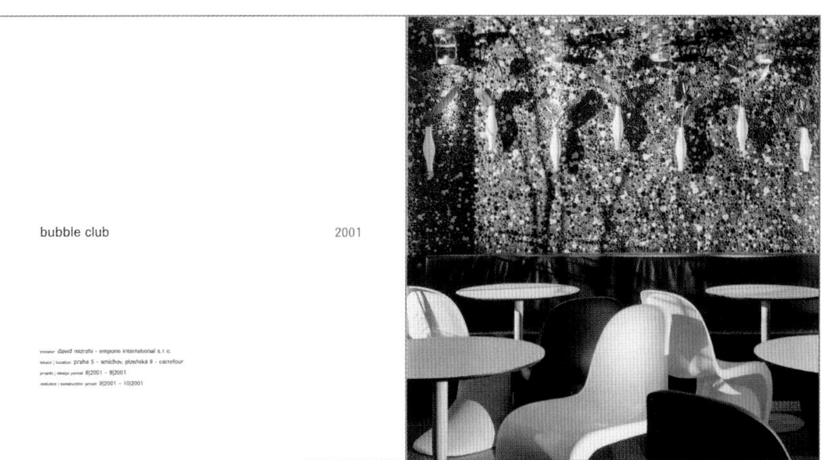

bubble club 2001

| studio najbrt | A minimal design is supported by a simple structure. The limited amount of content is suited to a nine-unit modular grid. Modular grids offer consistency for the placement of visual elements. For example, the dominant typographic content falls from the top of the second set of horizontal modules, whereas the subordinate text hangs from the third.

visual balance

No grid (or rules) are absolute. There are numerous paths that lead to appropriate, dynamic, and effective visual solutions. Grids provide the basis, as well as innumerable options, to construct strong layouts. Although grids provide the foundation to build the design, the designer must recognize that grids are symmetrical and are visually static. Because grids are constructed by dividing a space equally, the result is a symmetrical division of space. By its very nature, symmetry generates a balance of identical parts.

symmetry There are a variety of symmetry operations. The most common symmetry operations are bilateral and radial. Bilateral symmetry is a mirror reflection along a central axis and radial symmetry is an arrangement of uniform parts around a central axis. This results in a proportional system of one-to-one relationships or a 1:1 ratio. The principle of proportion may be stated as the comparative relationship of one surface area to another surface area.

breaking the grid Control the composition using the grid as a guide. As such, the designer must break the grid in small or large proportional increments for the benefit of visual contrast in scale. The term "breaking the grid" may be misinterpreted as purposefully abandoning the regular uniform divisions of the image area. In fact, the underlying uniform grid structure provides the framework to divide the space proportionally along axes generated by the uniform grid resulting in dynamic symmetry. However, if the grid is broken too often, it may indicate that too many variables have been applied resulting in visual clutter. Dynamic symmetry promotes visual balance by using a uniform grid to create large and small units of a system. Exercising restraint by controlling the numerous variables is a manifestation of the designer's intelligent hand.

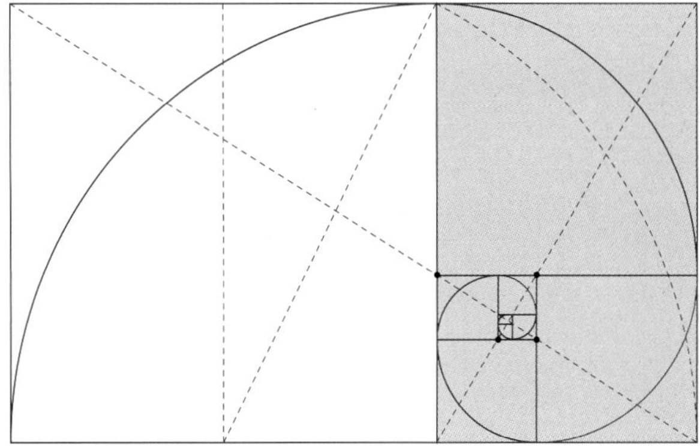

the golden section

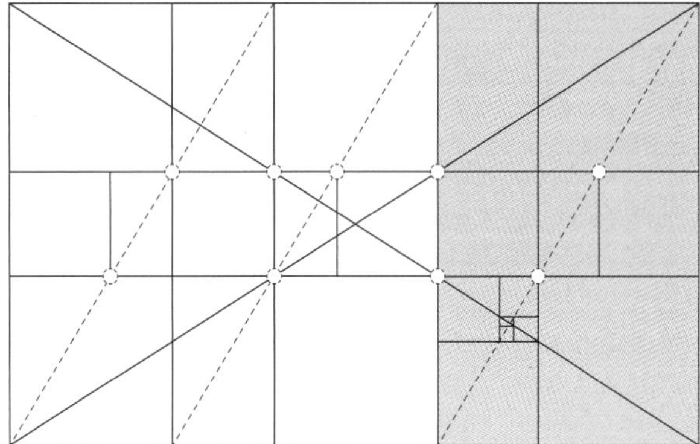

modular division of the divine proportion

dynamic symmetry embodies visual balance in an orderly system of proportion. By contrasting small and large parts, visual balance is achieved through harmonious divisions of space. Systems of proportion have been incorporated in the visual arts since the 5th century. The golden section is found in the architecture and artifacts of the century. The Fibonacci numerical sequence is also known as the divine proportion, found in the architecture and artifacts of the Renaissance. The numerical sequence of the Fibonacci Sequence is [1,1, 2, 3, 5, 8, 13, 21]. Remarkably, the golden section and the divine proportion both share the same proportional division of space (1:1.6). Expressed literally, the ratio reads: *the lesser part is to the greater part as the greater part is to the whole surface area*. Even now, this proportional system may be found in images, icons, page layout, and interface design.

The rule of thirds is commonly found in the grid of the camera viewing area. The nine parts form rectangles approximately similar to the divine proportion.

Practicing in thirteenth-century France, Villard de Honnecourt devised page proportions, margins, and type areas based upon the Van de Graaf Canon—a methodology of geometry and harmony in medieval book design.

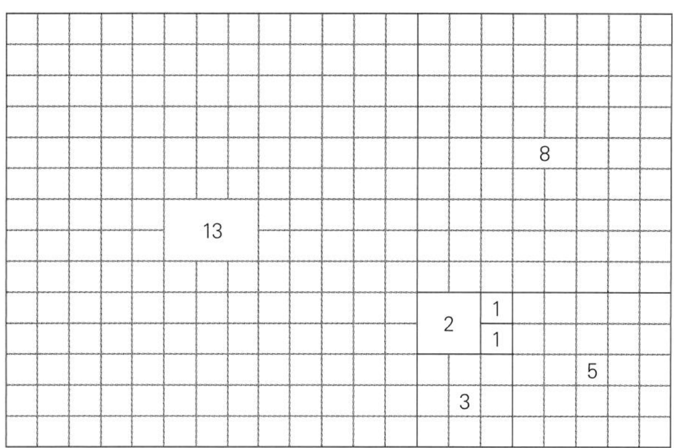

the fibonacci numerical sequence

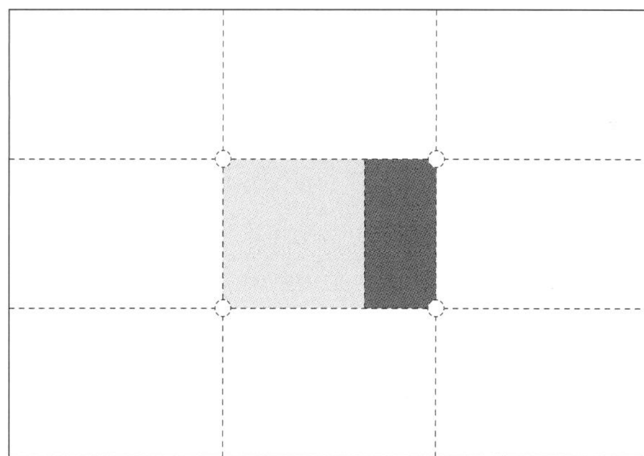

the rule of thirds

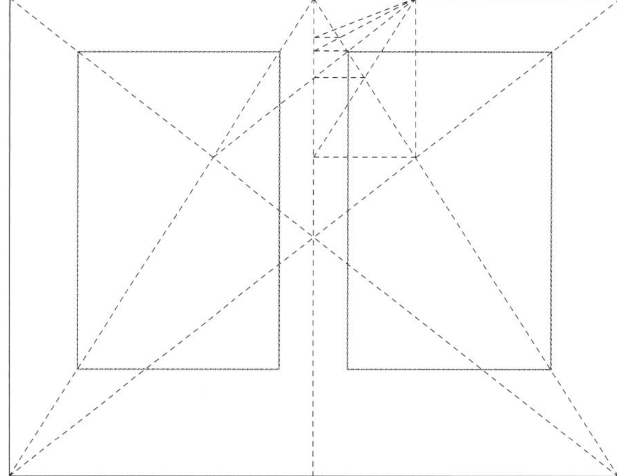

villard de honnecourt proportions

dynamic rectangles Another system of defining proportional relationships is the method of creating root rectangles, also called dynamic rectangles. To create the proportion, the diagonal of a square is the first step in the process that generates the first rectangle. The successive diagonal of each new rectangle determines a mathematical progression of increasing rectangles. The successive increasing size of each new rectangle results in a square root 1, 2, 3, 4, 5... sequence. At the root 4 point, the square is doubled. At the root 5 point, a derivative of the divine proportion (1:1.6) occurs.

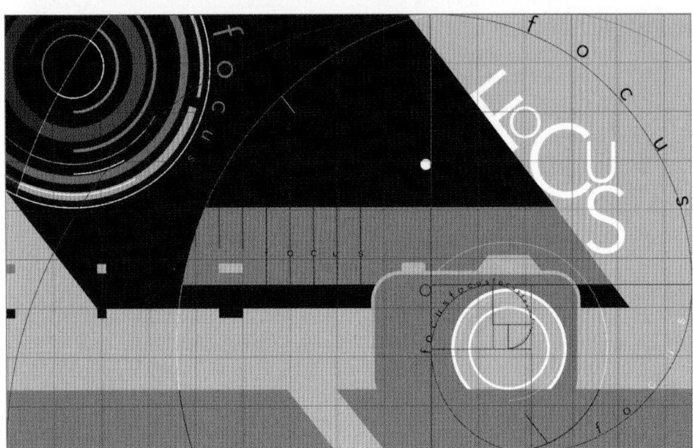

| **bailey reinhart** | The divine proportion system is used for a composition incorporating image, type, and graphic elements.

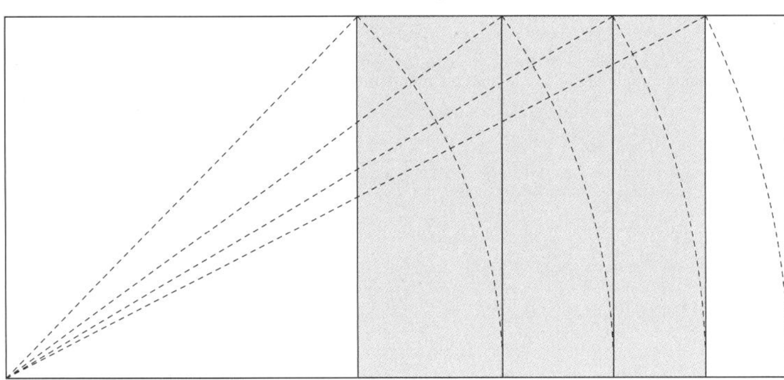

Successively increasing rectangles in a square root 1, 2, 3, 4, 5, sequence

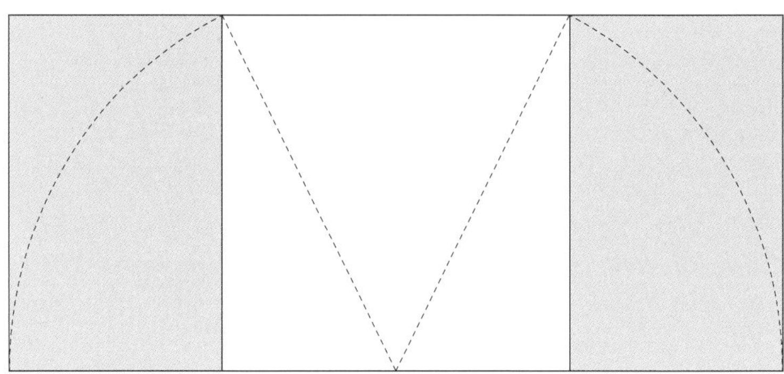

Derivative of the divine proportion equals the root five rectangle

structure methodology Proportional divisions of a rectangular area begin with the square. Square units found within the rectangle produce diagonal axes. Intersections and alignments of axes found within a rectangle enable similar proportional relationships. Accordingly, proportional divisions within the rectangle remain integral to the whole surface area. Applying this method, a diverse number of proportional harmonies is possible. This concept is demonstrated in a rectangle with a 1:2 ratio and a rectangle with a 1:1.5 ratio. The same method could be actualized for rectangles varying in size. The underlying symmetrical grid structure yields endless opportunities to divide space in a logical and systematic method that initiates a balanced asymmetrical appearance.

key points In these proportional systems, visual balance and order is determined by the logical inherent structure of the parts. The role of the square and the diagonals of the rectangle are invaluable fundamental tools for the designer to consider and apply. The well-conceived grid and proportion system should be a flexible mechanism of organization that drives the information hierarchy and fosters the structural integration of type, image, and graphic elements.

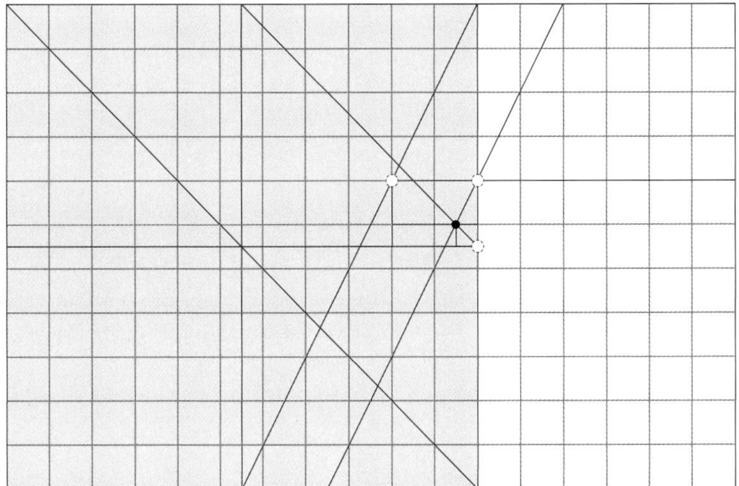

Rectangle in a 1:2
height-to-width ratio

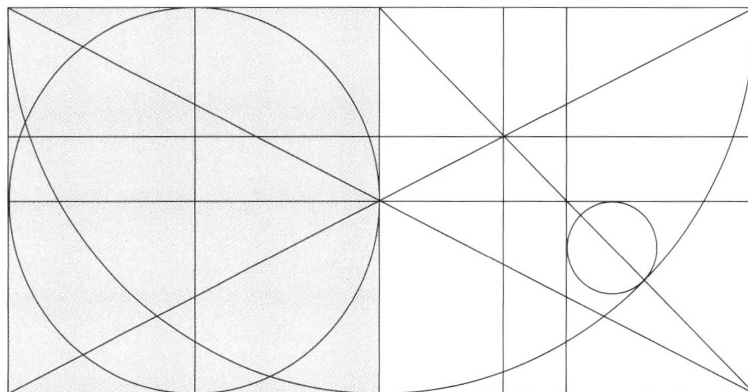

Rectangle in a 1:1.5
height-to-width ratio

alternative grids are often loose and organic and rely heavily on the intuitive placement of the visual elements. Intuition plays an important role when working with all grids—it helps the designer make choices and keeps them attuned to what works and what does not. They are often used when basic grids are not needed or if the content requires more spatial complexity. Alternative grids can evolve from any of the basic grids by taking them apart and adding, deleting, overlapping, or shifting the spatial divisions.

All visual elements are inherently structural. In alternative grids, the visual elements define the architecture of the page, as well as the spatial relationships between elements. For example, the compositional structure is built around the dominant visual element, or focal point, using its lines, orientation, and position as alignment points for additional elements. Alternative grids require attention to ensure that the visual elements are working together. The use of an alternative grid, or lack of a grid, does not negate the need for an ordering system. Spatial relationships and visual connections are imperative in all grids and help the viewer navigate through the design.

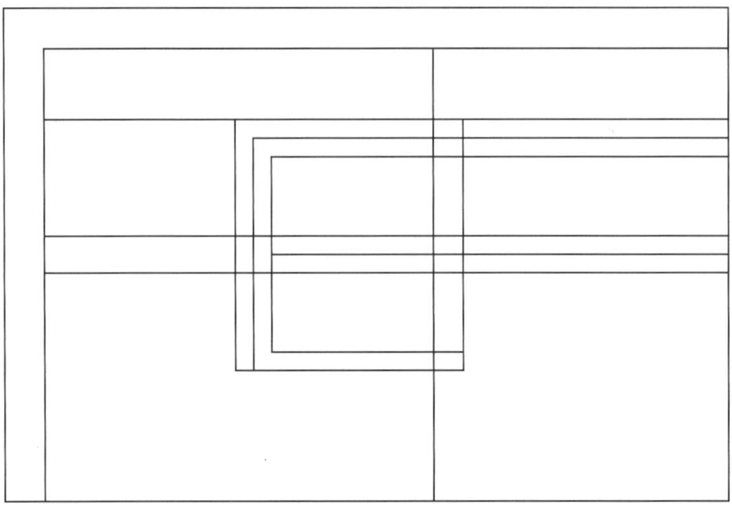

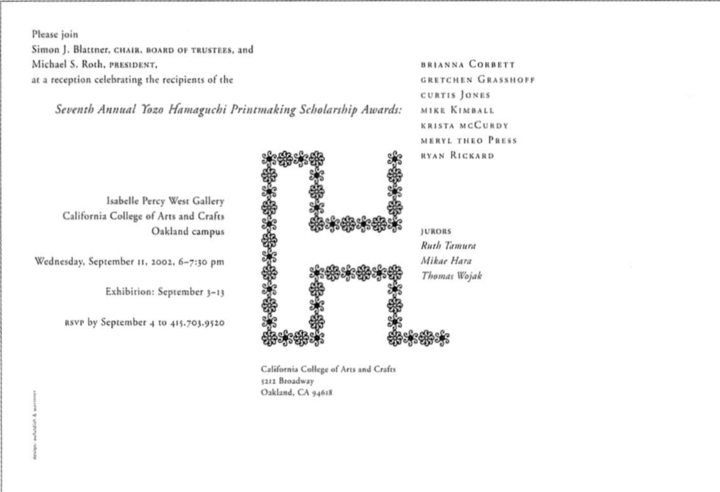

| **aufuldish & warinner** | The 'H' is a decisive focal point and provides the structure around which most of the textual content aligns. The basic grid is reinvented. The edges and lines of the dominant shape create horizontal and vertical divisions of space.

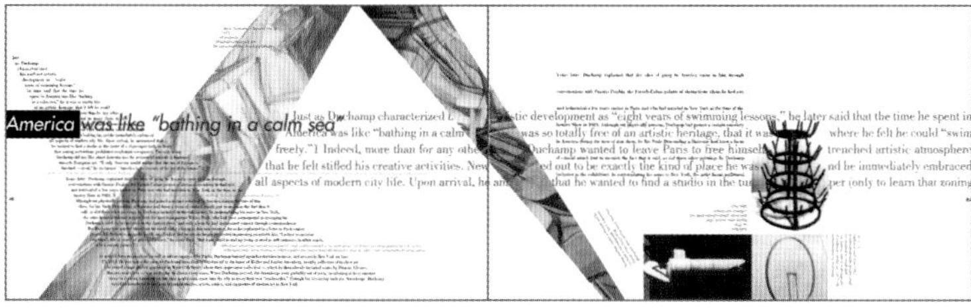

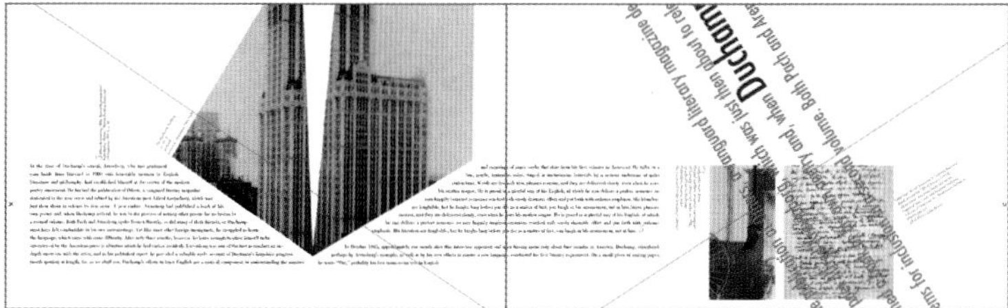

FINAL THOUGHTS Grids are tremendous assets to layout development, but they are not the definitive answer to successful design solutions. They must be used with acute skill, in conjunction with decisive hierarchy, typographic application, and interaction of visual elements. The designer should use grids freely, adhere to spatial divisions to create dynamic relationships, and intelligently break them, when appropriate. If viewed as restrictive, the grid (and the designer) will never be used to its fullest potential.

| **jennifer hoverman** | Strong diagonal alignment points are established and become the dominant structural force of this experimental student design project. Typography, imagery, and graphic shapes are integrated and create activity and movement.

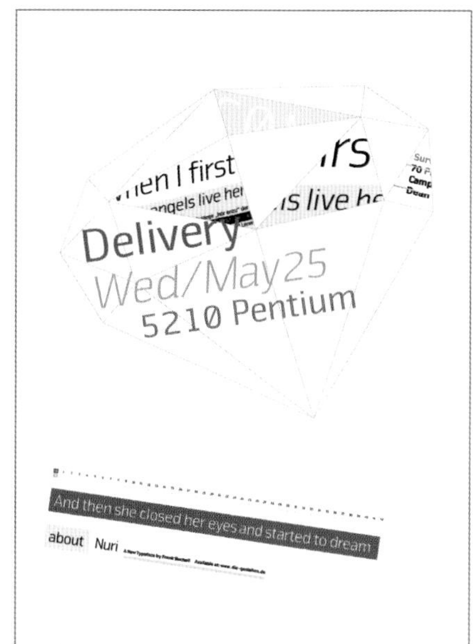

| **kearneyrocholl** | The traditional grid is challenged in this poster. Playing off the angular diamond form, typographic elements are composed within, and on top of, triangular shapes.

THE INTERACTION

The white surface of the paper is taken to be 'empty,'

an inactive surface,

despite visible structures that are present.

With the first appearance of a dot, a line,

the empty surface is activated.

ADRIAN FRUTIGER
illustrator, teacher, type and graphic designer, typographer

OF VISUAL ELEMENTS

ESTABLISHING HIERARCHY

The blank page is dull, meaningless, and static, yet full of potential. To the designer, it is an empty canvas used to create meaning. Color, form, image, space, and typography collaborate to convey an intended message. When the designer activates the page through the placement of the visual elements, he or she needs an ordering system to help the viewer make sense of the design. The ordering system, or hierarchy, defines the level of activity and importance for every visual element and determines their sequence through the design. Dominant and subordinate visual elements are composed decisively to achieve clarity. No visual element is insignificant; each one contributes in overt and subtle ways to the communication of the message. A strong, systematic hierarchy provides accessibility, continuity, integration, navigation, and variety within the design.

hierarchical development

Hierarchy depends on the complementing and contrasting relationships of visual elements. It is established by creating a clear focal point that attracts the eye to initiate viewer interaction with the design. Supporting the focal point, the melding of subordinate visual elements allows for in-depth analysis, interpretation, and understanding. When dominant and subordinate elements coalesce, the design maintains the fixed attention of the eye. The viewer begins to recognize the ordering system and is led through a logical and meaningful journey. If the visual elements demand equal attention, the eye is distracted and moves continuously around the surface of the page without direction. This type of design lacks impact, legibility, and usefulness. Nothing is communicated, and the result is a visual muddle.

Revealing messages through an integrated hierarchy is an effective approach to organizing content and enhancing the value of the design. Hierarchy is inherent to the comprehensive function of the design, whether it is simple or complex, conservative or expressive, quiet or loud. Developed and controlled by the designer, a methodical system synthesizes the design.

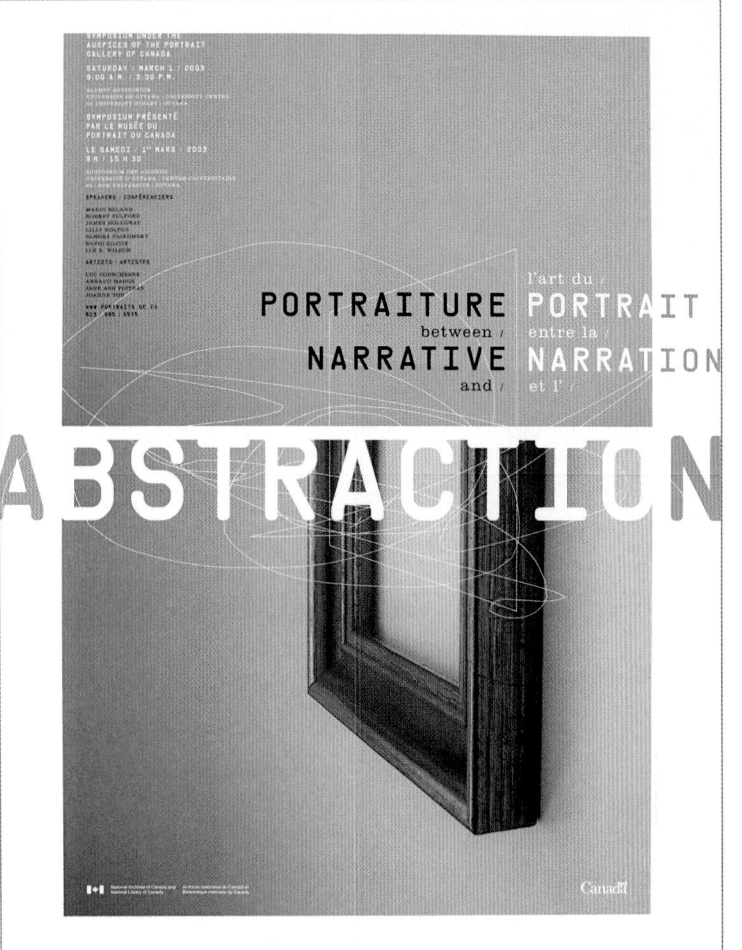

| **kolégram** | The hierarchy of this poster is dictated by its centrally located title, *Abstraction*. Providing initial impact, the title divides the design into halves, which connotes the contrast between abstraction and reality. The subtitle, set in English and French, is proximate to the title, yet distinct, in a smaller type size. The tertiary text sits modestly in the top-left corner.

Hierarchical development begins by ranking the visual elements by importance. Simply, the designer must determine what he or she wants the viewer to see first, second, third, and so on. By giving the visual elements an order, or level of importance, the designer defines the role each element will play in the delivery of the message. Dominant elements will reside in the foreground and demand attention, whereas subordinate elements will activate the middle ground or background in support of the dominant elements. For example, on the chapter title spreads in this book, the titles dominate the page—they are the primary focal point. In support, graphic shapes and linear elements punctuate the compositional space, and additional text, including subtitles, body copy, and page numbers, are subordinate to the titles. All elements are carefully considered because their roles are critical in effectively shaping the page.

Initial hierarchical considerations also include determining which visual elements are the same (or closely related to each other). The designer groups the elements to forge consistency and visual relationships throughout the design. For example, the designer groups together all headings or body copy. When the layout of the visual elements begins, the content is already dissected and prepared in groups for use. It is clearly defined at the beginning of the design process which elements are partnered. During the design phase, the designer must establish the strongest visual treatment for each group and apply it universally throughout the design. Once the viewer recognizes the repeated treatments, comprehension is enabled—the viewer becomes aware of the ordering system and can easily access primary, secondary, and tertiary information.

| **no.parking** | The image of the hand creates a strong visual impression. Although it fills the cover, it does not dominate the composition. The reduced value of the image contrasts with the white title treatment, which elevates the typography to the focal point. In addition, the use of subordinate textural type in the middle ground of the design adds depth.

Die Titelredaktion

Texte in Sachbüchern lassen sich meist leichter lesen und verstehen, wenn sie strukturiert sind.

Sachtexte sind nicht immer leicht verständlich. Oft fehlt erklärendes Bildmaterial, oft ist der Text kompliziert und kaum gegliedert. Präsentiert sich eine Buchseite solcherart, wird das Buch häufig weggelegt.
Es gibt einfache, doch umso wirkungsvollere Wege, die einen Text für den jugendlichen Leser interessant machen. Eines dieser Mittel ist der Zwischentitel.
Als Redakteure erfahren die Schüler, wie Autoren ihre Leser motivieren und ihren Stoff verständlich machen. Sie untersuchen Zwischentitel und versuchen, selber welche zu finden. Sie lernen die Variationsmöglichkeiten bei Zwischentiteln kennen und anwenden.
Bei Redaktionsschluss rauchen die Köpfe, und alle wundern sich, wie viele neue Informationen in kurzer Zeit erfasst und vielfältig gestaltet geworden sind.

Zubereitung

1 Die Lehrerin präsentiert der Klasse zwei aufgeschlagene Sachbücher. Die Doppelseite des einen Buches zeigt einen strukturierten Text mit mehreren, leicht lesbaren Zwischentiteln: „Uns interessieren an diesen beiden Sachbüchern nicht die Bilder, sondern der Text. Was fällt euch auf den ersten Blick auf?" Je nach Altersstufe gibt die Lehrerin Artikulationshilfen: „Wie sieht hier der Text aus? Ist er eingeteilt? Gibt es Absätze? Haben die Absätze Überschriften?"

2 Nach dieser ersten kurzen Gesprächsrunde gehen die Schüler zu einem Tisch mit Sachbüchern. Zu zweit sollen sie nun zwei Bücher aussuchen und entscheiden, ob die Texte darin im Block oder in Bausteinen gestaltet sind. Eine Sache von fünf Minuten.

3 Dann schlagen sie bei beiden Büchern je eine ausgewählte Doppelseite auf und legen die Bücher auf den Boden, entweder zur Karte „Fließtext" oder zur Karte „strukturierter Text".

→

Zutaten

- 30 Sachbücher, die Hälfte davon mit strukturiertem Text
- Zwei Karten: „Fließtext" und „strukturierter Text"
- Schreibzeug
- Eineinhalb Stunden Zeit

52 53

| **no.parking** | An interior spread features changes in typographic scale and weight to denote the textual hierarchy of the design. A colored rectangular shape breaks the monotony of the white page and interrupts the horizontal motion of the typography. The contrast in orientation effectively leads the eye across and down the page to access all content.

the principles of spatial organization

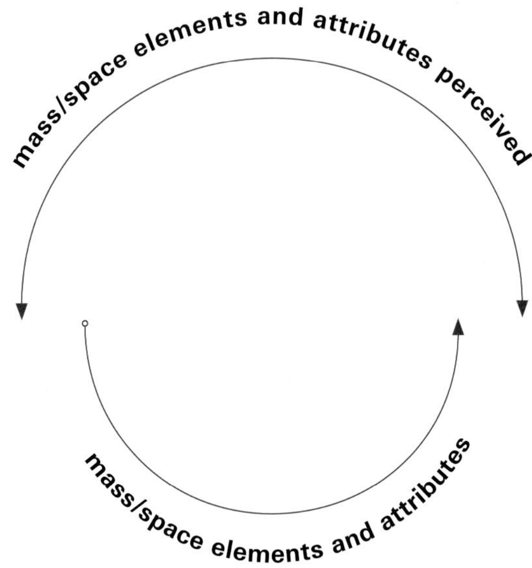

components of visual elements

mass/space elements

attributes of the mass/space elements

the mass/space elements and attributes perceived (the holistic interaction of the visual parts)

The designer works with principles of visual organization to achieve a composition with structural order and hierarchy throughout the layout. The harmonious integration of the visual elements and spatial organization plays a critical role when shaping the page.

The visual elements are comprised of three components:

1. mass/space elements

2. attributes of the mass/space elements

3. The mass/space elements and attributes perceived (the holistic interaction of the visual parts)

mass/space elements consist of point, line, plane and volume/space. The mass/space elements have visual attributes or characteristics. The visual attributes of the mass/space elements consist of color, size, shape and texture. Controlling the elements and their attributes in a composition depends upon how these elements are cognitively perceived. There are numerous factors that influence perception. Several of these factors are found in Gestalt psychology—the holistic interaction of the visual parts. The most common factors are figure/ground, closure, balance, alignment, quantity/number, repetition, direction, sequence, orientation, position, proximity, tension, and rotation. Additional compositional factors to be considered include proportion, symmetry, dynamic symmetry, grids, image, typography and hierarchical arrangement of parts. Mass/space elements equip the designer with a language to objectively analyze the strengths and weaknesses of a composition.

The designer must experiment and determine which factors effectively contribute to and define the ordered presentation of textual and visual information. When the visual elements have been ranked and grouped, the design process begins. To continue developing a strong, composition, the designer must activate the compositional factors by balancing similar parts and contrasting part—too much similarity creates monotony, too much contrast creates chaos. The principles of spatial organization grant the designer a method to evaluate a composition objectively.

The designer must thoughtfully control and finesse the compositional factors to avoid monotonous or overactive visual fields. Monotony will ensue if all elements share equal importance and visual strength. The design will lack hierarchy, and it will be impossible for the viewer to determine the most important content from the least significant. On the other hand, if the design is overactive, the visual elements will compete for attention. Although the composition may make a strong first impression, it will be too energetic and lack function and will not provide a starting point to engage the viewer. The designer must remember that all elements cannot be visually equal.

Contrast is the essential factor needed to achieve successful hierarchy within the design. It effectively distinguishes all the visual elements that interact in the compositional space. By creating visual differences, juxtaposed elements efficiently communicate their intended meaning. The visual contrast that exists between the elements makes them identifiable and comprehensible to the viewer, who notes the differences and deciphers the dominant and subordinate levels of information. Decisive contrast between disparate visual elements makes the hierarchical system visually apparent and the design effectively communicates its intended messages in a logical progression.

The three categories that comprise the principles of spatial organization establish the language of visual form. The language of visual form provides the basis for objective criteria to analyze the strengths and weakness of a visual composition.

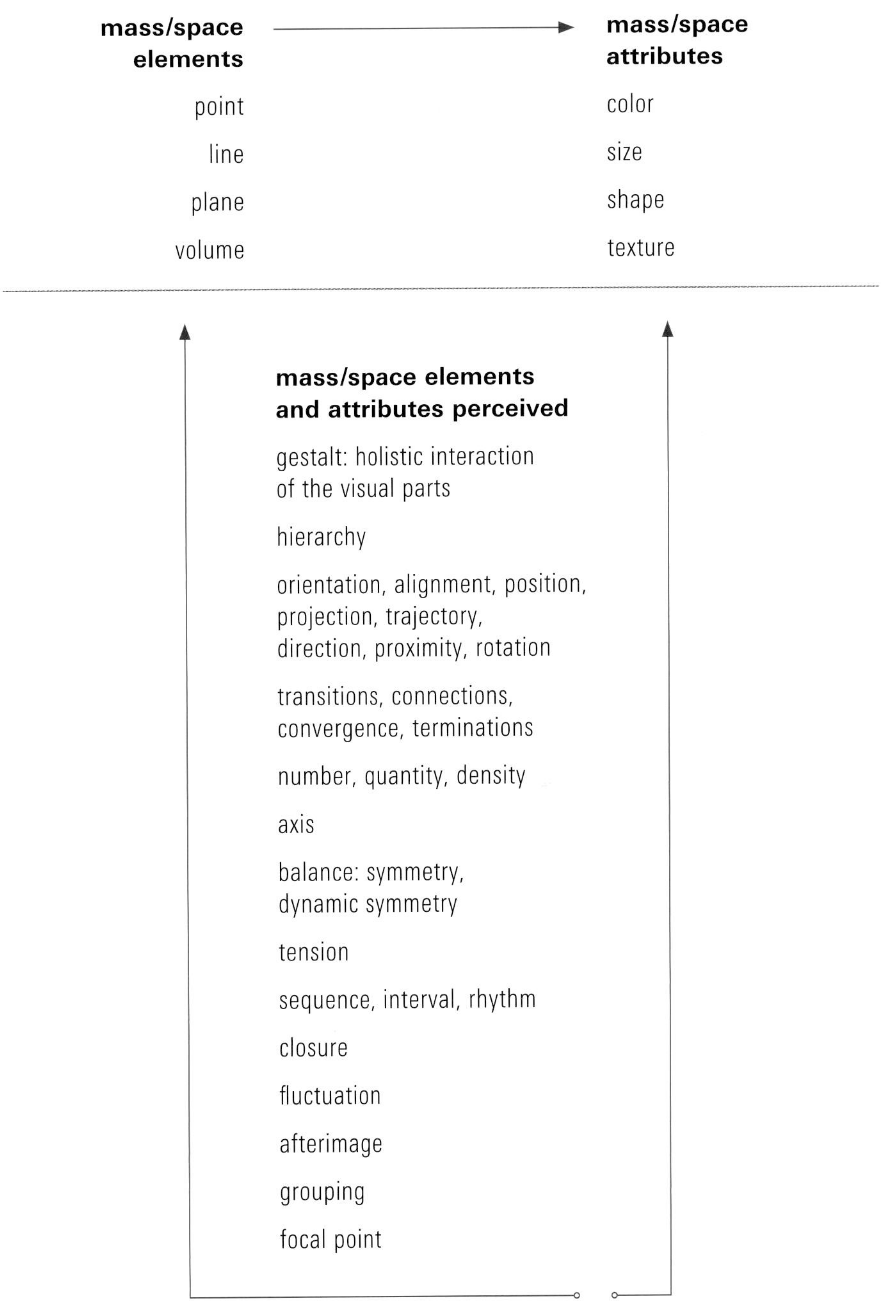

mass/space elements

point

line

plane

volume

mass/space attributes

color

size

shape

texture

mass/space elements and attributes perceived

gestalt: holistic interaction of the visual parts

hierarchy

orientation, alignment, position, projection, trajectory, direction, proximity, rotation

transitions, connections, convergence, terminations

number, quantity, density

axis

balance: symmetry, dynamic symmetry

tension

sequence, interval, rhythm

closure

fluctuation

afterimage

grouping

focal point

space is an important factor that the designer must consider. If used competently, space provides visual contrast and contributes to an effective ordering system. The empty compositional space brings the visual elements alive; it is the invisible energy of the design and must be considered a dominant element. The designer must focus attention toward the activity (or inactivity) of the negative space to activate the visual elements that reside within it. Space is needed in all compositions—it is imperative to accessibility and navigation. It provides pathways, or channels, that lead the eye through the design, while directing the focus toward the positive areas of the compositional space.

The designer can take advantage of space in several ways. On a simple level, visual elements can be grouped together by limiting the amount of space between them to create a focal point. Increasing space between elements separates them. The extra space leads the eye to the isolated elements. In other cases, space affects the visual elements based on their position. For example, centering a visual element in the middle of the page equalizes the space around it, rendering the space ineffective. On the other hand, positioning a visual element to the right or left of center, as well as near the top or bottom of the page, creates weighted, asymmetric space. For example, if a larger amount of space is on the bottom of the composition and the visual elements rise to the top or above the optical center of the page, the design feels grounded. Space secures the element in place.

Excessive amounts of space that are used ineffectively do not activate the page because the visual elements fade into the background, and space dominates. If the amount of negative space is limited because the design is overfilled, it is unclear to the viewer how to navigate through the design in a logical progression. The visual elements are trapped within the edges of the page, and the design does not deliver its message.

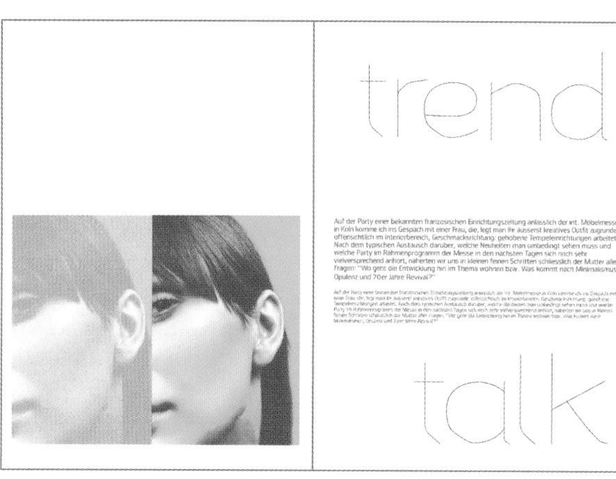

| **kearneyrocholl** | Delicate rectangles frame the body text of this catalog. Their pale hues make them barely apparent. In addition, large headings, set in the typeface Nya, direct the eye. Three type sizes indicate primary, secondary, and tertiary text, while color changes provide contrast.

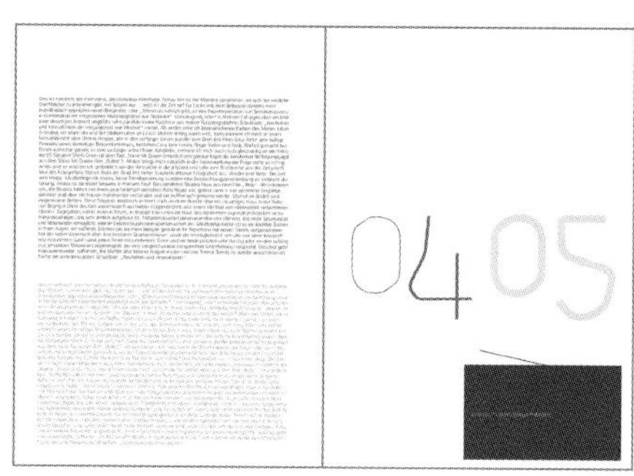

| **kearneyrocholl** | A text-heavy page contrasts its facing page, which is light and open. Balance created between pages makes the design approachable.

scale relationships produce immediate contrast. If the visual elements demonstrate changes in scale, both large and small, the contrast between them establishes an adequate hierarchy. If all the elements are the same size, or visual weight, they will negate the hierarchical force of each other. The compositional field is optically even and lacks a decisive focal point. Each element demands the same amount of attention and nothing is subordinate.

When adjusting the scale of visual elements, the designer must use consistency and progression. Randomly changing scale is inadequate and leads to chaos because nothing is related. It is important that all scale changes be considered in relationship to every element of the composition. A clear, hierarchical distinction exists between small, medium, and large visual elements, and progressive scale variations also give the design rhythm. Varying scale relationships define the appropriate and logical order of the visual elements while improving navigation through the design.

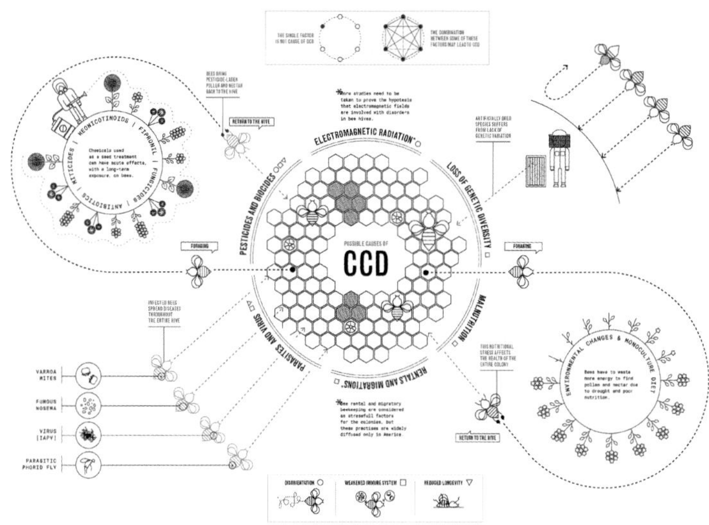

| **densitydesign** | Giulia DeRossi's representation of the possible causes of colony collapse disorder reflects the relevance of contrasting scale in type, image, and graphic elements to share effective and accurate scientific content.

| **kearneyrocholl** | The quantity of information on the spread is plentiful, and progressive changes in the size of the photographs create depth. The negative space complements the layout because it is proportionately related to the size and shape of the images. Clear spatial pathways lead the eye through the composition.

number, quantity, and density The quantity of elements also affects the designer's ability to produce effective visual contrast and hierarchy. Incorporating unnecessary visual elements beyond the project requirements can result in visual clutter and a lack of order. The designer must be cautious not to add unnecessary imagery, graphic shapes, or linear elements unless they have a specific function. For example, if too many elements (no matter how subordinate) are present in the design, they will confuse the order of the presentation. In this case, it is helpful to reduce the visual elements to the bare essentials. Editing or eliminating information—a subtractive method—adds clarity and impact. Although additional elements are beneficial in some cases, the designer must always remember that excessive noise in addition to the required elements of the design, may often distract the viewer and negate the ordering system.

Counter to subtractive methods, the designer may choose to intentionally increase the quantity of visual elements on the page—an additive method—to enhance the delivery of the message. The added elements, which can include graphic shapes and linear elements, add visual impact and variation to the required elements of the design. For example, a graphic shape or linear element that directs the eye toward the dominant text effectively strengthens hierarchy. It can be a positive addition to the design without adding visual noise. Additional elements that are incorporated into the design must reinforce or support the primary message. Every design project differs, and the designer must attain balance and learn when to appropriately add or edit information to benefit the communicative function of the design.

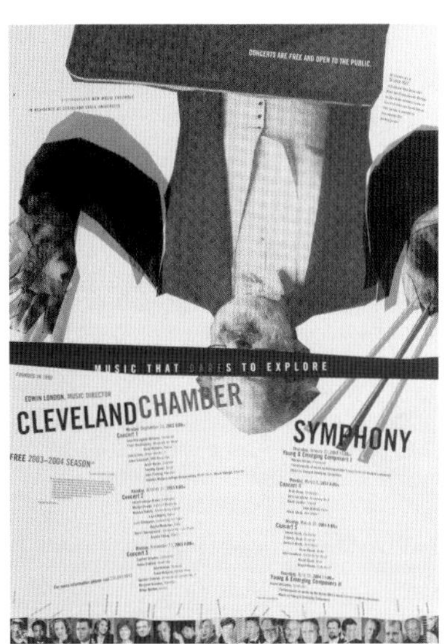

| **visocky o'grady** | The angular orientation of the visual elements enlivens this poster. The inverted image of the conductor provides immediate visual impact—it is a decisive focal point. Intentional shifts in the orientation and color activate the design.

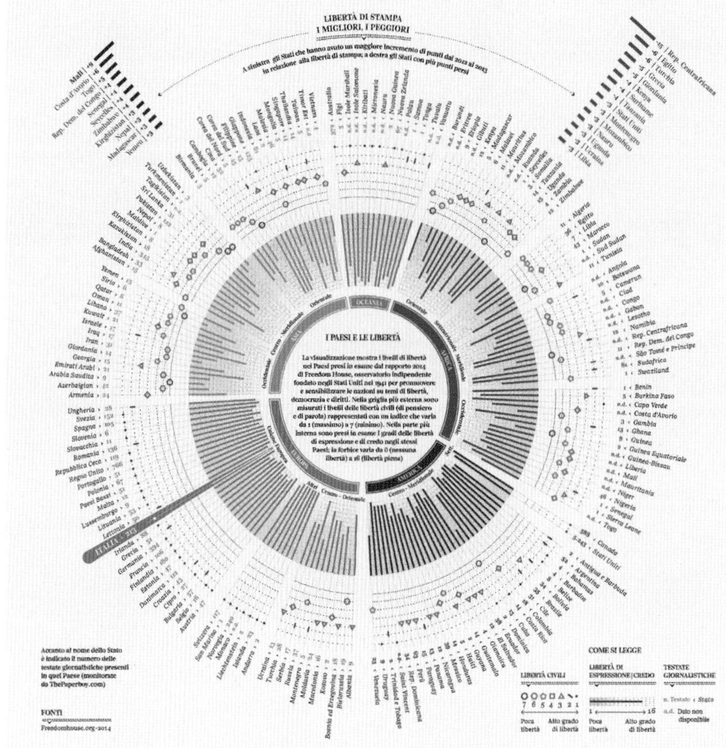

| **sara piccolomini** | This data visualization explores the levels of freedom in countries. The title of the visualization is the central focal point. Graphic elements and color support the hierarchical levels of meaningful substance.

orientation, alignment, and position

are additional factors that foster contrast and distinctive hierarchy. These factors are influenced by the interactions of projection, trajectory, direction, proximity, and rotation. When composing the page, the designer positions the visual elements throughout the design along the top, bottom, and sides of the page as clustered groups or isolated elements in horizontal, vertical, or diagonal axes orientations. Shifting orientation and position of visual elements is an effective way to command attention. For example, if all the elements are horizontally oriented, a strong vertical element draws attention. Or, if a composition is composed along a diagonal axis, rotating one or a series of elements at an opposing angle leads the viewer to that distinct area of the design. (Diagonals are dynamic and directly contrast the rectilinear shape of the page. They add immediate drama and movement.) In addition, the intersection points of horizontal, vertical, and diagonal axes are active, providing focal points by leading the eye to the area where all elements meet. Positioning visual elements near the edge or running off the page creates visual tension, which also leads the viewer to specific areas of the composition.

| **visual dialogue** | Layered, repeated photography commands attention, scale provides impact and movement, and transparency and value add depth. The photography is also directional; note how the bent knee of the figure points to the starting point of the typography on the front of the design. Changes in typographic scale, as well as orientation and position, help to structure the organization of the text.

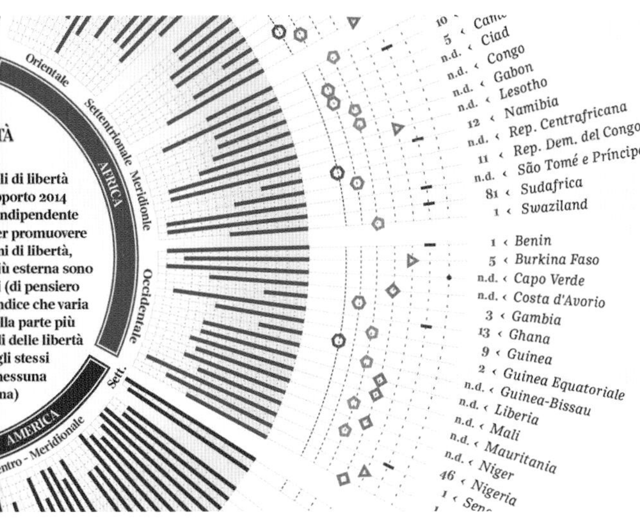

| **sara piccolomini** | This detail from the *Freedom of Countries* data visualization demonstrates the importance of linear elements to define the data and enhance the structure of the design.

volume: depth, dimension, and perspective

Perspective is a unique way to engage the compositional space of the page while contrasting and distinguishing visual elements. The use of perspective shifts the two-dimensional surface of the design into the third dimension—depth and the illusion of spatial volume are created. Now, the compositional field is extended. Elements positioned in perspective recede or move out toward the viewer. In addition, the implied lines moving toward vanishing points are directive and lead the eye toward visual elements positioned along that distinctive line. (Use perspective carefully. Be cautious and avoid skewing imagery or typography in an inappropriate way that alters its character or integrity.)

| **nb: studio** | A conservative, yet well-considered, hierarchical structure is seen in the typographic system of this catalog. The order of the text is distinguished by changes in type size, weight, and color. A blue heading calls attention to the top of the page. Space between the heading and the body copy reinforces the dominant hierarchy.

Layering visual elements also helps achieve depth and dimension on the page. Layering occurs when planar elements overlap one another. The designer can take advantage of foreground, middle ground, and background to expand the visual environment of the composition. In addition to layering, size/scale influences the depth dimension of the page. Generally, large elements project forward while smaller elements recede in the background. Also, primary, secondary, and tertiary levels of importance can be easily organized in the foreground, middle ground, and background areas of the composition. Repetition creates depth and dimension as well as rhythm throughout the design while emphasizing the specific visual elements that are repeated. In addition, patterns and textures can be used to draw attention or create interest in specific areas of the composition.

closure effect and the figure/ground

The effect of closure occurs when an image is complete in its appearance even though parts of the figure are not connected. It is important to note that the trajectory of line endings form a predictable, implied path.

The figure is a positive shape on a negative background. When the figure/ground relationship reverses, the figure becomes the ground and the ground becomes the figure. The phenomena of figure/ground reversal and closure are visually powerful tools. Examples of closure and figure/ground reversal are often found in symbols and logotypes.

| **andrio abero** | A subtle image of a landscape establishes the foreground of this poster. Though the typographic content is in the background, it is still a dominant element. White type contrasts with the dark, solid field and commands attention. The typography also shows a scale progression that orders the text.

The effect of closure occurs when an image is visually completed, even though parts are not connected. The figure is a shape on a background. Figure/ground reversal occurs when the shape becomes the background and the background becomes the shape.

for in-depth typographic information, refer to *chapter 7: typography*

typography Like all considerations throughout the design process, typographic application needs careful attention and consistent application to be effective and contribute to the hierarchical system. Initially, the text needs to be broken into levels of importance and then purposefully set to visually distinguish all typographic variables and clarify their order of presentation. The designer's goal is to create consistency with enough visual contrast that the viewer can discern the typographic differences and access the content efficiently. A uniformly applied system allows the viewer to make visual connections. For example, the consistent treatment of headings enables the viewer to recognize easily the typographic organization because of its repetitious treatment.

Innumerable options for distinguishing one level of textual information from the next are available. A simple method to achieve contrast and emphasis is changing the type size. However, changes in size are often predictable, and other methods of contrast and emphasis are sometimes more desirable, especially in text-heavy compositions. (Too many changes in type size can be confusing and can lead to disorder.) When considering alternative options to scale changes, the designer can use italic (also oblique) or bold styles of a single typeface to create emphasis within limited quantities of textual content. Also, areas of text that demand attention can be set in full or small capitals, as well as lowercase settings. A broad typeface family with diverse styles, weights, and widths will provide a range of visual options, including condensed and extended typefaces. Combinations of serif and sans serif typefaces are also distinctive and provide effective contrast, if used together competently. The designer must explore the possibilities and discover the range of available choices.

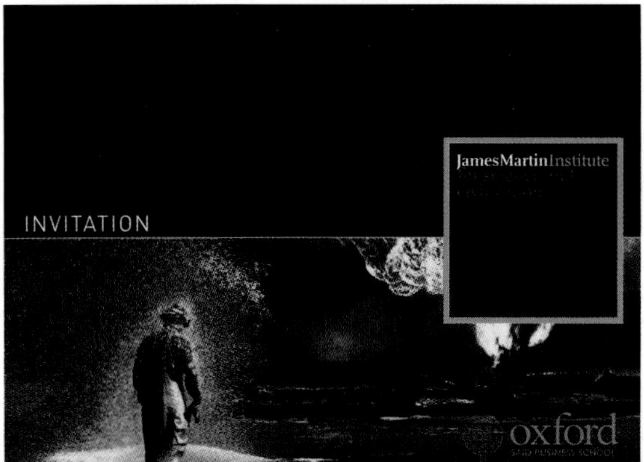

| **wilsonharvey/loewy** |
The word 'invitation' is visually dominant because of its isolated position on the page and the stark contrast of white type on a black field. A yellow linear element reinforces the baseline of the text and leads the viewer across the page.

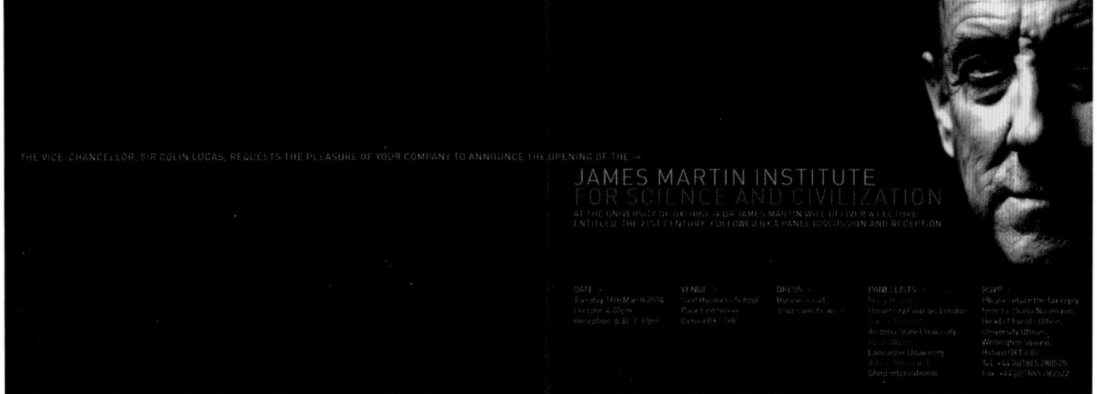

| **wilsonharvey/loewy** |
Mimicking the yellow rule on the cover, a single line of typography leads the eye across the interior spread toward the dominant area of the design. Typographic color and scale effectively call attention to 'James Martin Institute.' It is surrounded by dramatic negative space, which is the backbone of the composition.

color is a compositional factor that provides visual interest and emphasizes specific elements of the design. It can be added to graphic shapes and other visual elements, as well as typographic content. Color can also be used to fill large fields to create rich backgrounds or it can be used to isolate select areas of the design that need attention. For example, color can be applied to all the headings to make them identifiable. Or, a colored bar can surround the headings; this technique also effectively distinguishes the content. Careful consideration of color and its balance on the page is a critical component of the design process. The designer can establish a comprehensive color palette or use only one or two colors. Often, the designer works with several colors to test the hues that evoke the best overall impression and lead the viewer through the design effectively.

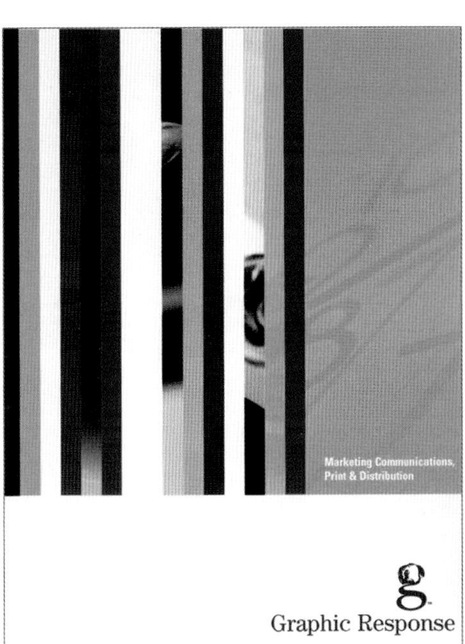

| **the jones group** | Bands of color create a bright field and direct the eye down the cover toward descriptive text. They also provide alignment points for typography. The smallest piece of text commands visual attention because it is the only element within a field of color. Its separation makes it distinctive.

| **the jones group** | Interior spreads feature bright, warm colors that activate the foreground. Yellow text rises to the surface of the page, and the effect is appropriate for the large headings *Imagine* and *Your Peace of Mind*. Graphic shapes and linear elements also support the design. Notably, a star accents the center of an image, drawing attention toward shaking hands, reinforcing the image's message.

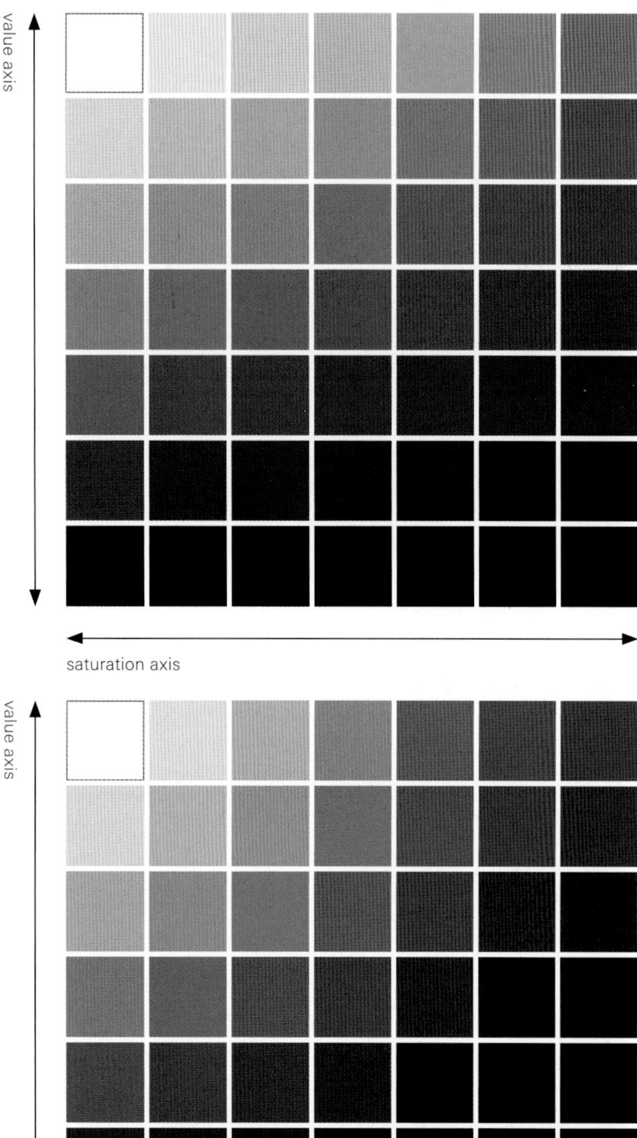

color theory The attribute of color has three properties—hue, value, and chroma/saturation.

1. **Hue** is the generic or family name of color. A red hue, for example, is the root of all reds that appear light, dark, bright, or dull.

2. The **value** of a color is expressed by its relative lightness or darkness. Generally, light colors that appear to have white in them are called tints, while colors that appear to have black in them are called shades.

3. **Chroma** is the third property of color. Saturation and brightness are two chroma characteristics. Colors at full saturation cannot be made more colorful. Desaturated colors appear to have a gray added to them and are called tones. Therefore, a tonal color is derived from a fully saturated color that has been modified with gray. As colors appear grayer they become dull or less bright.

These three properties of color are utilized and identified as HVS, in most visual software applications. In a software application with color selection options, one single hue will yield a magnitude of derivative colors in various degrees of value and saturation.

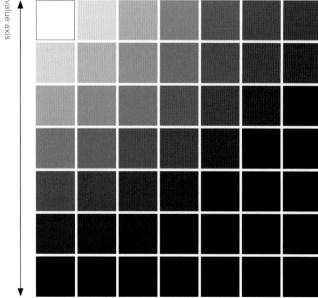

color space is also defined as a color model. The most commonly referred to color models are RGB (red, green, and blue); RYB (red, yellow, and blue); and CMYK (cyan, magenta, yellow, and black).

RGB is an additive color space, merging red, green, and blue. The RGB additive mixing process produces white light or colors of the visible spectrum.

RYB (red, yellow, and blue) color system is a subtractive model. Red, yellow, and blue are the primary colors of the commonly known color wheel. The secondary colors—violet, orange, and green—make up a secondary triad. In theory, the secondary colors are produced by mixing red and blue, red and yellow, and blue and yellow. Since this is a subtractive process, this method of mixing produces desaturated secondary colors.

CMYK (cyan, magenta, yellow, and black) is a subtractive model used in printing.

Additive color space creates the appearance of white light when mixing red, green, and blue (RGB) wavelengths of light. Subtractive color space creates the appearance of black or dark gray when mixing red, yellow, and blue pigments (RYB).

HSB (hue, saturation, and brightness) is a color model found in software applications. HSB transformations may also be defined as HSV (hue, saturation, and value), and HLS (hue, lightness, and saturation).

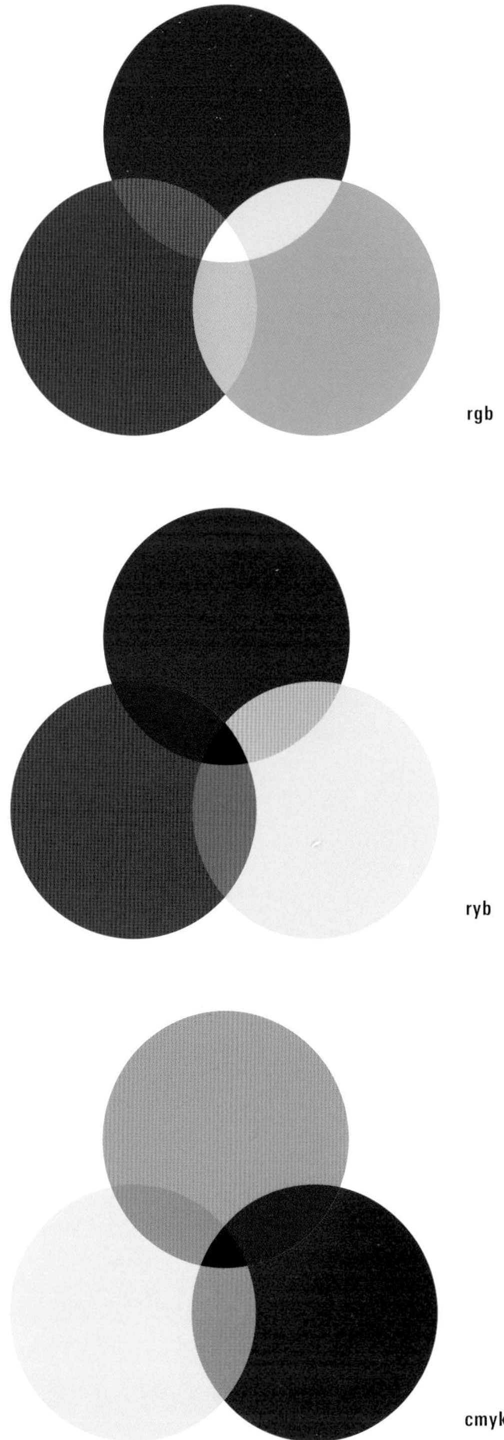

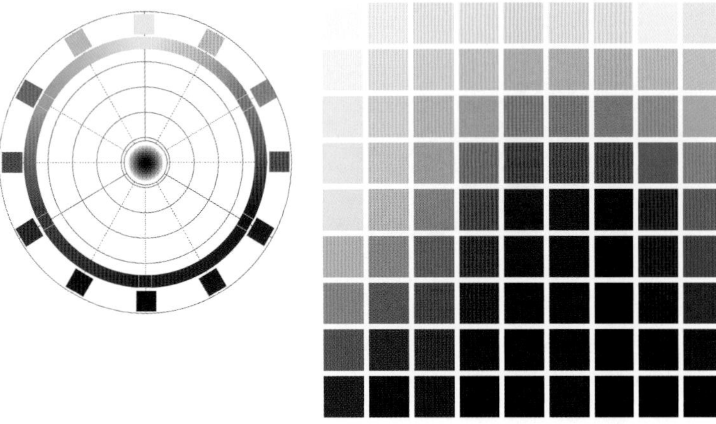

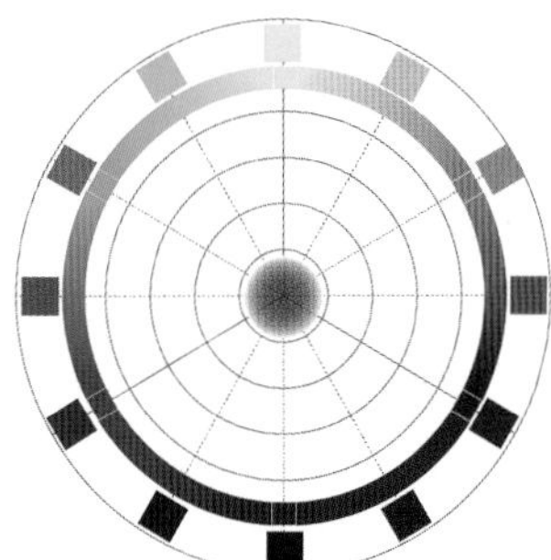

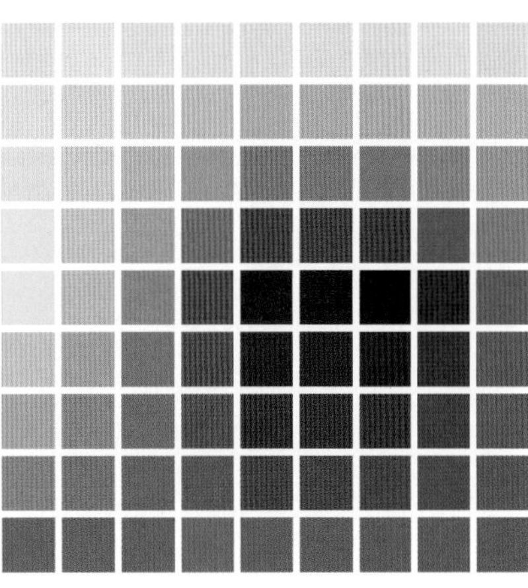

monochromatic harmonies

color harmony is an internal orderly structure encompassing a dynamic balance between similar and contrasting parts. Selecting a color palette based upon a conventional color harmony can be a useful visual tool. The application of a color harmony tends to generate a congruent and agreeable arrangement of color parts.

Conventional color harmonies are based upon the RYB color space. Similar harmonies are found in the RGB color space. Recognizing the difference between the two is essential. The RYB color space harmonies will yield the most visually pleasing results, since it is the system employed in painting and illustration.

Conventional Color Harmonies

1. *Monochromatic Harmonies*
Derivative colors of one hue. These colors appear to be modified by white, black, or gray.

2. *Primary, Secondary, Tertiary Triad Harmonies*
Colors equally distant on the color wheel.

3. *Analogous Harmonies*
Colors directly adjacent on the color wheel.

4. *Complementary Harmonies*
Colors directly opposite each other on the color wheel.

5. *Split Complementary Harmonies*
Two colors adjacent to one of the complementary pairs.

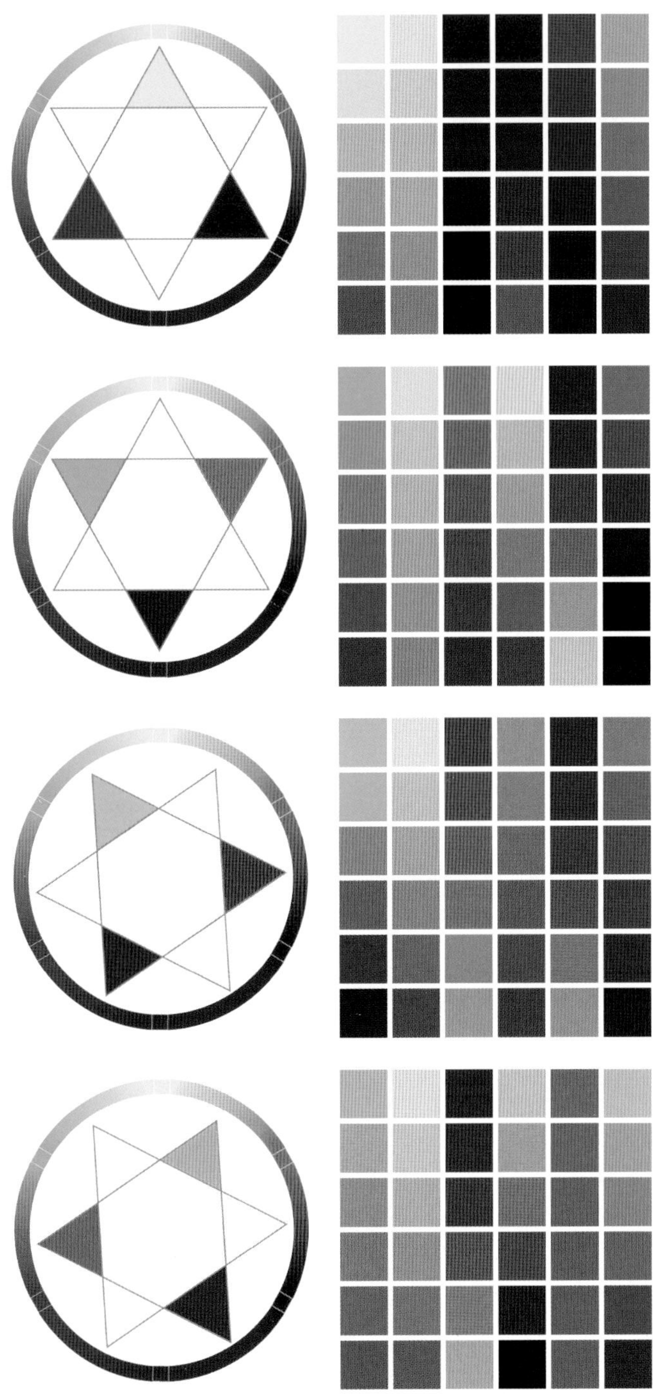

primary, secondary, tertiary triad harmonies

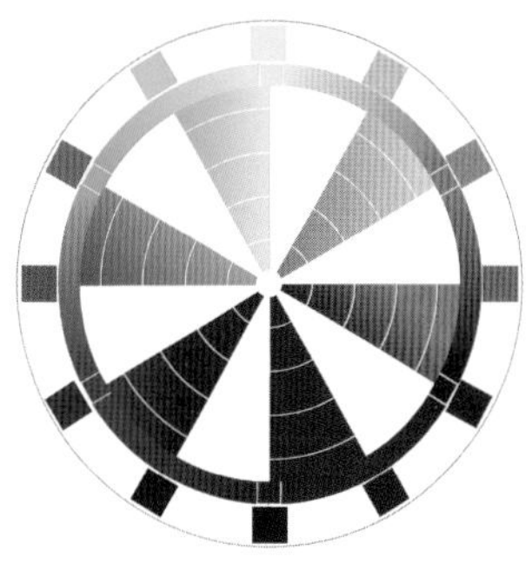

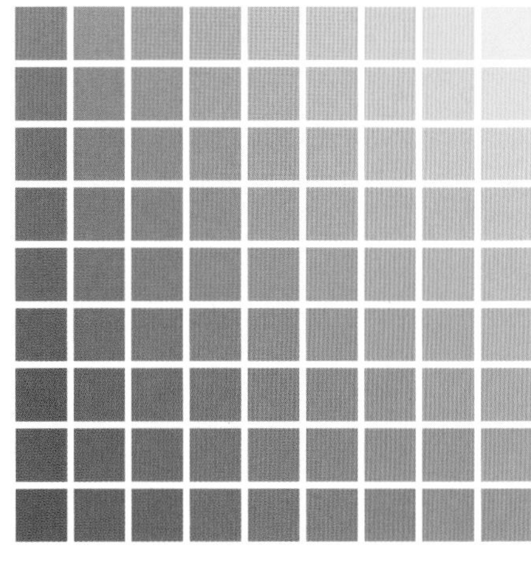

analogous harmonies

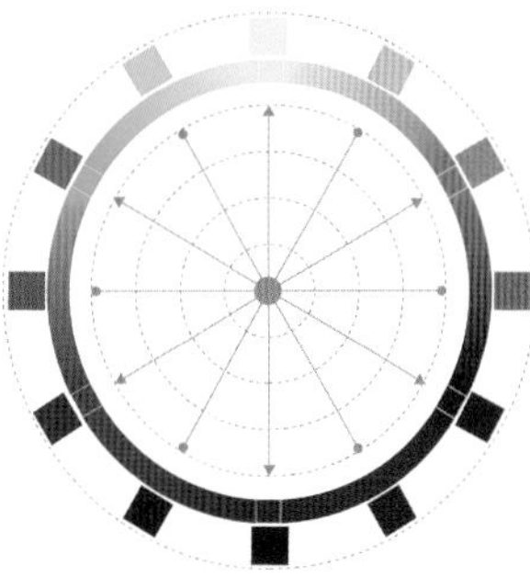

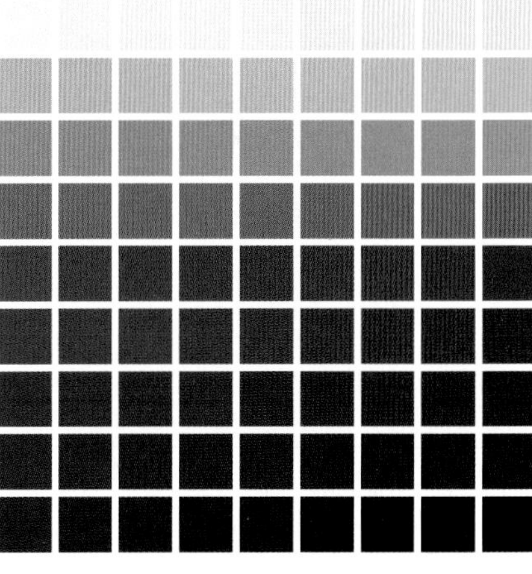

complementary harmonies

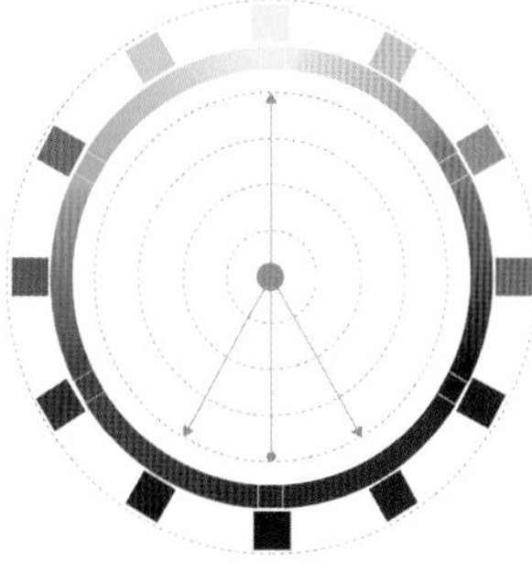

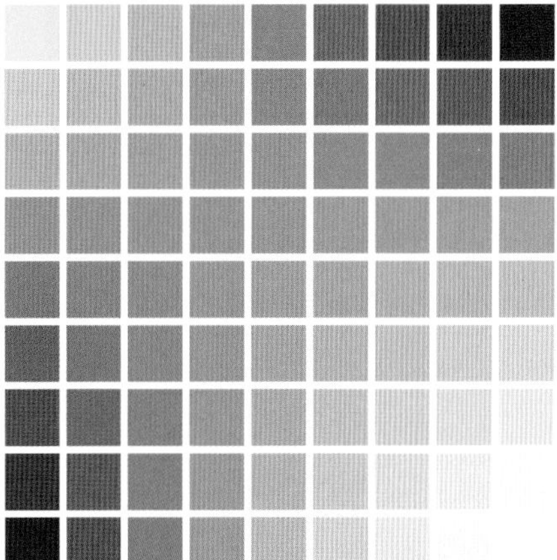

split complementary harmonies

color application By adjusting the color of the visual elements, the designer can reinforce content and heighten its meaning. He or she must consider the tone of the design and use colors that complement or contrast the attitude of the piece. In some cultures, for example, red connotes heat, passion, and urgency, whereas blue is cool and quiet. Warm colors (red, orange, and yellow) rise to the surface of the composition and effectively command attention. Generally, cool colors (green, blue, and purple) recede; their quiet impression is evident but often secondary to warmer colors. Even if using one color, the designer can create impressions of depth using value. Whereas darker values move to the foreground, lighter values recede in a monochromatic composition. In addition, pairing contrasting colors draws the eye toward specific sections of the composition. Bright and saturated colors will have an immediate impact, if used sparingly. If everything is bright or heavily saturated, the composition will lack focus. Experimentation will help the designer understand the effectiveness of color and its impact on hierarchy.

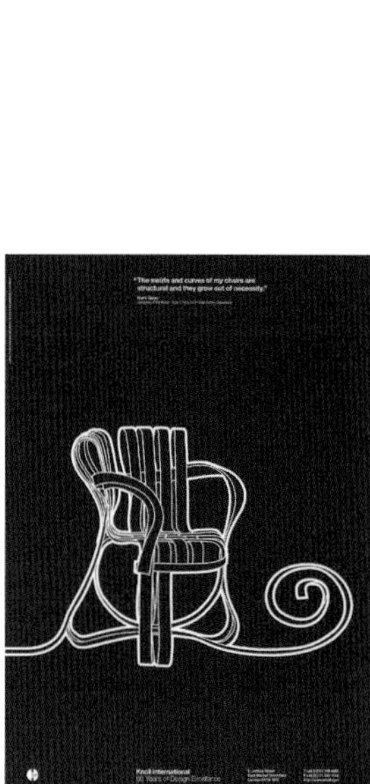

| **nb: studio** | The Knoll posters feature minimal illustrations that create impact and communicate the individual characteristics of the furniture. Their dominant scale visually contrasts the type. Color adds strong and inviting backgrounds that distinguish the posters from each other.

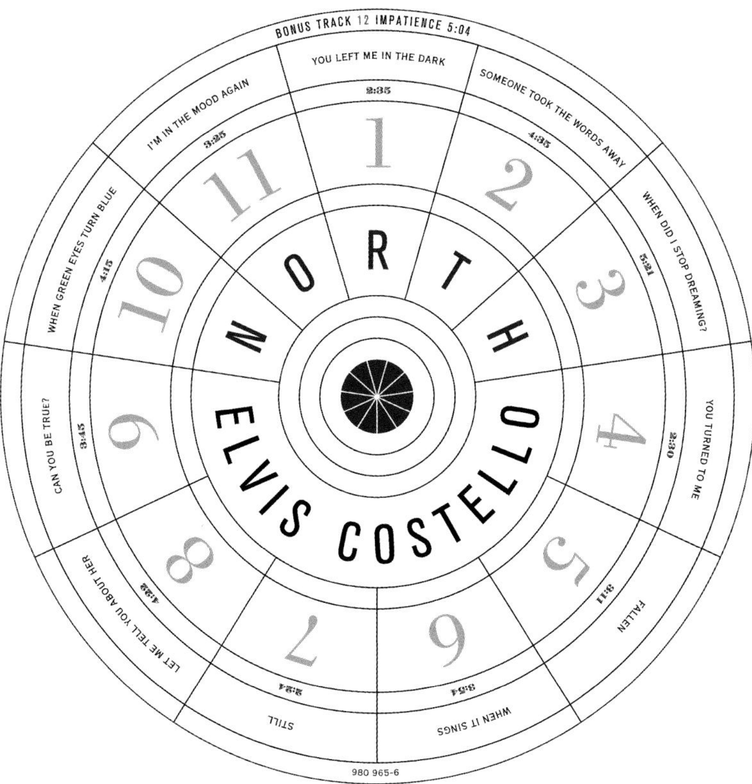

| helicopter | Limited space on the inlay of this CD does not negate an effective hierarchy. The composition moves out from a central focal point. Beginning with the title of the album and name of the performer, content progresses from dominant to subordinate. Linear elements divide the circle and provide equal spatial intervals for type.

FINAL THOUGHTS Hierarchy is critical to the appropriateness and effectiveness of the visual solution. Without it, the design lacks purpose, and the communicative function is lost. The designer must order and control the design, using contrast to establish the visual levels of dominance and subordination. Using compositional forces, including color, graphic shapes, and linear elements, effectively and with purpose, the designer will be able to integrate all the elements harmoniously. However, it is important to remember that some elements will lead the design, whereas others should intentionally follow. These elements represent the essential components of a visual language that provide structure and organization for the embodiment of content.

| helicopter | An interior spread of the CD booklet demonstrates control over a large number of textual elements. The spread contains song titles, production information, and lyrics in four languages. Despite the quantity of information, the layout is clear and ordered. Linear elements are added to enhance the structure of the design.

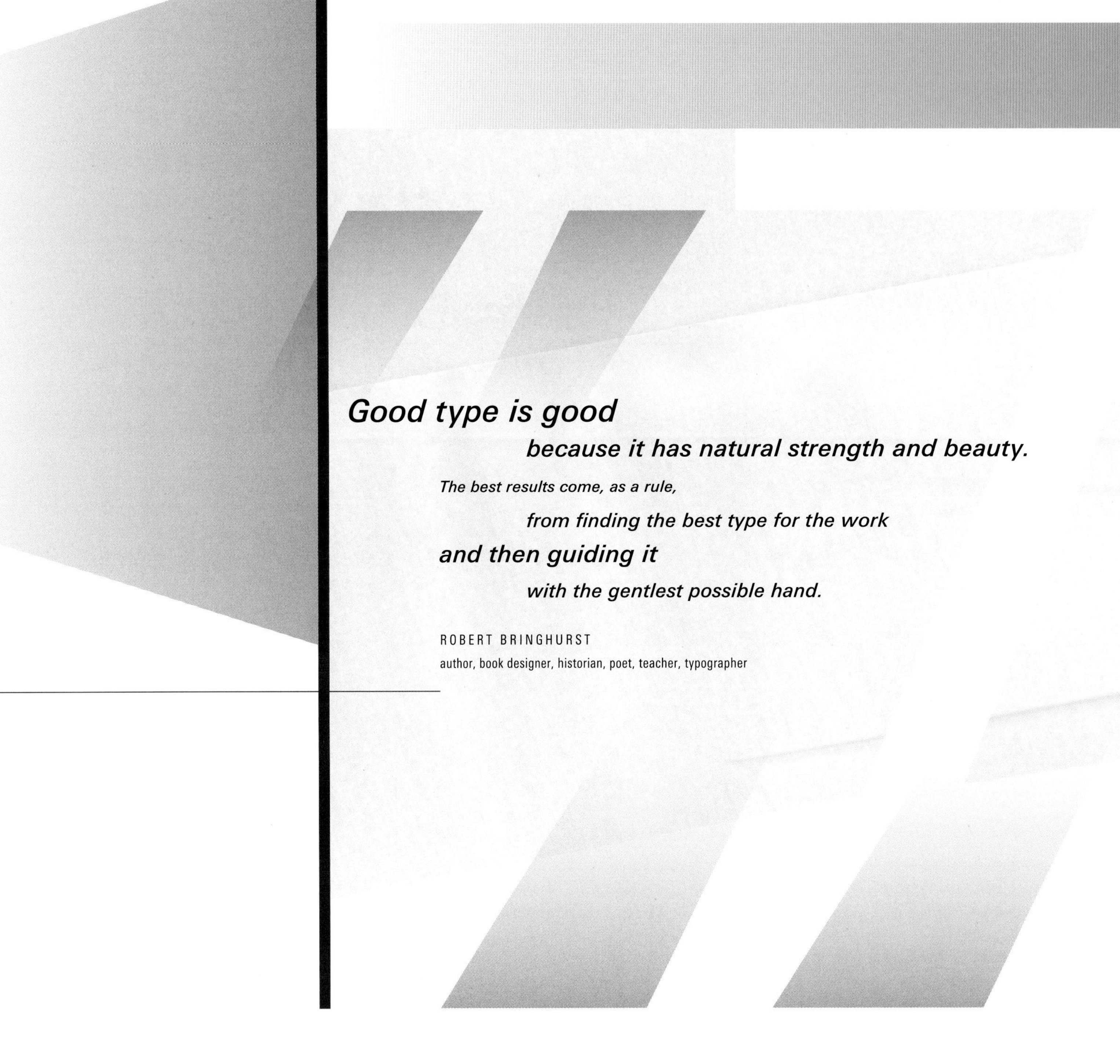

Good type is good

because it has natural strength and beauty.

The best results come, as a rule,

from finding the best type for the work

and then guiding it

with the gentlest possible hand.

ROBERT BRINGHURST

author, book designer, historian, poet, teacher, typographer

TYPOGRAPHY

SHAPING LANGUAGE

Typography is visible language. Representing human thoughts, it fosters exchange and preserves intellect through sight, speech, and sound. It is the foundation of visual communication. Typography delivers an array of information from insignificant memos to life-sustaining facts that is essential to daily function and understanding.

It is beautiful and ugly, engaging and irritating, meaningful and trivial. Indelibly linked to everyday experience, it is ubiquitous. Typography enlivens communication. It is a voice that resonates on the surface of the page, setting the tone of the design.

the function of type
typographic characteristics

Typography unifies the design through its complementary and contrasting juxtaposition with all the visual elements. The designer composes type to invite the viewer into—and cultivate their relationship with—the design. A decisive, well-planned system encourages readability and comprehension. Type is the leading factor (the conductor of the orchestra) that controls the activity of the page (the symphony) and enables sequential flow. Nurturing order and structural harmony, typography aesthetically invigorates text with meaning. It is the framework for the exchange of ideas.

Designing with type is an artful, detail-oriented activity that demands competence and patience. Nothing can be overlooked—from the overall composition to all of its subtleties. Whether type exists as letters, words, lines, and paragraphs, or image, texture, and graphic form, typographic expression is unlimited. Any text, in any form and environment, can be made meaningful through intelligent application. Working with typography is a delicate balance of understanding and intuition, conformity and rebellion. The designer is limited only by his or her imagination.

| **hendersonbromsteadartco.** | This poster is a successful union of expressive lettering and illustration. Creating visual interest from a distance, the design incites interaction. Hand lettering mimics the shape and movement of a scarf through changes in orientation and scale.

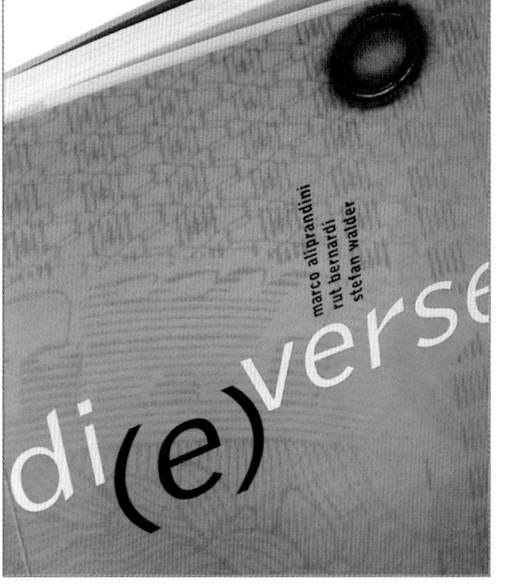

| **no.parking** | The cover and title page of *di(e)verse*, a book of poetry, presents a subtle shift in the baseline that drops the '(e)' from alignment with the rest of the title. The x-height of the title is used to position the authors' names in a vertical orientation.

All typefaces have personalities—such as cold, sophisticated, or friendly—that establish the attitude of the design. They provide an immediate first impression that is critical to the delivery of messages and, oftentimes, the emotional connection the viewer has with the design. Type has the power to engage (or disengage) the viewer. Typefaces must possess the proper character to connote the spirit of the design, while also supporting legibility and readability. It is a constant rule that the function, content, and end user define the typeface selection process. If typefaces are chosen carelessly, they will not serve the communicative function of the design. It is not a process to be overlooked or considered lightly.

classification systems organize typefaces into similar groupings that allow for identification based on unifying characteristics. Though a range of typeface styles exist, often crossing or even defying classification, most typefaces can be organized simply into the five basic classifications discussed here: Old Style, Transitional, Modern, Slab Serif, and Sans Serif. Display and Script classifications often categorize decorative styles not fitting into other areas. (The designer may also consider custom lettering, such as hand drawn, calligraphic, or computer-generated forms, which provide alternatives to typefaces in some situations and with distinctive style.)

Old Style
bembo

Transitional
baskerville

Modern
bodoni

Slab Serif
clarendon

Sans Serif
trade gothic

Display
cooper black

Script
zapf chancery

Typefaces are organized into different classifications according to their unifying characteristics, including stroke weight, serif or sans serif style, and vertical stress, or axis, of rounded forms, such as the 'o.'

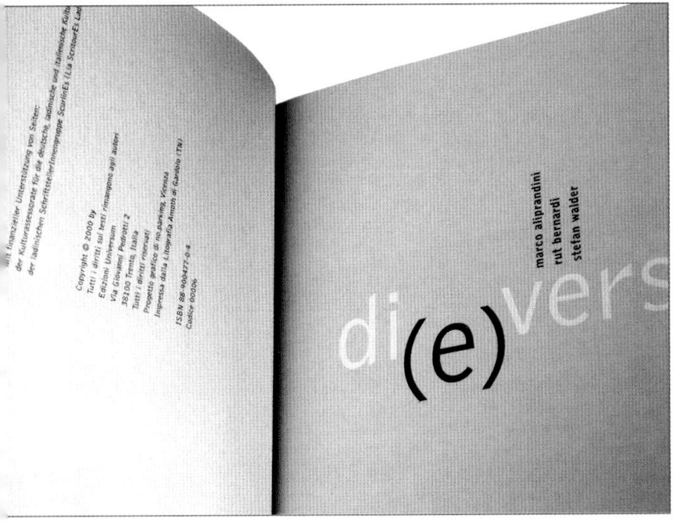

| **no.parking** | An interior spread provides alternative settings for the poetry. Contrast between the open, gridded letterforms (verso) and dense, justified paragraph (recto) adds typographic color to the stable composition.

style: posture, weight, and width The style of a typeface indicates its posture, weight, and width. Posture refers to the angle of characters relative to their baseline. Roman (also regular) characters are upright with a vertical stance. Posture also includes italics (also oblique), which usually have a 12–15° slant variation as compared to their roman counterparts.

Weight refers to stroke thickness and defines the lightness or darkness of characters. Regular and bold are weights common to most typeface families. Additional weights found in typefaces may include hairline, thin, light, medium, semi-bold, black, or heavy.

Width refers to how wide characters sit. Width variations include condensed, compressed, or extended.

Changes in type posture, weight, and width add depth and variety to typographic systems. They can be used to differentiate information, order text, and contribute to the overall typographic color of the page or screen.

Typefaces are carefully designed by type designers. Changes within a typeface to posture, weight, or width are carefully considered as a complete system (or family) Avoid relying on software conversions or manual modifications to change typeface styles. For example, choose italic fonts from within a typeface versus arbitrarily slanting roman styles. Select a light or bold font rather than adding strokes to change the typeface weight. Forgo skewing or stretching characters; this diminishes their intended shape and proportions.

x-height and cap height X-height refers to the height of the lowercase letters without ascenders and descenders. Ascenders rise up from the baseline above the x-height to the cap height and sometimes higher. Descenders fall below the baseline. X-height is determined by looking at the height of the lowercase x. Cap height refers to the height of the capital letters. It is measured from the baseline—the line on which the letters sit—to the capline—the line at the top of uppercase letters. Because the x-height and cap height vary with each typeface, it can be useful to compare them when combining typefaces.

counterforms (counters) are enclosed white spaces located inside of, and partially enclosed within, characters that affect legibility, readability, and the density of forms. Counterforms vary with each font, depending on its size, height, weight, and width.

small capitals are specially designed capital letters that share the same weight (and approximate height) as lowercase letters. SMALL CAPITALS can be used when elements, such as acronyms or abbreviations, appear in body or continuous text. In such cases, SMALL CAPITALS replace FULL CAPITALS in body text to avoid unwanted emphasis that FULL CAPITALS command due to their larger appearance. SMALL CAPITALS allow body text to flow continuously without distraction. Not all typefaces contain small capitals. If they are needed, choose a typeface that has them. Avoid improvising small caps by reducing the size of full capitals. This often results in a thinner stroke weight and an awkward appearance that is not visually cohesive with the lowercase letters.

Ultra Light, *Italic*
Regular, *Italic*
Medium, *Italic*
Demi Bold, *Italic*
Bold, *Italic*
Heavy, *Italic*

Ultra Light Condensed, *Italic*
Regular Condensed, *Italic*
Medium Condensed, *Italic*
Demi Bold Condensed, *Italic*
Bold Condensed, *Italic*
Heavy Condensed, *Italic*

Avenir Next and Avenir Next Condensed, designed by Adrian Frutiger with Akira Kobayashi, is a contemporary sans serif typeface with a number of style variations. A broad typeface family provides unlimited options to add depth to compositions.

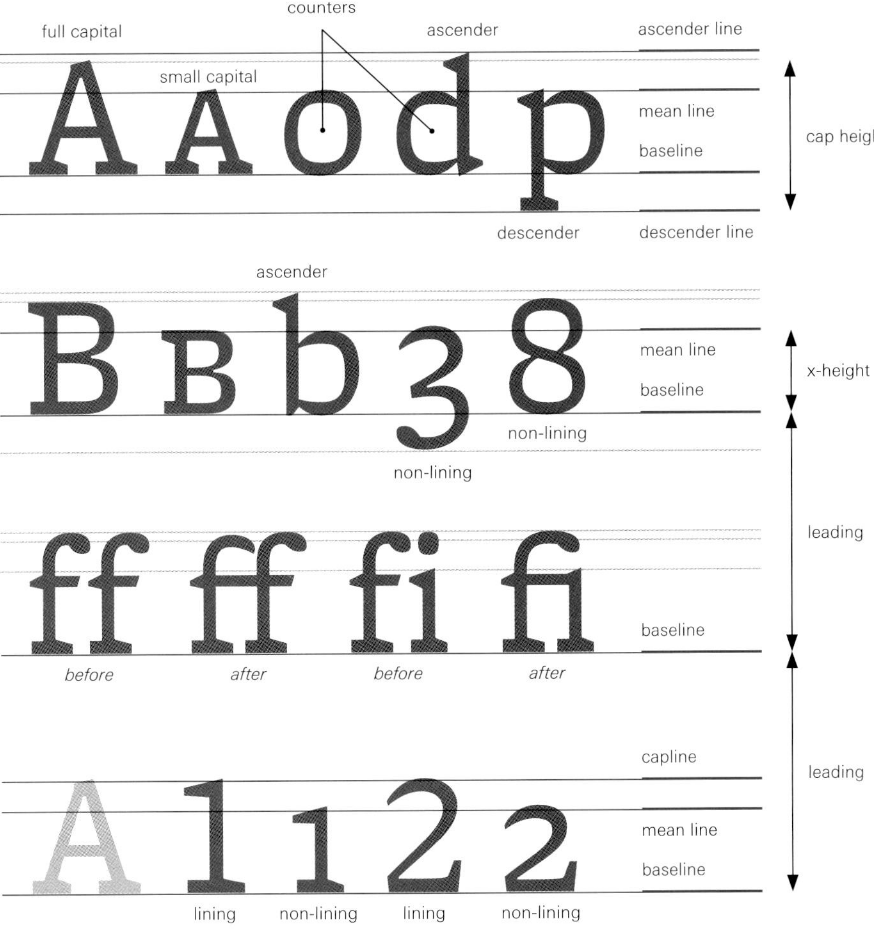

A basic framework of typography, which includes terms and anatomy, is learned and used consistently in the designer's vocabulary.

numerals Typefaces contain different styles of numerals: lining, non-lining, proportional, and tabular. Lining figures, which are also known as title figures share the same height as full capitals. They do not have ascenders or descenders.

Non-lining figures, also known as old style or text figures, share the same x-height as the lowercase letters and feature ascenders, descenders, and variable widths. Non-lining numerals work effectively within continuous text, eliminating unwanted attention that lining numerals can often produce. Non-lining figures also pair perfectly with small capitals, though they will appear too small next to full capitals.

Proportional figures are numerals with a variable width or body size. For example, a *1* has a narrower width than a *8*. They accommodate many types of texts—except numerical data or columns of numerals that require vertical alignment (in these cases, tabular figures excel). Proportional figures may be lining or non-lining.

Tabular figures are monospaced numerals, which means that all of the numerals share the same character width; they have a fixed width. They accommodate numerical data or columns of numerals that require vertical alignment, as required when designing tables or charts. Tabular figures may be lining or non-lining. It is advantageous to choose typefaces with all sets of numerals to have the broadest range of typographic options.

ligatures are specially designed forms produced by the considered union of two or three letters into a wholly new character. Ligatures offer refinement and often resolve collisions that occur when certain pairs of letters appear next to each other. For example, in some typefaces, the lowercase *f* may extend into the space of the letter following it, including the lowercase *i*. Common ligatures include ff, ffi, ffl, fi, and fj.

typeface selection

With an understanding of the characteristics of typefaces, the selection process begins. The first step is to evaluate the function and longevity of the design. Is it a book with a large body of text and a long shelf life? Is it an invitation or poster for a special one-time event with limited text? Is the design geared toward a broad or specific audience? In all scenarios, it is critical to examine the text provided and determine all of its typographic variables—from heads and subheads to body and caption sizes. No text is to be left unconsidered. Understanding the typographic needs for specific texts is important because not all typefaces work in every situation. Choose typefaces that best serve the content and the delivery of its message. For example, a typical spread from this book contains headings, subheadings, body, captions, headers, footers, and folios. This is a considerable number of variables that need individual attention in relationship to the entire typographic system. The diversity of text dictates the need for a flexible and reliable typeface family with full character sets (alphabet, numerals, punctuation, and diacritics) and a range of fonts to establish hierarchy.

Topic Portfolio
LUCINDA DEVLIN
9 **Where Death Becomes Us**
A view of "The Omega Suites"

Letters to the Editor
12 **Fads Everywhere!**

From the Editor
13 **What Makes A Magazine**

KENNETH HARTMAN
16 **Life Without Parole**
The long, protracted death of a life sentence

JULIA ROCHESTER
21 **Brazil's Big House**
And the campaign to shut it down

JEAN TROUNSTINE
26 **Family Drama**
Framingham Women's Prison presents "The Scarlet Letter"

TOM PRESTON
32 **The Life Sentence**
When the hereafter isn't soon enough

DIANE BOONE
41 **Dragon Lady**
She cooks with fire in a prison kitchen

DAN TAMIR
44 **Out of Line**
Refusing to serve in the Israeli Army

Topic Portfolio
RAHIMULLAH SAMANDER
48 **Faces From Guantanamo**
Paying a visit to former detainees

CHESA BOUDIN
57 **Making Time Count**
Looking back on a childhood of visiting hours

LAURA HERSHEY
62 **Disability Prisons**
Wheeling oneself to jail

KRISTINE MCNEIL
69 **Girl, Interrupted**
A decade spent in an Egyptian prison

JACK BLACK
75 **The Big Break**
Escaping the horrors of Folsom

Topic Portfolio
ALIX LAMBERT
81 **Killing Time**
Russian prisoners and their tattoos

| giampietro+smith |
The typeface Gotham is set in a range of weights to establish hierarchy and add typographic color. A combination of fonts, as well as upper- and lowercase settings, distinguishes author names, articles, and descriptions. Gotham features open counters that enhance readability and add white space to the page.

| giampietro+smith |
A strong image commands the cover; it nicely contrasts the clean and elegant masthead, *Topic*, which establishes the typographic tone of the magazine and alludes to the design within.

The next step is to select and preview a range of serif and sans serif type families, as well as display faces, if applicable. Evaluate historical and contemporary connotations as they relate to the content. Typefaces that are innovative one year might be appropriate and timely, or they could be outdated. Traditional faces that go beyond fashion could be classic and timeless, or they could be too conservative. Examine type families in a variety of settings that match the requirements of the design. To help narrow the options, compare the selections side by side and determine which evoke favored emotions, demonstrate maximum legibility and readability, and reflect the needs of the client and viewer.

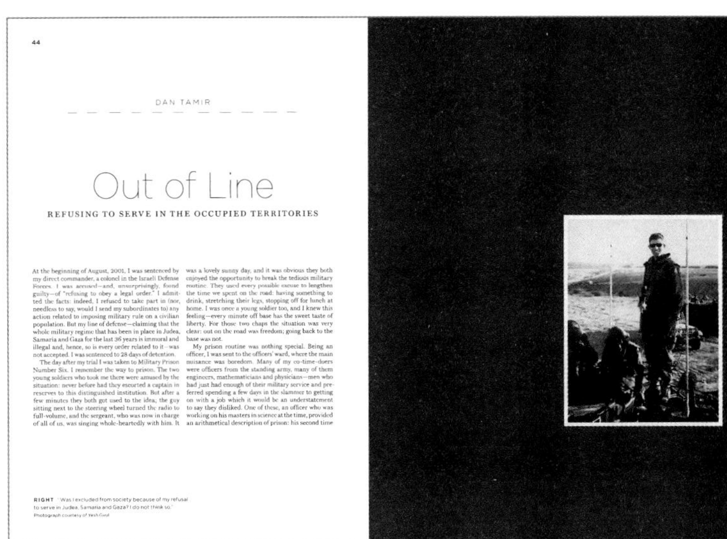

44

DAN TAMIR

Out of Line

REFUSING TO SERVE IN THE OCCUPIED TERRITORIES

At the beginning of August, 2001, I was sentenced by my direct commander, a colonel in the Israeli Defense Forces. I was accused—and, unsurprisingly, found guilty—of "refusing to obey a legal order." I admitted the facts: indeed, I refused to take part in (nor, needless to say, would I send my subordinates to) any action related to imposing military rule on a civilian population. But my line of defense—claiming that the whole military regime that has been in place in Judea, Samaria and Gaza for the last 36 years is immoral and illegal and, hence, so is every order related to it—was not accepted. I was sentenced to 28 days of detention.

The day after my trial I was taken to Military Prison Number Six. I remember the way to prison. The two young soldiers who took me there were amused by the situation: never before had they escorted a captain in reserves to this distinguished institution. But after a few minutes they both got used to the idea; the guy sitting next to the steering wheel turned the radio to full-volume, and the sergeant, who was now in charge of all of us, was singing whole-heartedly with him. It was a lovely sunny day, and it was obvious they both enjoyed the opportunity to break the tedious military routine. They used every possible excuse to lengthen the time we spent on the road: having something to drink, stretching their legs, stopping off for lunch at home. I was once a young soldier too, and I knew this feeling—every minute off base has the sweet taste of liberty. For those two chaps the situation was very clear: out on the road was freedom; going back to the base was not.

My prison routine was nothing special. Being an officer, I was sent to the officers' ward, where the main nuisance was boredom. Many of my co-time-doers were officers from the standing army, many of them engineers, mathematicians and physicians—men who had just had enough of their military service and preferred spending a few days in the slammer to getting on with a job which it would be an understatement to say they disliked. One of these, an officer who was working on his masters in science at the time, provided an arithmetical description of prison: his second time

RIGHT "Was I excluded from society because of my refusal to serve in Judea, Samaria and Gaza? I do not think so."
Photograph courtesy of Yesh Gvul

| giampietro+smith |
An interior spread introduces the serif typeface Miller, which harmoniously contrasts with the sans serif Gotham. Used for subheadings and justified body text, Miller contrasts nicely with the clean sans serif.

"I was crucified by Soviet power."
"I won't stand on my knees before the authorities." (Eight-pointed star worn below the kneecap.)
"What we love destroys us."
"As long as I live, I hope."
"I'm a slave to fate, but no lackey to the law."
"And life will teach you to laugh through tears."
"I love my one friend strongly."
"Alyonka, I ask and beg for one thing, don't leave me alone."
"I hate lies in people."
"Don't wake." (On the eyelid.)

A SAMPLING OF PHRASES TATTOOED ON PRISONERS

| giampietro+smith |
A close-up details a centered alignment of text that is simply set and readable. The quiet presentation is subordinate to the black-and-white photograph on which it sits. Note the use of the fi ligature in the word "crucified" on the first line.

combining typefaces A single typeface family with a range of styles, weights, and widths will typically satisfy the needs of most projects. For a broader typographic palette, the designer may also explore combining typefaces. Multiple type families, typically up to two or three (though this all depends on the content), extend the typographic possibilities. Not only do multiple typefaces provide visual contrast, they also help the designer establish hierarchy and distinguish information. Typeface combinations—when used wisely and with a delicate hand—can also serve to enhance typographic color, rhythm, and texture while adding perceived value and sophistication.

Typefaces are often combined based on their comparative visual characteristics. For example, serif and sans serif typefaces with similar widths and x-heights, such as Sabon and Syntax, are comfortable pairings. Type families that have been designed by a single designer and share proportional relationships are strong matches. A harmonious combination is Meridien and Frutiger designed by Adrian Frutiger. Some typefaces, such as Rotis and Thesis, are designed with sans serif, semi sans, and serif variations that are consistently designed throughout the extensive family.

Additionally, serif or sans serif typefaces that are unrelated by their comparative characteristics or type designer, and have considerable visual differences, might be combined. Most often, these combinations should be notably distinct to provide enough contrast to justify the union. If a combination looks too similar, it might look like a mistake, rather than an intentional decision. Bodoni with Didot or Helvetica with Akzidenz Grotesque are two examples of less than desirable combinations due to their marked similarities. Finally, when considering typeface combinations, do not forget about display and script typefaces that can add unique style to the treatment of content in support of body text, such as titles, headings, subheadings, or folios. Display and script faces suitably combine with serif and sans serif typefaces.

No matter the typefaces used, all merit the respect and attention of the designer to maintain the integrity of the typeface design as carefully crafted by type designers. If a typeface is not a perfect fit, find another with the desired characteristics.

| **concrete [the office of jilly simons]** | This announcement for Hinge, a sound studio, reveals information through transparent sheets. The layout relies on type to carry the message and bring the viewer into the design. Layers of letters and numbers create intrigue by sharing a consistent baseline that blends the pages.

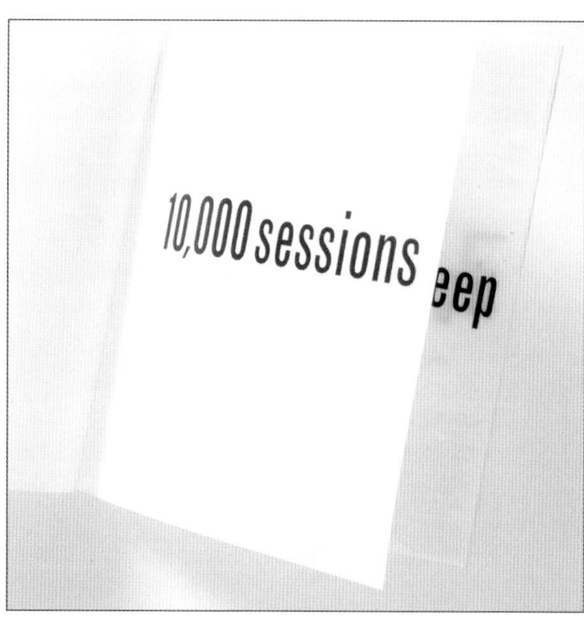

Thesis
TheSans
TheMix
TheSerif

Rotis
Sans Serif
Semi Sans Serif
Semi Serif
Serif

Typeface superfamilies, such as Rotis and Thesis, include sans serif, semi sans, semi serif, and serif variations, all of which share similar proportions throughout the family and provide multiple typographic options that cross classifications.

Sabon
Syntax

Meridien
Frutiger

Examining the characteristics of letterforms with comparable widths and x-heights (Sabon and Syntax), are considerations when combining typefaces. Additionally, typefaces that share proportional relationships and are designed by one designer often combine well, as seen with Meridien and Frutiger by Adrian Frutiger.

Bodoni
Didot

Grotesque
Helvetica

Typefaces that fall within the same classification often share comparable features and result in poor combinations due to their notable similarities and lack of visual contrast.

| **concrete [the office of jilly simons]** | On the fourth spread, typefaces change to surprise the viewer and contrast the tone of the previously seen condensed face. The design loosens up with the energy brought to the page through the arrangement and combination of typefaces.

designing with type

It is critical for the designer to be intimately familiar with any text before working with it. Every project is unique and demands different approaches based on the content. Determining the function of the design before shaping the page or screen influences its typographic presentation. Is it an annual report that contains several charts and lists that demand easy access? Is it a poster with limited textual content that needs visual impact? Is it a book with large amounts of continuous text? The designer develops, composes, and controls a typographic system that leads the viewer through the design without visual roadblocks that prevent accessibility and comprehension.

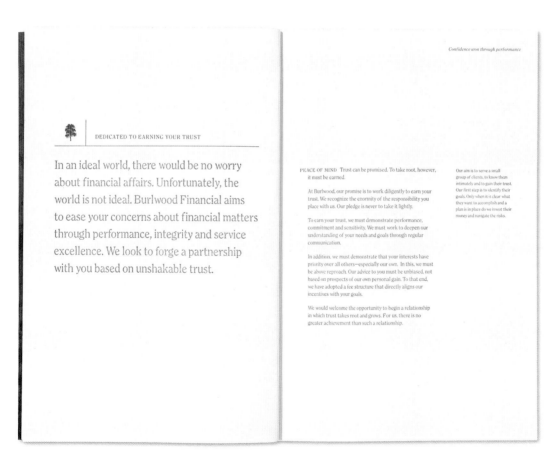

Confidence won through performance

DEDICATED TO EARNING YOUR TRUST

In an ideal world, there would be no worry about financial affairs. Unfortunately, the world is not ideal. Burlwood Financial aims to ease your concerns about financial matters through performance, integrity and service excellence. We look to forge a partnership with you based on unshakable trust.

PEACE OF MIND Trust can be promised. To take root, however, it must be earned.

At Burlwood, our promise is to work diligently to earn your trust. We recognize the enormity of the responsibility you place with us. Our pledge is never to take it lightly.

To earn your trust, we must demonstrate performance, commitment and sensitivity. We must work to deepen our understanding of your needs and goals through regular communication.

In addition, we must demonstrate that your interests have priority over all others—especially our own. In this, we must be above reproach. Our advice to you must be unbiased, not based on prospects of our own personal gain. To that end, we have adopted a fee structure that directly aligns our incentives with your goals.

We would welcome the opportunity to begin a relationship in which trust takes root and grows. For us, there is no greater achievement than such a relationship.

Our aim is to serve a small group of clients, to know them intimately and to gain their trust. Our first step is to identify their goals. Only when it is clear what they want to accomplish and a plan is in place do we invest their money and navigate the risks.

| **capsule** | One typeface applied with shifts in scale and position achieve an ordered design. Large type commands presence without cluttering the layout, which features a strong horizontal grid line from which primary text hangs. Subordinate typographic information is set in smaller sizes that progressively move across the page.

legibility and readability are inherent to successful communication. Although the terms are used interchangeably, differences between them do exist. Legibility refers to the recognition of individual letterforms and their relative position to other letters in word formation. The design of the typeface determines legibility. An illegible typeface will not be readable. Readability refers to how typography is presented to the viewer as words, lines, and paragraphs. It is influenced by the typographic arrangement, including factors such as line length, leading, and spacing. Readability is dependent on the designer and his or her ability to work with typography effectively. If a text is unintentionally unreadable, it is likely that it is poorly composed or the typeface is illegible; its application needs reconsideration or new typefaces should be chosen.

In some applications, intentional illegibility for aesthetic—not communicative—reasons may be desirable. For example, any typographic element, or combinations of them, can be carefully constructed into layers, textures, and graphic forms that are intended for expression and visual interest—not legibility or readability.

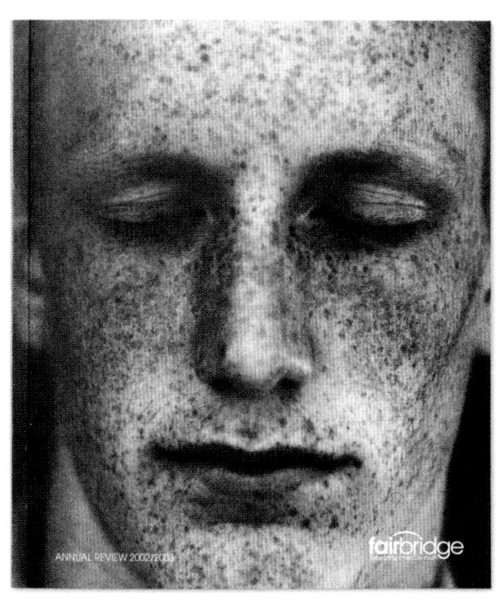

| **hat-trick design** | A dominant photograph commands attention on the cover of this annual review. Subtle typography is composed simply along the bottom margin. It is diminutive yet easily distinguishable within the dark areas of the image by knocking out of the paper stock.

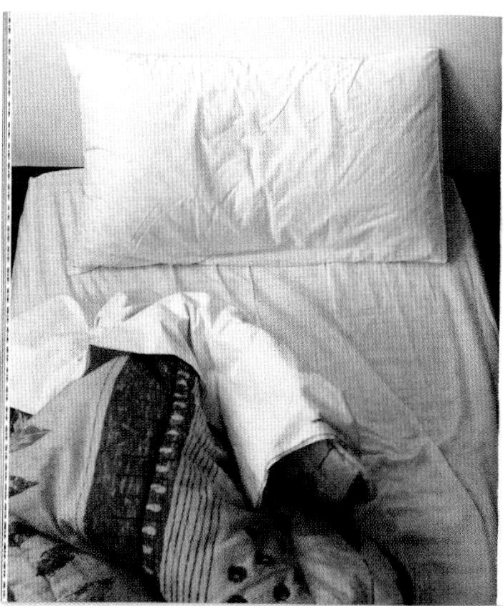

| **hat-trick design** | Hand lettering, an alternative to typefaces, adds distinction to the spacious interior spreads of this annual review. Even when not using traditional typefaces, it is important that all lettering maintain legibility and readability to convey the message of the design effectively.

objective and subjective representation

Although many methods of designing with type exist, most approaches fit into two categories of representation: objective and subjective. Objective representation is straightforward and practical. It is characterized by a clear (sometimes viewed as conservative) presentation of content and text that is visualized directly and efficiently. The typographic design shares messages without relying on conceptually driven applications of type and form that imply deeper meanings. Objective representation is neutral in tone without imposing on the viewer a specific graphic style, point of view, or emotional impact. Examples of objective representation include maps, charts, diagrams, and timetables.

Subjective representation reflects an idea-based, conceptual, and interpretive visualization of text. Subjective solutions may also be called poetic or expressive. They are heavily focused on a theme or idea that creates a unique experience for the viewer. Often allowing for greater complexity in the design, subjective representation can be layered or textural, creating a considered integration of type and form on the page or screen. Subjective representation appeals to the emotions of the viewer and offers multiple levels of navigation through the design.

Whether a design is objective or subjective (or somewhere in between), the designer's task is to read, understand, and approach the text with a critical eye and design with type compositions that are engaging and readable, while also appropriately reflecting the content.

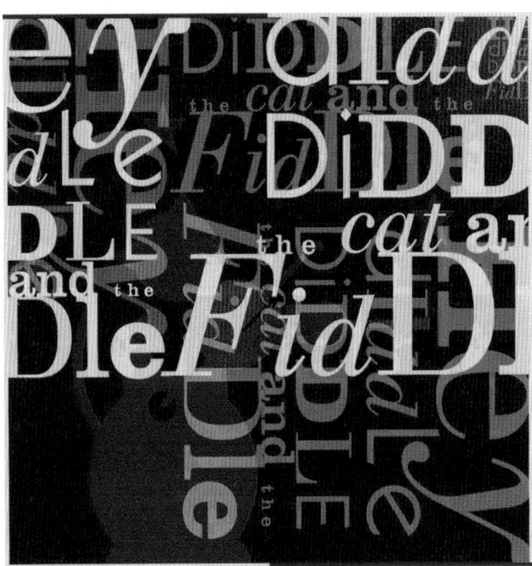

| **meghan eplett** | The type seen in *The Cat and the Fiddle* is musical. By using multiple type sizes and typefaces (Clarendon, Walbaum, and Kabel), the designer has made the text rhythmic. Type tells the story via dense textures that fill the page and connote volume.

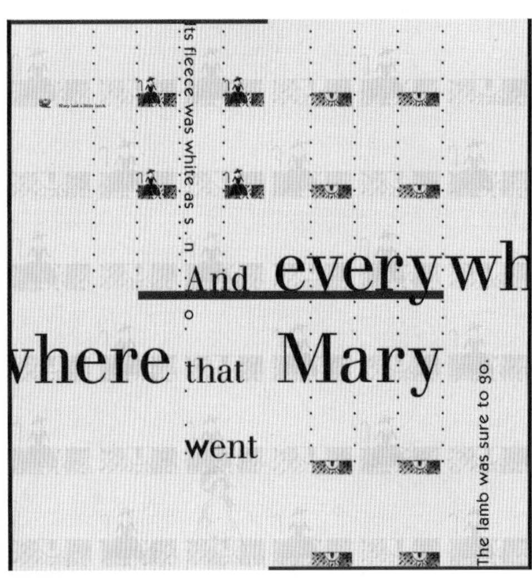

| **meghan eplett** | The viewer is led down and across the spread for *Mary Had a Little Lamb*. The type forms a path for the viewer to follow in the same way that the lamb follows Mary.

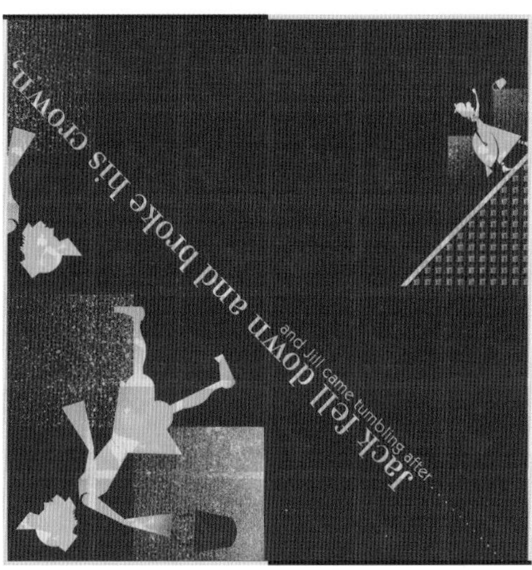

| **meghan eplett** | The type in *Jack and Jill* is composed along a dynamic angle. The unnatural reading direction encourages the viewer to make connections between the position of the typography and its connection to the story.

macro and micro perspectives The designer views the process of designing with typography via the lens of macro and micro perspectives—seeing the design holistically. One view (macro) is concerned with the overall composition; the other view (micro) applies to the typographic details. The macro view is concerned with the whole body of type—the typographic system—that makes up the design. Seeing all content at once, the designer establishes the format of the composition, its hierarchy, and the placement of the visual elements. Within the macro lens, each element needs attention. With a micro perspective, the designer concentrates on typographic details, such as kerning, spacing, and ragging, to ensure a clean presentation and consistent use of type throughout the design. Such attention to detail touches all type in the design, refining it and contributing to the success of the whole. Attention to macro and micro perspectives is critical—they are interdependent and equally important.

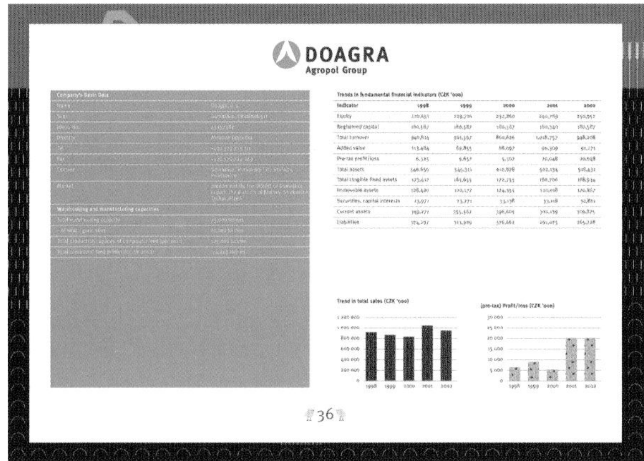

| **studio najbrt** | A page from this annual report features a number of tables and graphs, which are common examples of objective representation. Facts and figures lend themselves to clear, ordered presentations that express information directly.

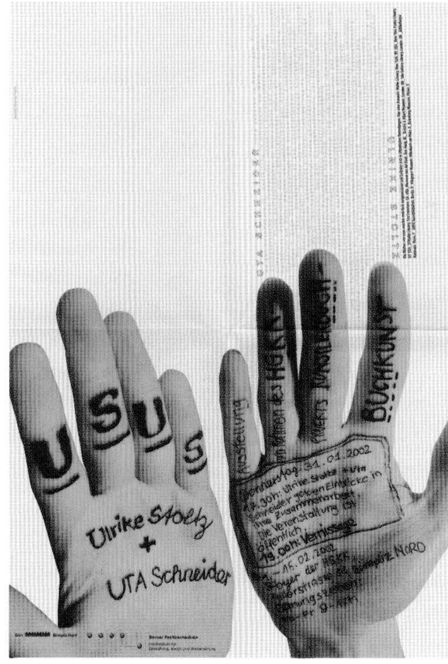

| **superbüro** | Alternative type treatments distinguish this set of posters. Unique letterforms draw attention and communicate with impact. Constructed out of plants and written on hands, the letters are conceptually appropriate; the plants symbolize Holland (home of Irma Boom), whereas the hands connote the left and right pages of a book (USUS are book designers).

| **nb: studio** | A more traditional, symmetrical composition demonstrates balance through the use of a single typographic column and contrasting black-and-white pages. Changes in type size provide variety, while the unusual structure of the book promotes interaction.

symmetry and asymmetry There are different ways to compose the typographic page or screen: symmetrically or asymmetrically. Symmetrical compositions offer balance and harmony. They possess inherent stability that is approachable and understandable. However, symmetry may also be static, which can lead to passive, lifeless typography that falls to the background. It can sometimes be difficult, though not impossible, to work with multiple typographic elements and achieve balance. Regardless, the designer must find ways to create variety and visual emphasis within a symmetrical structure to keep the design interesting.

Asymmetrical compositions generate activity and motion—desired qualities in most applications. They typically support compositions with numerous typographic variables. Multiple alignment points provide unlimited options for the arrangement of the visual elements. Like symmetrical layouts, the designer still needs to achieve optical balance. The visual elements should not feel like they are falling down or tipping over. There are many options when working asymmetrically: Use visual tension. Push typography to the edge of the page. Contrast large elements with small ones. Turn type on its side and mix orientations. Vary the depth of columns. Use graphic shapes and imagery to offset the typographic elements. With the designer in control, the compositional possibilities for enriching the design are limitless—without overcomplicating it and doing too much.

| **lichtwitz** | An underlying structure provides vertical alignment points for the placement of text columns, which feature the use of type weight to distinguish information. The left margin serves as the leading edge for dominant typography.

alignment refers to the horizontal and vertical positioning of typography within the margins. The edges of the page or screen can also serve as alignment points, if the type is strong enough and will not be trimmed off during production or beyond safe areas on screens. The designer uses alignment to create relationships between the elements of the design. Alignments helps unify the composition. The precise alignment of typography across and down the page cultivates harmonious spatial relationships and consistency. Connected sight lines lead the viewer through the design. Grids and systems of proportions provide the divisions of space to achieve alignment. It is critical to note that typographic settings often need subtle adjustments to create proper optical alignments.

typographic color refers to overall type lightness and darkness based on perceived gray value, not on hue. Typographic color is affected by how a typeface is used—its size, style, and spacing (leading and tracking). Different values of type affect its appearance and hierarchy, while providing depth, rhythm, and variation. A lack of typographic color may be dull and result in a static design. The contrast of typographic elements creates dynamic, rich compositions with dark and light values.

| **kontour design** | The variable density of the justified text blocks demonstrates perceived gray values. Typographic color is affected by the range of styles, weights, and widths of the typeface Cholla.

| **344 design, llc** | This book spread is carefully structured and composed along horizontal, vertical, and diagonal alignment points that create optical connections between the visual elements, strengthening and unifying the design.

type size is measured in points. Large and small shifts in type size can make a significant difference between clarity and confusion, elegance and clumsiness. Changes in type size are effective methods to create hierarchy and add contrast to the page. In addition, remember that typographic application relies heavily on optical settings. For example, typefaces that are the same point size generally do not match in visual size. Adjustments are needed to harmonize their appearance. In addition, it is sometimes helpful to develop a proportionate scale of type sizes that foster relationships and provide a range of options for all variables throughout the design. Though not all design projects require such detailed consideration of type sizes, it is useful to do studies and develop a system based on the hierarchical needs of the content before beginning to design.

case Uppercase and lowercase settings have individual characteristics that make them useful in typographic applications. Lowercase letters are typically more readable than uppercase because of their variation in form, as well as the white space in and around each character (counters). Ascenders and descenders also assist with word recognition. Because uppercase characters share a cap height, recognition is emphasized letter by letter, which slows down the reading process. This often makes it impractical for large amounts of text, including paragraphs. Uppercase settings can be used for emphasis and to denote text hierarchy.

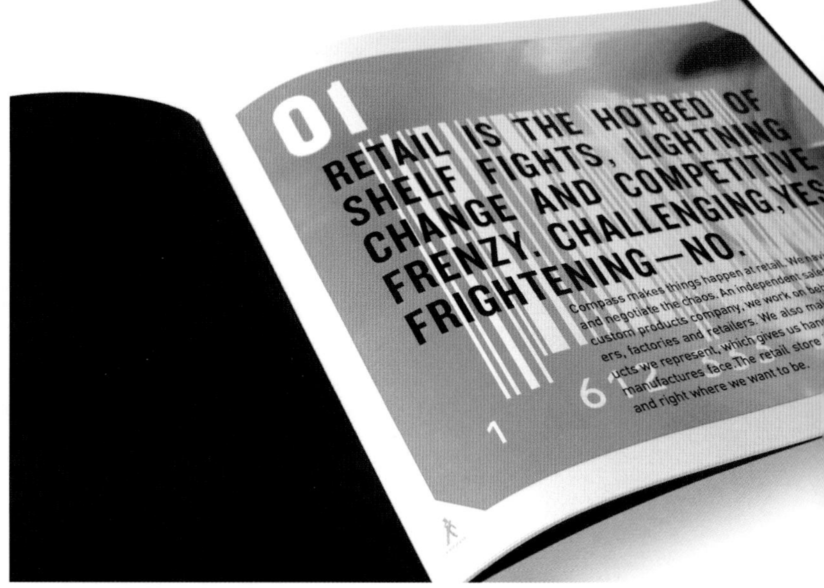

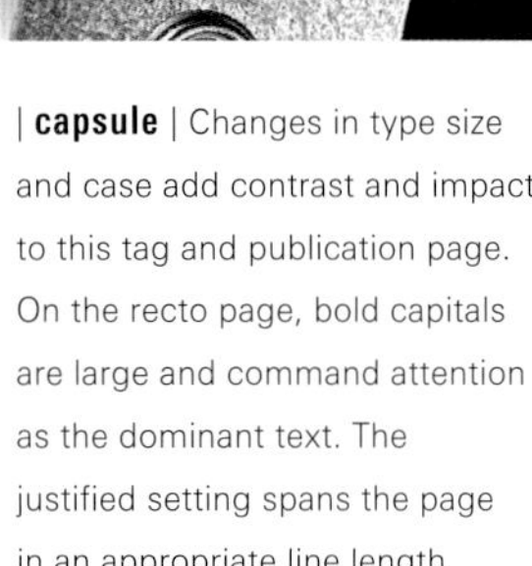
| **capsule** | Changes in type size and case add contrast and impact to this tag and publication page. On the recto page, bold capitals are large and command attention as the dominant text. The justified setting spans the page in an appropriate line length.

kerning and tracking *Letterspace* refers to the spaces between letters, whereas *word space* is concerned with the spaces between words. Adjusting letterspace and word space improves legibility and finesses letter-to-letter and line-to-line relationships to achieve optically even type settings. With any adjustments, whether loose or tight, always be consistent.

Kerning, also known as letterspacing, is used to adjust the slight distances between letters to avoid character collisions and irregular and unwanted spaces. Kerning fosters a uniform typographic texture that allows the text to flow and read smoothly. It is critical when setting text in large type sizes, because the spacing irregularities are more apparent. Common character combinations, including *Ty*, *Va*, *Yi*, *11*, and *19*, almost always require attention.

Tracking is concerned with the overall spacing of words, lines, and paragraphs and can improve readability. It also affects typographic color; tightly spaced text appears heavier and darker on the page, whereas open text appears lighter and gray. However, as letters get closer, collisions occur. As they move further apart, they lose their identity as words. A general rule is to avoid tracking lowercase letters, especially (almost always) in paragraph settings. The text becomes less legible and readable as spacing increases. However, very slight amounts may improve readability, especially with bold and condensed typefaces. Uppercase settings most always demand tracking with a careful eye to increase legibility and readability.

"Typography is the basic grammar of graphic design, its common currency."

"TYPOGRAPHY IS THE BASIC GRAMMAR OF GRAPHIC DESIGN, ITS COMMON CURRENCY."

The variation in the shapes of lowercase letters, particularly ascenders and descenders, allows them to be recognized easily. Uppercase letters, which are uniform in height, require additional spacing—tracking—to enhance recognition.

quote from
Mixing Messages: Graphic Design in Contemporary Culture
by Ellen Lupton
Princeton Architectural Press, New York, 1996

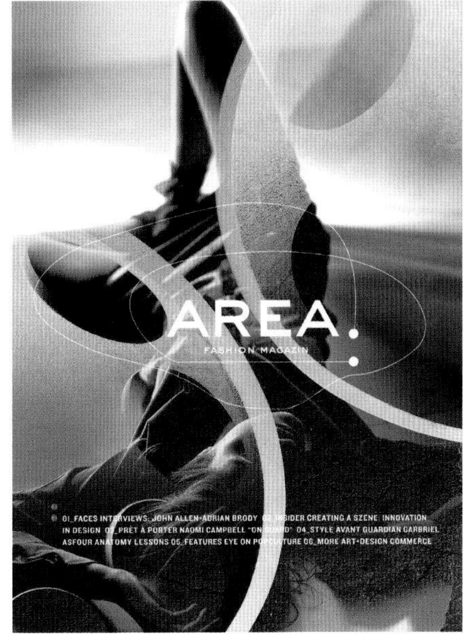

| **kearneyrocholl** | An uppercase setting is used on this cover of *Area* magazine. Attention to tracking is imperative to improve readability when working with capitals.

Type

Type

corrected spacing

TYPE

TYPE

corrected spacing

Kerning and tracking are used to achieve optically even type, notably in larger sizes and uppercase settings. Spacing fixes collisions and creates optical balance, while improving the readability of all capitals. Relying on default settings is often ineffective.

line length refers to the width of a text line. It is measured in picas. Like most typesetting factors, line length depends on the typeface, type size, leading, spacing, and column width. The quantity of text also needs to be considered. An ideal line length contains forty-five to seventy-five characters per line. If the line length is too short, the number of words per line is limited and the movement from one line to the next happens too quickly. If the line length is too long, the viewer's eyes travel a great distance to read one line of text, which is tiring; they can easily lose position or have difficulty moving down to the start of next line. Generally speaking, large type sizes often work best with wider line lengths, while small type excels with narrower line lengths.

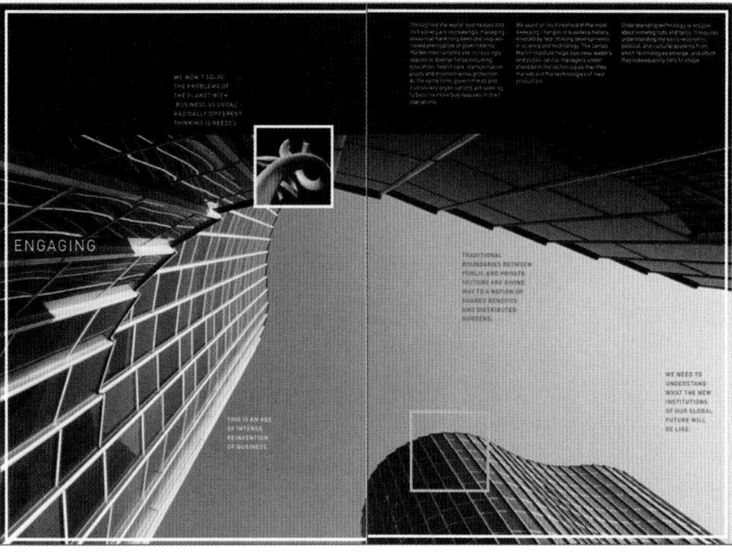

| **wilsonharvey/loewy** | Brochure spreads demonstrate an evident structure defined by three primary spatial intervals containing body text with comfortable line lengths. The divisions of space provide alignment points for other visual elements, including photography and secondary typography.

leading, which is measured in points, refers to the vertical distance from one baseline to the next. Leading is positive, negative, or solid. Positive leading is greater than the type size used, such as 8 point type size with 12 point leading. Negative leading is less than the type size used, like 9 point type with 6 point leading. Solid leading equals the type size that is being used. In most situations, positive leading works well. Negative leading can work with larger type sizes, like in display settings not body text.

Type size, x-height, and line length influence leading. For example, typefaces with tall x-heights and ascenders, as well as long descenders, often require more leading to avoid lines colliding into one another. Texts with longer line lengths benefit from more leading to accommodate the horizontal motion of reading. If leading is too tight, it is easy to jump to the next line without finishing the first. If it is too loose, the text no longer appears continuous and may be read as individual lines, not connected thoughts. In some cases, it is helpful to develop a system of leading intervals that unite all of the type elements in a design with a number of typographic variables, such as a book or magazine.

| kinetic singapore |
The business cards are designed to allow each designer to express his or her voice by controlling the presentation of the message using variations in content and color shifts in the typography.

Leading refers to the vertical distance from one baseline to the next. When leading is greater than the type size used, it is called positive leading, for example 9 point type over 12 point (9/12). When leading is less than the type size, it is called negative leading, such as 9/7. Leading can also be set solid, which means that the leading equals the type size (9/9). When two pieces of text intersect between lines, it is called overlapping text. This typesetting technique can integrate select texts.

"No matter how admirably we plan our work or how fine in design are the types we select, its appearance when printed depends on good composition—the combination of type into words, the arrangement of words in lines, and the assemblage of lines to make pages."

positive leading (9/12)

"No matter how admirably we plan our work or how fine in design are the types we select, its appearance when printed depends on good composition—the combination of type into words, the arrangement of words in lines, and the assemblage of lines to make pages."

negative leading (9/7)

"No matter how admirably we plan our work or how fine in design are the types we select, its appearance when printed depends on good composition—the combination of type into words, the arrangement of words in lines, and the assemblage of lines to make pages."

solid leading (9/9)

"No matter how admirably we plan our work
quote from
or how fine in design are the types we
Typographers on Type:
select, its appearance when printed depends
An Illustrated Anthology from William Morris
on good composition—the combination of
to the Present Day
type into words, the arrangement of words
by Rauri McLean, editor
in lines, and the assemblage of lines to
W. W. Norton & Company, New York, 1995
make pages."

overlapping text (9/24 and 8/12)

| **evelock design** | This brochure features a series of heads and flush left paragraphs that move across the front of each panel. The layout structure is based on the accordion fold, which divides the layout into six sections.

paragraph settings are determined by the content, which includes the different kinds of text and its quantity. The designer selects appropriate measures—type size, line length, and leading—that will best accommodate the text, promote interaction with the design, and fit comfortably within the space of the page or screen. The measures should activate the compositional space and encourage reading. Setting type in awkward arrangements with poor measures results in limited function, reduced readability, and strained viewer comprehension.

There are four styles of paragraph settings, also known as typographic alignments: centered (C), flush left/ragged right (FL, FL/RR), flush right/ragged left (FR, FR/RL), and justified (J, FL&R). Centered text is ragged along both sides. It often connotes formality and is useful in limited settings rather than for continuous text (running paragraphs). Flush left text is evenly aligned along the left side, and the right side of the text is ragged. Used often, flush left text is typically highly readable. Flush right text is set solid along its right edge with a ragged left. Readability is lessened because the beginnings of each line are ragged without the same starting point. Justified paragraphs settings are flush along both right and left edges. They create clean lines and strong left and right alignment edges, but pose challenges when the variable word spaces cause gaps, or holes, called rivers. Rivers are undesirable because they distract the eye.

centered (c)

Determining paragraph settings depends on the content,
which includes the different kinds of text and its quantity.
The designer selects appropriate measures—type size,
line length, and leading—that will best accommodate the
text, promote interaction with the design, and fit comfortably
within the space of the page or screen. The measures should
activate the compositional space and encourage reading.
Setting type in awkward arrangements with poor measures
results in limited function, reduced readability, and
strained viewer comprehension.

flush left, ragged right (fl, fl/rr)

Determining paragraph settings depends on the content,
which includes the different kinds of text and its quantity.
The designer selects appropriate measures—type size, line
length, and leading—that will best accommodate the text,
promote interaction with the design, and fit comfortably
within the space of the page or screen. The measures should
activate the compositional space and encourage reading.
Setting type in awkward arrangements with poor measures
results in limited function, reduced readability, and
strained viewer comprehension.

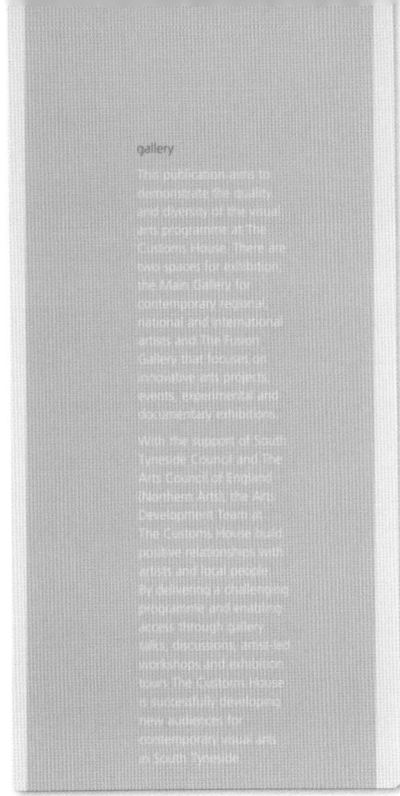

| founded design | Interior spreads can be viewed horizontally and vertically. The type is clean and simple. On the inside front cover, a narrow column of flush left text mimics the shape of the format. Another interior spread pictures quiet and small type playing a secondary role in support of the imagery.

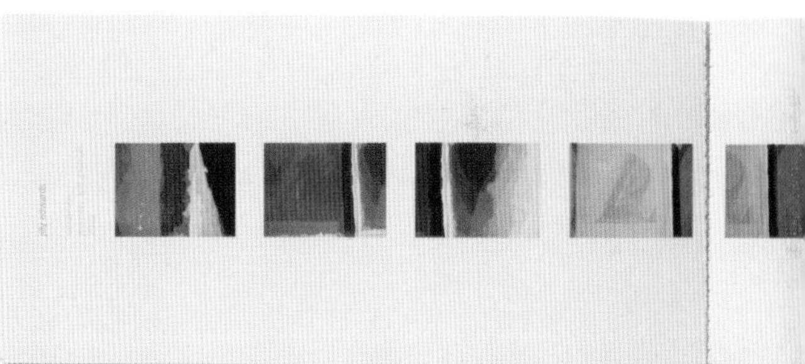

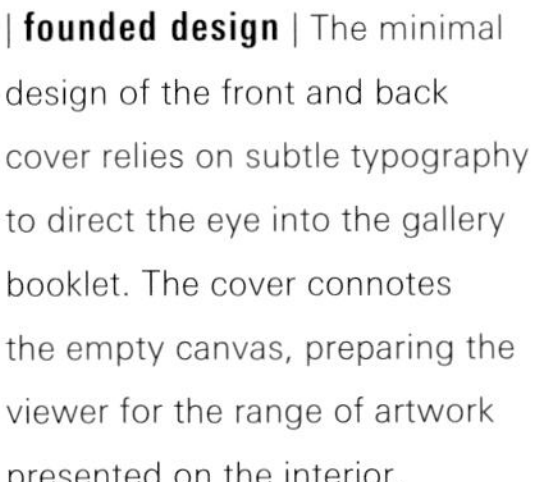

| founded design | The minimal design of the front and back cover relies on subtle typography to direct the eye into the gallery booklet. The cover connotes the empty canvas, preparing the viewer for the range of artwork presented on the interior.

flush right, ragged left (fr, fr/rl)

Determining paragraph settings depends on the content, which includes the different kinds of text and its quantity. The designer selects appropriate measures—type size, line length, and leading—that will best accommodate the text, promote interaction with the design, and fit comfortably within the space of the page or screen. The measures should activate the compositional space and encourage reading. Setting type in awkward arrangements with poor measures results in limited function, reduced readability, and strained viewer comprehension.

justified (j, fl&r)

Determining paragraph settings depends on the content, which includes the different kinds of text and its quantity. The designer selects appropriate measures—type size, line length, and leading—that will best accommodate the text, promote interaction with the design, and fit comfortably within the space of the page or screen. The measures should activate the compositional space and encourage reading. Setting type in awkward arrangements with poor measures results in limited function, reduced readability, and strained viewer comprehension.

All paragraph settings, except justified, have fixed spacing, which means that the word spaces are consistent. Justified settings have variable spacing. The word spaces are flexible when justified, depending on the number of words per line, as well as the length of the line. Working with justified text can be challenging. Without careful attention to type size and line length, visible holes, called rivers, may appear. Rivers are a series of inconsistent word spaces that create distracting open holes that run vertically through justified paragraphs. Flush left, flush right, and centered paragraphs are typically easier and more flexible to work with because they require fewer adjustments to achieve proper settings. Compositions may feature the use of one or a combination of paragraph settings. However, take caution if mixing paragraph settings. Using inconsistent alignments could lead to disorder and a scattered presentation of content that may be difficult for the viewer to follow.

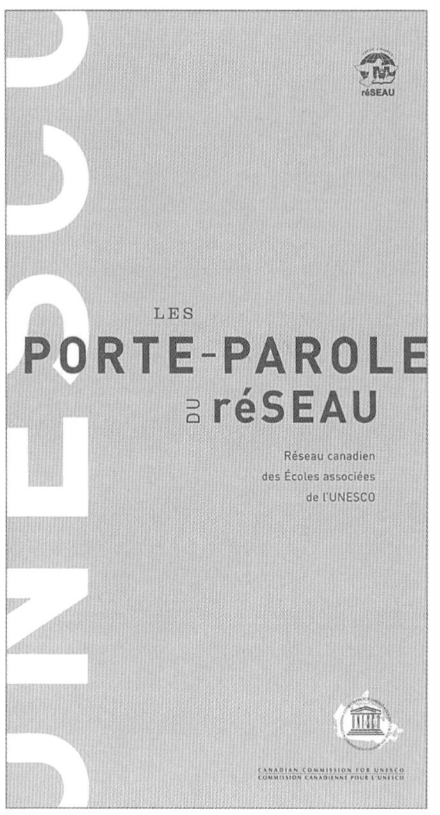

| **kolégram** | The cover of *Les Porte-Parole du réSeau* is composed in an optically centered, asymmetric layout. The title is a solid unit that features well-spaced capitals and shifts in scale and orientation. White letterforms on the left break the color field and demonstrate how type can function as graphic form and provide impact.

| **kolégram** | The first interior spread is composed with decisive hierarchy. A single justified column falls from the top margin. Its alignment, height, and width mirror the book format to create a harmonious relationship. A bold, uppercase title sits to the left of the body text with dominance, whereas a small page number rests on the bottom of the page.

"A good typographer is
one who can arrange type so as to produce
a graceful, orderly page that puts no strain on the eye.
This is the first and last
fundamental requisite of book design,
and like most operations,
it is a matter of years of training."

quote from
The Form of the Book: Essays on the Morality of Good Design
by Jan Tschichold
Hartley & Marks,
Washington, DC, 1991

Select lines of text, such as a quote or short poetry, may be composed in an asymmetric configuration, which adds visual interest to the arrangement of the text. Although not appropriate for all content, this method offers flexibility and potential for typographic invention.

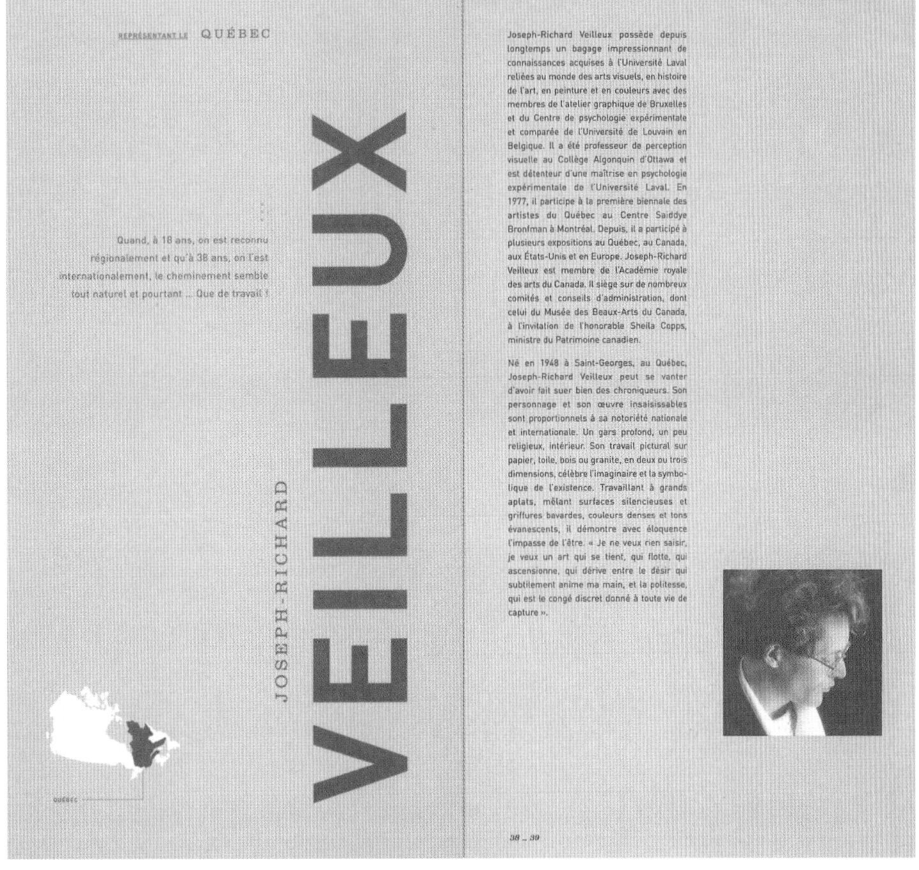
REPRÉSENTANT LE QUÉBEC

Quand, à 18 ans, on est reconnu régionalement et qu'à 38 ans, on l'est internationalement, le cheminement semble tout naturel et pourtant ... Que de travail !

JOSEPH-RICHARD

VEILLEUX

Joseph-Richard Veilleux possède depuis longtemps un bagage impressionnant de connaissances acquises à l'Université Laval reliées au monde des arts visuels, en histoire de l'art, en peinture et en couleurs avec des membres de l'atelier graphique de Bruxelles et du Centre de psychologie expérimentale et comparée de l'Université de Louvain en Belgique. Il a été professeur de perception visuelle au Collège Algonquin d'Ottawa et est détenteur d'une maîtrise en psychologie expérimentale de l'Université Laval. En 1977, il participe à la première biennale des artistes du Québec au Centre Saiddye Bronfman à Montréal. Depuis, il a participé à plusieurs expositions au Québec, au Canada, aux États-Unis et en Europe. Joseph-Richard Veilleux est membre de l'Académie royale des arts du Canada. Il siège sur de nombreux comités et conseils d'administration, dont celui du Musée des Beaux-Arts du Canada, à l'invitation de l'honorable Sheila Copps, ministre du Patrimoine canadien.

Né en 1948 à Saint-Georges, au Québec, Joseph-Richard Veilleux peut se vanter d'avoir fait suer bien des chroniqueurs. Son personnage et son œuvre insaisissables sont proportionnels à sa notoriété nationale et internationale. Un gars profond, un peu religieux, intérieur. Son travail pictural sur papier, toile, bois ou granite, en deux ou trois dimensions, célèbre l'imaginaire et la symbolique de l'existence. Travaillant à grands aplats, mêlant surfaces silencieuses et griffures bavardes, couleurs denses et tons évanescents, il démontre avec éloquence l'impasse de l'être. « Je ne veux rien saisir, je veux un art qui se tient, qui flotte, qui ascensionne, qui dérive entre le désir qui subtilement anime ma main, et la politesse, qui est le congé discret donné à toute vie de capture ».

38 _ 39

| **kolégram** | Interior spreads feature the same text: the name of a person or group, their country, one callout, body copy, and imagery. To maintain order, a consistent layout is applied. The last name (or group) is the focal point running up from the bottom of the page. It identifies each spread while giving it an individual spirit that breaks the monotony of the pages. The name also provides an edge for the callout text and country name, which sit in alignment.

indents are used to signal a change from the paragraph preceding it. (The first paragraph of any text does not require an indent because there is nothing that comes before it.) Indents vary in depth, depending on the type size and line length. Traditionally, indents are the size of an em, which is a measure of horizontal distance equal to the type size used. For example, if 8-point type is used, the em measure is 8 points. However, many alternatives are available. For example, add an extra line space between paragraphs. Even without an indent, the empty space is a visual cue indicating a new paragraph. Instead of adding space, insert typographic devices at the beginning of the paragraph, such as bullets, ornaments, or symbols. Hanging indents, also known as outdenting, feature the first line set outside of the other lines that are indented below it. It is a good idea for the designer to experiment with indents so that he or she gets a sense of what functions appropriately with different designs.

spacing With the paragraph positioned in relation to the shape of the page or screen, as well as the other typographic variables and visual elements, it is necessary to hone its finer details. For example, consideration of overall spacing is important; all type must be tracked and kerned as needed. For multiple page layouts, be aware of the sequential flow of the text. Do not leave a short line with one or two words—a widow—at the end of the paragraph. This leaves too much white space on the last line and attracts attention because it is the only isolated element of the paragraph. Do not begin a spread with the last line from the previous spread. On a similar note, do not end a spread with the first line of a paragraph that runs onto the next page. Both of these situations are known as orphans.

Hyphenation and ragging also require careful attention. Some simple suggestions to improve the appearance of text include avoiding more than two hyphenated lines in a row. Be alert to how words split. If possible, try to break them into even halves instead of leaving a stump at the end or beginning of a line. Never hyphenate proper names.

It is also important to adjust ragged edges of a paragraph. Manual line breaks for all paragraph settings will help clean irregular edges. In limited cases, when manual breaks are not enough, very inconspicuous adjustments in column widths and slight spacing tweaks are also helpful. Anything that diverts attention from readability needs to be remedied. The eye should not be led to empty spaces, truncated words, short lines, or ledges that extend too far beyond the average line length. Take care to avoid angles, curves, holes, and shapes. Rags should appear even, but not so even that they look justified. The designer strives to achieve smooth ebb and flow through paragraphs without distractions.

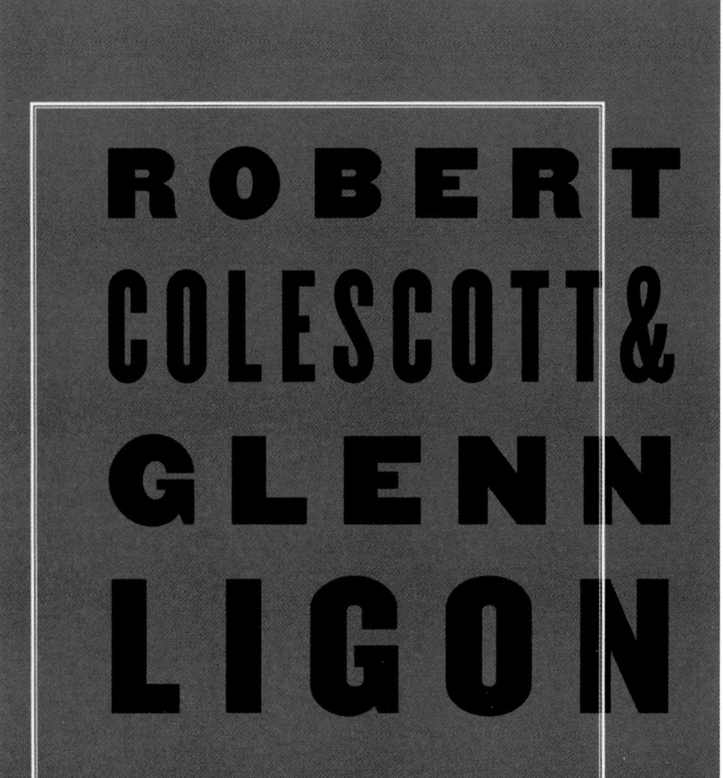

| **aufuldish & warinner** |
The *Robert Colescott & Glenn Ligon* catalog uses a mix of serif, sans serif, and display typefaces. The composition is clean and the type treatment elicits a contemporary tone.

hyphens, en dashes, and em dashes

Hyphens (-) appear in hyphenated or breaking (break-ing), words, as well as compound words (twenty-one, well-liked). En dashes (–) link items such as dates (2000–2018), times (6:00–8:00), page numbers (25–63), and other strings of numbers. Extra space does not need to be applied before and after en dashes. However, the designer may need to kern around en dashes to avoid accidental collisions. Em dashes (—) separate thoughts in sentences. No spaces are needed before and after—though slight kerning may be needed around the em dash. Depending on a client's house style, en dashes can replace em dashes when separating thoughts. In such cases, space before and after the en dash is required. Use either method consistently.

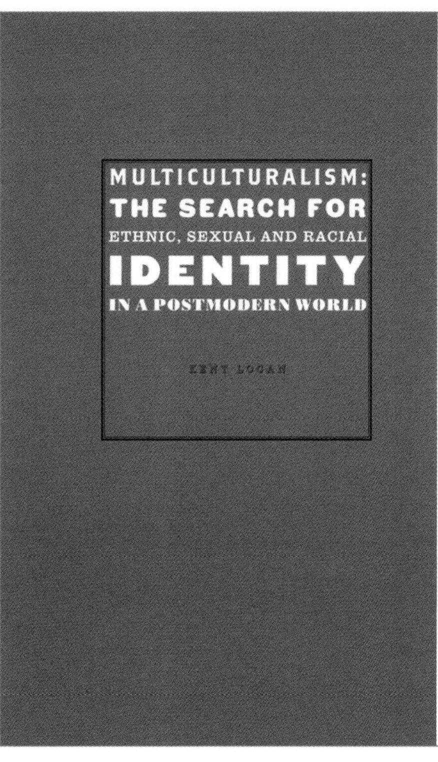

IT IS OFTEN SAID that "socio-political art" becomes dated very quickly and disappears from virtually all curatorial agendas. And while art that references overt, specific events or persons typically does not stand the test of time or memory, there have been several universal socio-political themes which have been a part of the fabric of society for the past thirty years and thus have transcended the narrow label of "socio-political art." In fact, art that is "relevant" to social issues is at the heart of the definition of postmodernism, and is often referenced under the umbrella of "multiculturalism."

As discussed above, Pop Art was a mirror on the popular culture of materialism and "keeping-up-with-the-Joneses" so prevalent in the 1960's. But as the decade drew to a close, darker issues clouded the horizon. The optimism of the early 1960's seemed to evaporate with the continued escalation of the Vietnam War and the concurrent growing antiwar sentiment at home; simultaneously, the Civil Rights Movement was in full swing, heightened by the assassinations of Martin Luther King, Jr., and Robert Kennedy in 1968.

Up to this point, mainstream artists only addressed socio-political issues obliquely. The first artist of stature who dared to do it directly was, ironically, the Abstract Expressionist painter, turned realist, Philip Guston. In 1970, Guston shocked the art world with his show of hooded Ku Klux Klansmen at the Marlborough Gallery. The evil images of Klansmen smoking, drinking, sitting around in empty rooms or patrolling streets reflected Guston's deep disenchantment with the Vietnam War, the oppression of minorities' civil rights and general political corruption and ineptitude. Leon Golub explored this same territory in a more graphic figurative manner. His paintings of torturers, mercenaries and thugs exposed the dehumanizing aspects of tyranny, abuse of power, oppression and the exploitation of the innocent. In a similar manner, the German artists Georg Baselitz and Anselm Kiefer held up a mirror to Germany's role in World War II and the Holocaust. Kiefer was often referred to as the "archaeologist of German guilt" and "as a kind of Pied Piper leading away from the demons of the Third Reich" (Bernard Marcade, *Flash Art,* Oct.-Nov. 1985). Baselitz's 1965 "hero" paintings of partisans and peasants rising out of the ashes of post-war Germany represented the hope that German society could rebuild and regain a sense of respectability and pride. In Britain, Gilbert & George's series of "photo-sculptures" referenced issues as far ranging as homosexuality, social stratification, racism, totalitarianism and the disillusionment of youth—all questions raging through British society at the time. In many ways these "legitimized" socio-political art for the artists of the 1980's and 1990's. In that regard, similar issues would be pursued by artists as diverse as Cady Noland, Ida Applebroog, Jean-Michel Basquiat, Jerry Kearns, Tom Otterness and the South African William Kentridge, as well as the whole first generation of contemporary Chinese artists.

Racism, segregation and black voter disenfranchisement had also reached a boiling point in the early 1970's. The artist who first embraced those issues was the "new image" painter Robert Colescott. His cartoonish, raucous images of blacks in distorted historical situations were a biting commentary on popular racial stereotypes. And despite progress in addressing the many aspects of African-American status within our overall society, this sub-

{07}

| aufuldish & warinner |

A sample spread presents a justified paragraph setting for the treatment of the continuous text. Skillfully set in Bulmer, the text is the ideal size and line length for justification. The paragraph exhibits even spacing, ample leading, and hanging punctuation.

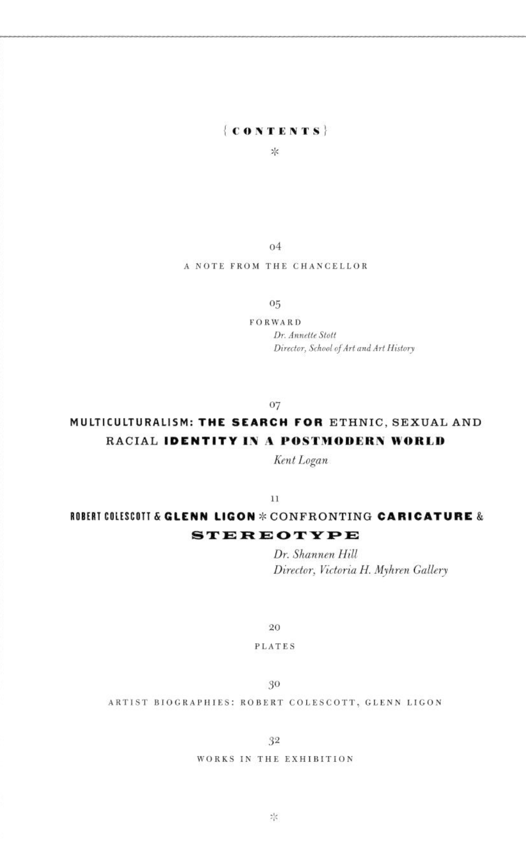

{ CONTENTS }

04
A NOTE FROM THE CHANCELLOR

05
FORWARD
Dr. Annette Stott
Director, School of Art and Art History

07
MULTICULTURALISM: **THE SEARCH FOR** ETHNIC, SEXUAL AND RACIAL **IDENTITY IN A POSTMODERN WORLD**
Kent Logan

11
ROBERT COLESCOTT & GLENN LIGON ✻ CONFRONTING **CARICATURE & STEREOTYPE**
Dr. Shannen Hill
Director, Victoria H. Myhren Gallery

20
PLATES

30
ARTIST BIOGRAPHIES: ROBERT COLESCOTT, GLENN LIGON

32
WORKS IN THE EXHIBITION

| aufuldish & warinner |

Old style numerals, spaciously set capitals, and italic type run down the contents page in a centered alignment. Fitting into the central axis, two essay titles exhibit distinct changes in typefaces, such as Clarendon, Bodoni, Champion, Brothers, Latin, and Gothic Round. The visual differences are varied and harmoniously composed. The density of the darkest letterforms contrasts with the lighter characters.

′ ′ ″ ″

‘ ’ “ ”

‘ ’ “ ”

Apostrophes and quotation marks may be inappropriately replaced with prime marks, which are used to denote feet and inches, minutes and seconds, and arcseconds and arcminutes. Depending on the typeface, apostrophes and quotations marks are angled or curved and open or closed, whereas prime marks are typically straight up and down.

5′5″

apostrophes, quotation marks, and primes

The correct use of apostrophes and quotation marks is a marked sign of the skilled and attentive designer. True apostrophes and quotation marks are curved (‘ “ ’ ”) or angled (′ ″ ′ ″), depending on the typeface. They are also open (‘ “ ′ ″) or closed (’ ” ′ ″) to signal beginnings or endings. Apostrophes and quotation marks are not straight up and down (' "). These forms are prime marks, which are typically straight or angled, represent measures such as feet and inches, minutes and seconds, and arcseconds and arcminutes.

The RSA Lecture Programme
For well over a century, the RSA has been organising lectures around the country to stimulate new thinking and fresh ideas about the challenges facing society. Not only do we attract the best speakers and attack the most diverse range of subjects, but we also promise a balanced and interactive debate.

Visit www.theRSA.org/events to see a complete listing of all RSA events, to listen to a lecture online, or to book yourself a place on a forthcoming lecture.

Events include:

Lisa Jardine, Professor of History, Queen Mary and Westfield College – Ingenuity and Commerce

Panel discussion on Music and Technology

Richard Kozul-Wright, United Nations Conference on Trade & Development

RSA at the Cheltenham Science Festival

“The sort of work the RSA does is broad, expansive… one of the few places that fosters genuine debate.”

Sonita Alleyne, Founder and Director, Somethin' Else

“When people with expertise in different areas talk to each other, everyone's a winner.”
Alex James, Bass player, Blur
www.theRSA.org

| **nb: studio** | Interior spreads feature sans serif typography that is legible in its compositional simplicity. Hanging quotes are present along the flush left edge of the text. The hung quotes maintain the straight edge of the text and avoid unsightly indents to achieve optical alignment.

hanging punctuation Optical alignment is a critical factor when designing with type. Anything that distracts the eye from reading needs subtle adjustments. This requires making minor adjustments to the type so it appears aligned. For example, when punctuation, such as apostrophes and quotation marks, falls along flush edges of text, a slight indent is created that is visually distracting; the marks need tending to ensure that the characters optically align. Punctuation marks moved outside of flush edges maintain optimal visual alignment of the text. Demonstrating a high level of typographic refinement, hanging punctuation is a detailed process. However, software often provides features that easily support it. Hanging punctuation typically applies to smaller forms such as asterisks, apostrophes, commas, and quotation marks. Forms that are the same optical weight as letterforms, like parentheses, question marks, and exclamation points, do not need finessing.

FINAL THOUGHTS Designing with type can be tedious and time consuming but ultimately rewarding. Education, practice, and experimentation allow the designer to make intelligent, thoughtful decisions about typographic selection, application, and refinement while achieving a high level of visual intrigue and sophistication. Although there are many rules when designing with type, there is also a tremendous amount of flexibility to break the rules capably. Typography expressed with aesthetic grace is essential to clear communication and adds a level of sophistication to any design.

| **nb: studio** | Type is used as texture and shapes the letters 'RSA' that run across the front and back cover of the Royal Society of Arts brochure. An interesting graphic, the texture is also functional. It is a running list of the 22,000 fellows of the organization.

"There are two sides to typography. First,
it does a practical job of work; and, second,
it is concerned with artistic form."

"There are two sides to typography. First,
it does a practical job of work; and, second,
it is concerned with artistic form."

corrected setting

Designing with type demands attention to details, such as hanging punctuation. To achieve the optical appearance of a flush edge, marks that include apostrophes and quotes are positioned just outside of the text alignment.

quote from
Typography: A Manual of Design
by Emil Ruder
Hastings House Publishers, Inc.,
New York, 1967

DESIGN

Form follows function—
that has been misunderstood.

Form and function should be one,
joined in a spiritual union.

FRANK LLOYD WRIGHT
architect

ANALYSIS

SEEING THE WHOLE AND ITS PARTS

The design process is evolutionary. It develops slowly over time and shapes the final design. The designer is actively involved with every aspect of the design process—from research and information gathering to brainstorming and conceptualization, as well as experimentation, development, and execution. When the design nears completion at the end of the execution stage, the designer must analyze the design to determine its success or failure, asking several important questions:

Is the design engaging and informative?

Is the delivery of the message appropriate and clear?

Does the design reflect its function and purpose?

Are the visual elements cohesive?

Is there a logical progression through the design?

the importance of analysis

Analysis is the final stage of the design process. Thoughtful attention to—and the considered evaluation of—the design ensures that all visual elements fit together like pieces of a puzzle. If one piece is out of place, the design is unresolved and the puzzle is incomplete. The missing piece could be found through careful examination. It helps to begin the analysis by seeing the design as a transparent medium. Look through the project and see all of its layers to identify if the visual elements are orchestrated harmoniously. The designer must evaluate the design considering numerous factors, including appropriateness, communicative value, effectiveness, and integration. Other form-based, critical assessment criteria are hierarchy, legibility, movement, organization, sequence, and structure. The designer also needs to examine the use of color, compositional space, and contrast, as well as image, scale, and typography.

The design can be analyzed further by carefully checking the interdependence of the parts to the whole. The whole is the culmination, or final product, of the design process. It creates initial impressions, encourages interaction, and establishes the pathway that leads the viewer toward understanding. The parts are the essential factors (the team players) that solidify the design. Inextricably linked to every visual element, the parts enable and support the communicative function of the design; they cannot exist independently of the whole. No matter how dominant or subordinate the role, all the visual elements are meaningful. However, they exist successfully only in their symbiotic relationship to everything else.

| **nielinger & rohsiepe** | A visual system of color, image, structure, and typography is introduced on this calendar. The layout initiates viewer interaction and creates interest while also establishing the mood of the design.

| **nielinger & rohsiepe** | Looking at two months of the calendar, it is evident that a visual system is flexibly applied. Distinct layouts for each month exist, yet all fit into a unified design scheme. Consistency is evident, as seen in the use of color.

| maggie gibbens | Characterized by a dramatic change in size, this poster effectively uses scale to achieve contrast. Active, layered, and implied letterforms lead the viewer through a sequence of pertinent information.

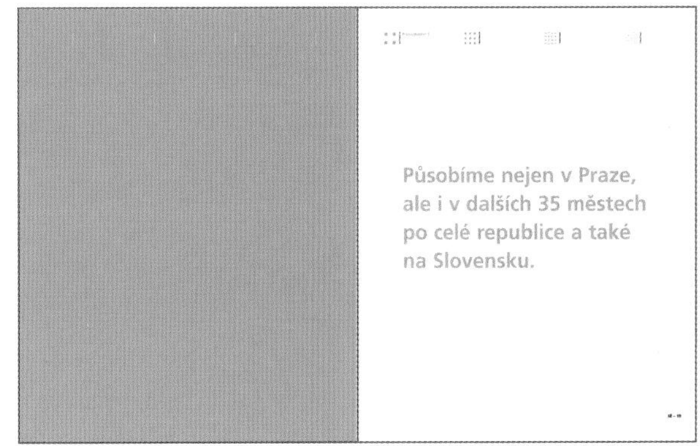

Působíme nejen v Praze,
ale i v dalších 35 městech
po celé republice a také
na Slovensku.

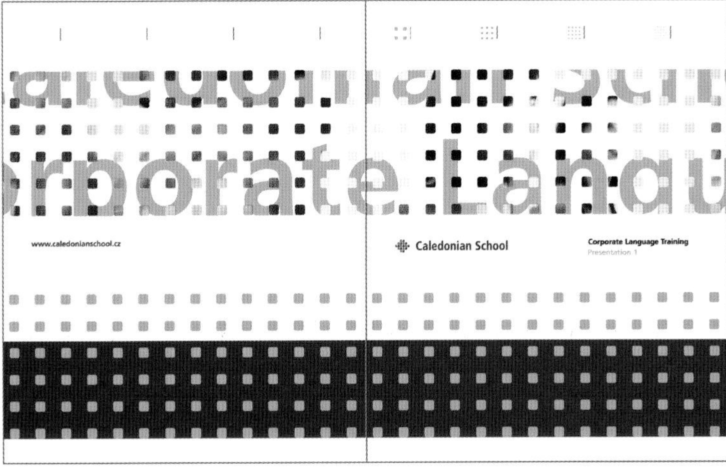

| studio najbrt | The *Corporate Language Training Presentation 1* brochure uses color (blue) as an identifier to separate it from the other brochures in the series. The brochures also feature repetitive square patterns and type that are uniformly applied to maintain consistency, which is critical to the unity of the series.

| studio najbrt | A series of four brochures for the Caledonian School is consolidated into one, harmonious package. Each of the brochures is distinguished by its content and photography, as well as a unique color seen on the spine.

evaluation considerations

Several analysis checkpoints are needed throughout the design process to keep the project on track. They ensure that the designer considers everything and does not jump to the final solution too quickly. The designer wants to avoid any surprises at the end of the process that would demand a complete overhaul of the design. At the end of the execution stage, the designer can expect to thoroughly analyze the design in preparation for its final production—this is the primary focus of the design analysis stage. The designer examines not only the big picture but also the function and success of its parts.

When the design reaches the analysis stage, the designer is intimately familiar with it and must examine the layout with a fine eye and calculated hand. It can be a difficult task to step away from the design and evaluate it objectively. It is critical to remember that the design is intended for a specific viewer. The designer must be objective and remove any personal preferences from the analysis for the benefit of the design. When analyzing a piece, it is sometimes helpful to ask colleagues, as well as targeted viewers, to assist in the process because outsiders can provide fresh perspectives and easily assess the success (or failure) of the design.

| **hendersonbromsteadartco.** | The use of color, texture, pattern, and expressive letterforms, makes this poster engaging and distinctive. Its first impression commands attention and leads the viewer into the piece.

| **hat-trick design** | A clean, elegant letterhead demonstrates a successful balance between the communicative and aesthetic functions of the design. Subtly accented with three lines of clean type, the spacious page allows room for correspondence while natural photography provides a soft background.

Critical analysis questions, which can be tailored to address individual projects, provide a starting point to begin the analysis of the design.

communicative function and purpose

Does the design reflect its function and purpose?

Is the delivery of the message appropriate, effective, and clear?

Does the design meet the client's objectives/goals?

Is there a balance between the design's communicative and aesthetic functions?

Is the design engaging, distinctive, and informative?

Does the integration of the visual elements create movement and rhythm?

Are the visual elements cohesive?

Does the design evoke the desired emotion, mood, and tone?

basic compositional factors

Is contrast used effectively to distinguish all visual elements?

Does the use of space direct the eye toward the positive areas of the design?

Are changes in scale of the visual elements effective?

Is the quantity of information in the composition too excessive or minimal?

Does the design exhibit depth, dimension, and perspective?

Are orientation and position of the visual elements used advantageously?

Is tension between the visual elements effective?

Is repetition used appropriately and without adding too many visual elements to the page?

Does the use of color add value without overpowering or distracting the viewer?

Do the graphic shapes and linear elements enhance the design?

Do the illustrations or photographs connote appropriate emotions and meaning?

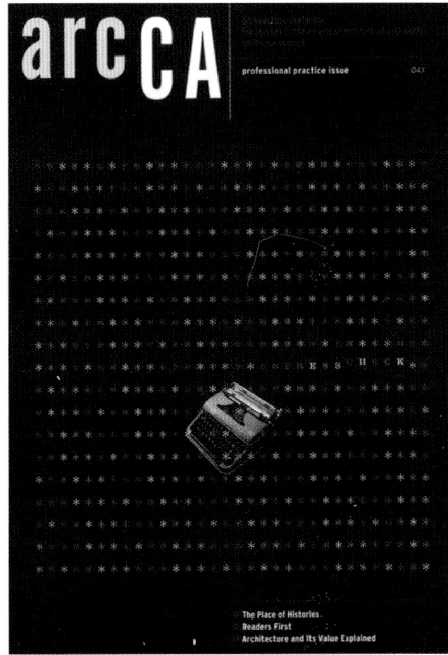

| **aufuldish & warinner** |

A bold type treatment commands the masthead of the architecture journal *arcCA*. Changes in case, color, and scale create contrast in the masthead and effectively distinguish content.

structure and organization

for in-depth structure and organization information, refer to *chapter 5: structure and organization*

Is an underlying structure or method of organization evident?

Do horizontal and vertical spatial divisions provide alignment points for the visual elements?

Do the margins activate the positive areas of the design rather than frame the page?

Do the number of spatial intervals, columns, or modules suit the quantity of information?

Is symmetry or asymmetry used advantageously?

Are the visual elements consistently aligned across and down the page?

hierarchy

for in-depth hierarchy information, refer to *chapter 6: the interaction of visual elements*

Is there a logical progression (sequence) through the design?

Is a strong systematic hierarchy evident?

Are the visual elements ranked and visually organized into dominant and subdominant levels?

Does a dominant focal point lead the viewer into the design?

Does the ordering system provide accessibility, continuity, integration, navigation, and variety?

Is there evidence of foreground, middle ground, and background?

Does the design avoid monotonous or overactive visual fields?

THE DESIGNER EXAMINES NOT ONLY THE BIG PICTURE BUT ALSO THE FUNCTION AND SUCCESS OF ITS PARTS.

typography

Does the typographic system encourage readability and comprehension?

Does the typography aesthetically invigorate the text with meaning?

Is the combination of multiple typefaces harmonious and optically matched?

Are the typefaces sending the appropriate attitude and personality?

Are true italic and bold fonts used, not improvised italic and bold styles?

Do the paragraph settings enhance the shape of the page?

Are changes in styles, weights, and widths distinguishing content effectively?

Is typographic contrast and color evident?

Are ligatures applied, if available, to the selected typefaces?

Are the typefaces legible and all text settings readable?

Are small capitals, as well as lining and non-lining numerals, used consistently?

Are all type sizes appropriate and not too small or large?

Are line lengths set in comfortable measures?

Is the leading between lines too tight or loose?

Does the typography need spacing (kerning and tracking) adjustments?

Do the paragraph settings suitably accommodate all the text?

Are all widows and orphans corrected?

Is attention paid to hyphenation and ragging?

Are indents used and consistently applied?

Are apostrophes and quotation marks used instead of prime marks?

Is attention paid to hanging punctuation?

Are hyphens, as well as en and em dashes, used correctly?

for in-depth typography information, refer to *chapter 7: typography*

FINAL THOUGHTS Analyze the design as a collective system versus an assortment of independent parts. Without a careful eye, the design may lack structure and organization, hierarchy, typographic proficiency, as well as clarity, value, and meaning. The designer pays close attention to every aspect of the design and makes numerous, thoughtful decisions along the way for its benefit.

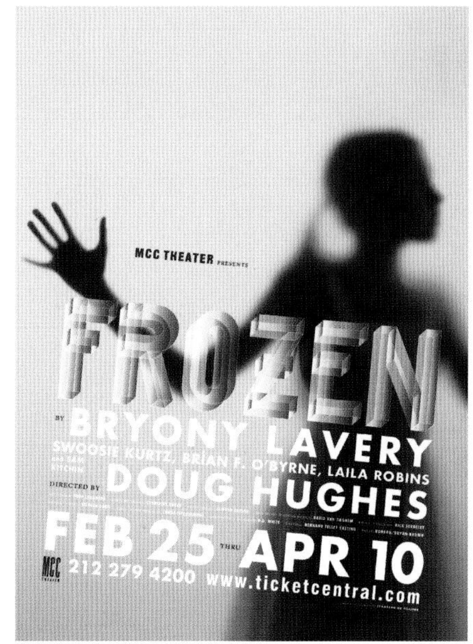

| **helicopter** | In the title treatment of the MCC Theater *Frozen* poster, letterforms create dimension. The stylized title is juxtaposed with sans serif type settings in a range of sizes to achieve hierarchy. The uppercase settings are aptly tracked with enough line spacing to enhance overall readability.

Design is a plan for arranging elements
in such a way as best
to accomplish a particular purpose.

CHARLES EAMES
architect, designer

PROFILES

LOOKING CLOSER

aufuldish & warinner 132
capsule 136
cheng design 138
ci studio 142
concrete [the office of jilly simons] 146
cook design 150
evelock design 154
renate gokl 158
hammerpress studio 162
hat-trick design 164
helicopter 168
hendersonbromsteadartco. 170
hoet & hoet 174
the jones group 176
kangaroo press 178
kearneyrocholl 180
kinetic singapore 184
kolégram 186
kontour design 190
lichtwitz 194
mitre agency 196
nb: studio 198
no.parking 202
noon 206
petrick design 208
rick rawlins/work and visual dialogue 210
rmac 212
samatamason 214
shinnoske design 218
studio najbrt 220
superbüro 224
visocky o'grady 228
wilsonharvey/loewy 232

AUFULDISH & WARINNER

California College of the Arts,
Master of Architecture Brochure and Poster;
Architecture Lecture Series Poster

art director, designer **bob aufuldish**
photographers **bob aufuldish, richard chang**

When the California College of the Arts added the Masters of Architecture (mARCH) degree to their program, Aufuldish & Warinner was approached to design materials announcing its inception. The first project in the series was a poster introducing the new program and establishing the visual language system that was applied to later designs. At the outset of the collaboration, art director/designer Bob Aufuldish consulted with the client to discuss the project objectives. "What I started with was what not to do," says Aufuldish. "The client pointed to a wall of posters for architecture programs and lecture series and said that they all looked the same to him. And they did—they all used a very narrow design vocabulary." It was critical to establish an initial design that would contrast existing architecture programs yet still reflect architecture, as well as the California College of the Arts, in a fresh, unexpected manner.

After meeting with the client, the design process moved into the visual realm. "The idea of using jellyfish came to me quickly. Jellyfish ended up being perfect on numerous levels—visually, they are beautiful and perfectly suited to their environment; conceptually they make a clear connection to the idea of architecture as experimental structure. As a bonus, they speak to the college's location on the West Coast," explains Aufuldish. "Pyrex glassware was used to suggest the more rational side of architecture. I also liked the glassware for its references to chemistry and alchemy. The jellyfish and Pyrex contrast with each other conceptually and formally but are both are translucent and liquid, which helps unify them. I especially like the inside of the brochure where a jellyfish hovers above a flask like a ghostly vapor." Aufuldish next composed a cohesive design that combined organic imagery with rectilinear shapes and type. "I was trying to communicate unconventional structure without showing a building or a model and without layering together imagery," adds Aufuldish.

The two-color brochure adapts the visual system designed in the poster. The typeface, Faceplate, is set consistently; the headings feature proficiently spaced capitals. Graphic shapes play a role in the structure of the composition. Transparent blue bars run across the cover and into the interior. Adding impact, they also provide baselines for headings, as well as alignment points for body copy.

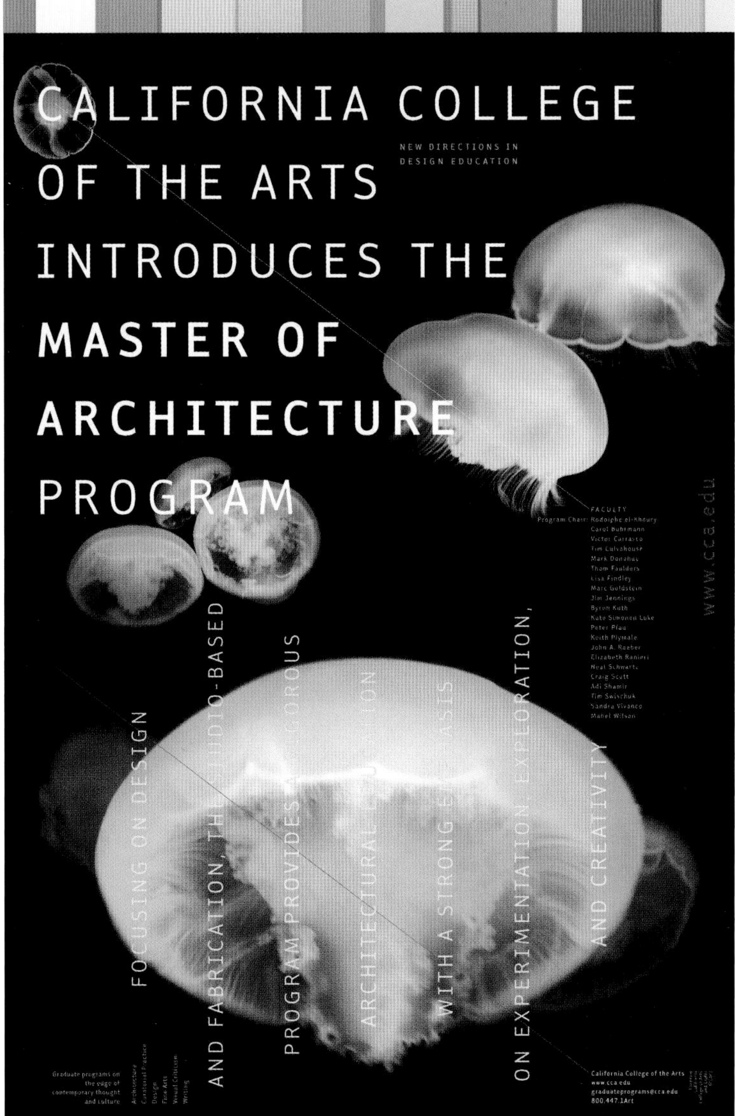

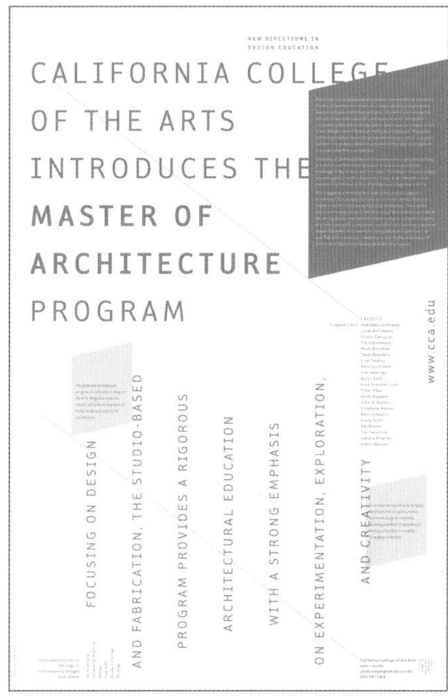

The California College of the Arts Master of Architecture poster takes an atypical approach toward the presentation of architecture. Using jellyfish as a metaphor, the design features organic imagery combined with clean typography. Orientation, position, and scale establish the hierarchy. Graphic shapes and linear elements offer structural reinforcement.

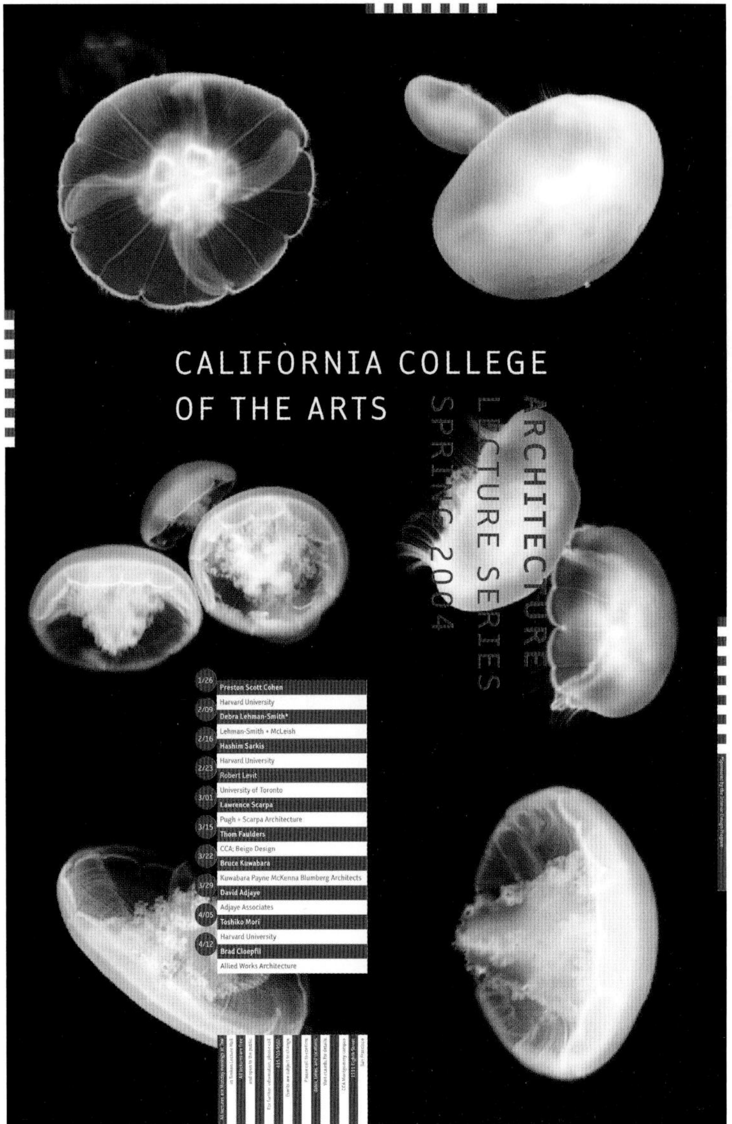

The fluid imagery glides on the surface of the brochure and posters, with graphic form adding color and providing the foundation for typography. Faceplate is the sole typeface; like the jellyfish, it is applied consistently and solidifies the visual system throughout all the pieces. Aufuldish further discusses the design: "The hierarchy is most complex on the master's poster because of the amount of text involved. Here, the hierarchy is controlled via color, size, position, and grouping. The brochure is a simpler matter because it's smaller and the majority of the text appears inside. The lecture series poster is structured functionally—the design and placement of photographs is based on the way the poster folds."

The California College of the Arts, Master of Architecture brochure and poster, as well as the Architecture Lecture Series poster, are compelling designs that effectively communicate the client's message in an exciting, distinctive presentation. Using the metaphor of jellyfish, as well the integration of color, form, and space, the work commands viewer attention. "The mARCH materials have been very successful," states Aufuldish. "The program completely filled its first class of thirty students."

The California College of the Arts Architecture Lecture Series poster combines imagery, graphic shapes, and typography. The jellyfish are distinctive, while the system of red and white rectangles adds visual interest, contains content, and defines the hierarchy.

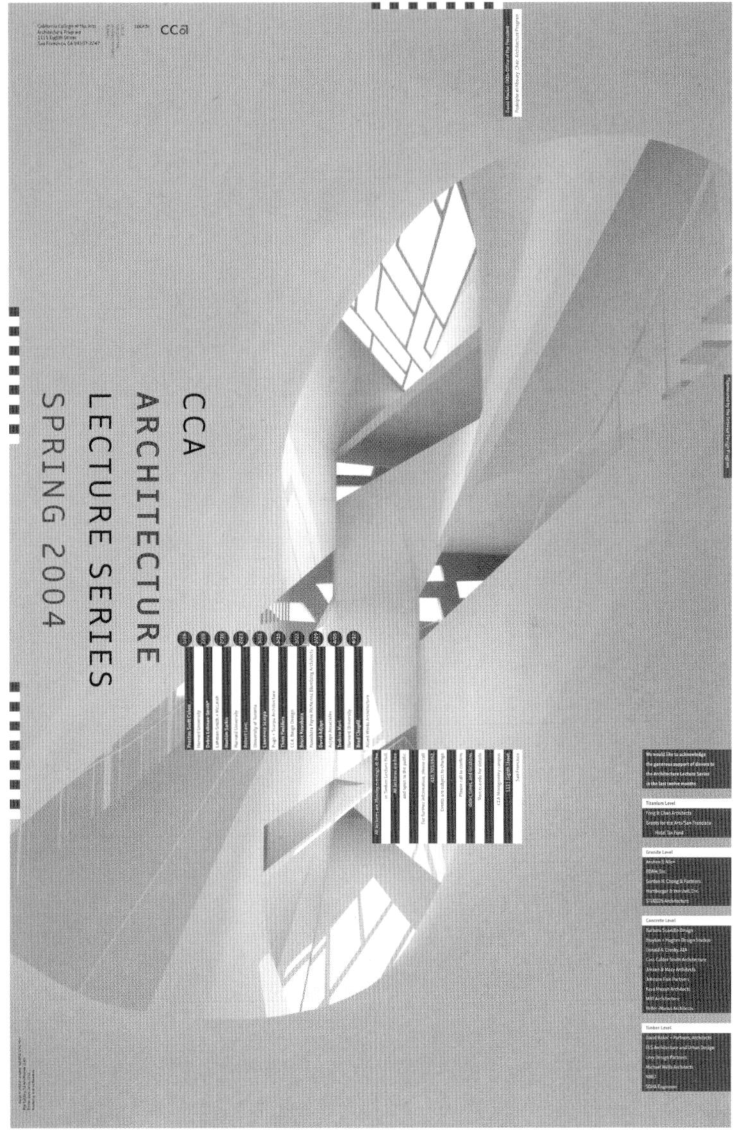

Capsule Letterhead System

CAPSULE

designers **brian adducci, greg brose, dan baggenstoss**

Capsule presents a dynamic image in their letterhead system, which includes envelopes, business cards, and mailing labels. "In designing our own stationery package, our goal was to develop a system that not only created a lasting impression but worked harder as a marketing tool than any brochure or website ever could," explains designer Greg Brose. Like all design projects, Capsule approached the project with a thorough methodology that included brainstorming, conceptualization, and exploration. "Once the name and philosophy was determined, we began by brainstorming metaphors that communicated explore, discover, and inspire," says Brose. (Explore, discover, and inspire are the primary themes of the identity system, as well as the philosophy of Capsule.) "Concepts were critiqued and refined until the final design was chosen to reflect the personality of Capsule."

The design process involved the development of a visual language system that is applied throughout all the materials produced. The visual elements used consistently include the typographic treatment, color palette, vertical orientation of the Capsule logotype, and the condensed 'C,' which is embossed on the letterhead and envelope and die cut on the business cards. Conceptually and aesthetically strong, the letterhead system also incorporates tactility and materiality into the design. "We wanted to use unique materials and textures to enhance the overall experience and engage the senses," adds Brose. Although textured paper is used, metal business cards demonstrate the most distinctive use of materials. Typography and linear elements are etched into both sides of the cards, and printed stickers allow for customization and the addition of color.

One of the significant elements of the Capsule letterhead system is its communicative value. Brose describes: "The design message comes to life in a way that creates a unique experience each time someone interacts with the stationery system. The recipient explores the artifacts and discovers the layers of meaning—a conversation is created around the meaning of the stationery system. For example, the golden section has been used as a fundamental design measure in art, architecture, and typography for centuries. In this context, we use it as a systematic element, which is sometimes confused with a ruler or decoration [on the business card]. Then, after a discussion around what the golden section measures—natural beauty—the participant learns something new. The result is an everyday example of our philosophy: explore, discover, and inspire."

The Capsule letterhead system engages the viewer and provides the opportunity to build a design dialogue among designers and nondesigners. The design is sophisticated and presents a contemporary image. "The conversation that the card starts is a great way to warm up a meeting, presentation, or almost any discussion," comments Brose. Through unique materials and presentation, it has created a memorable experience for anyone we meet."

Etched business cards distinguish the system. They incorporate the consistent elements of the visual system, including the logotype and typographic treatment. They also communicate Capsule's philosophy—explore, discover, and inspire. Nicely spaced capitals interact on the back of the cards. Stickers add color to the metal forms, contrast the reflective surface, and call attention to the name of the designer.

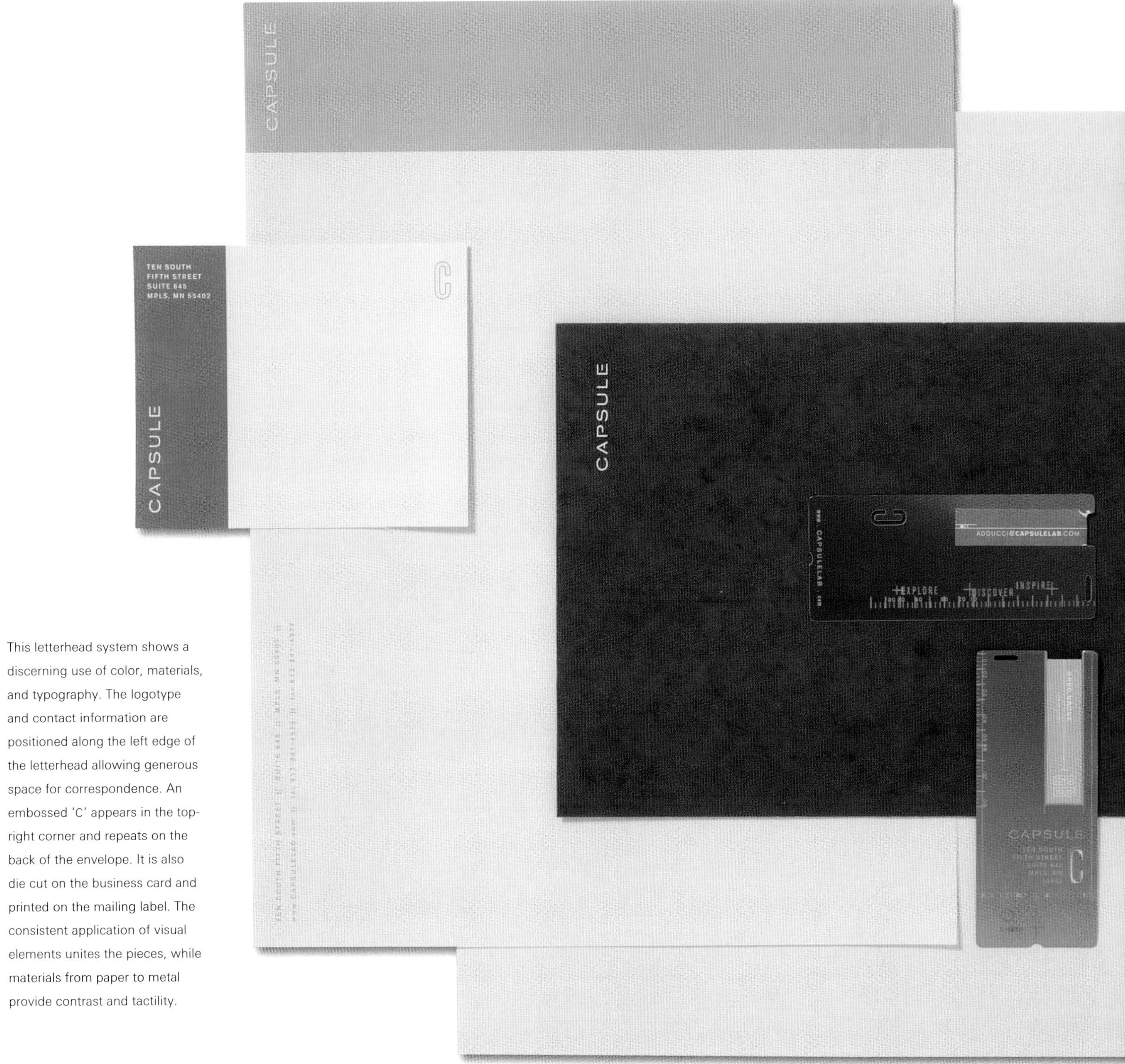

This letterhead system shows a discerning use of color, materials, and typography. The logotype and contact information are positioned along the left edge of the letterhead allowing generous space for correspondence. An embossed 'C' appears in the top-right corner and repeats on the back of the envelope. It is also die cut on the business card and printed on the mailing label. The consistent application of visual elements unites the pieces, while materials from paper to metal provide contrast and tactility.

CHENG DESIGN

Seattle Arts & Lectures Brochure Series

designer **karen cheng**

WORKING IN **TWO-COLOR** IS ALWAYS RESTRICTIVE, BUT FRANKLY, I WELCOME IT.

Seattle Arts & Lectures is a nonprofit literary organization that is "devoted to exploring ideas and imagination through language," describes designer Karen Cheng. They wanted to reinvent their "old-fashioned, even stodgy" image and produce collateral materials that would better reflect the variety of contemporary and prominent poets and writers participating with the organization. Seattle Arts & Lectures requested something "smart and fun," says Cheng, to complement their "intellectually challenging and interesting but not inaccessible or overly pedantic" events. The design was limited to two colors and inexpensive paper. Although these limitations may have excluded some possibilities, Cheng adds, "Working in two-color is always restrictive, but frankly, I welcome it. It helps narrow the design possibilities quickly."

The strength of the brochure series is the use of color and typography. Inspired by *The Interaction of Color* by Josef Albers, Cheng describes, "Each brochure is printed with only two colors. The colors are overprinted in a wide variety of screen combinations to create a four-color illusion." The brochure series adopts a modest yet rich color palette from bright yellow and warm orange to pale blue and deep green. Value and transparency are applied interchangeably throughout the series to distinguish typography, cast subtle light to photography, frame the page, and add graphic interest. The range of colors connotes sophistication and value from the series while also increasing their utility for Seattle Arts & Lectures.

2002-2003
the Simpson Center for the Humanities and Seattle Arts & Lectures present
wednesday university
philosophy/ history/ literature/ culture

Seamus Heaney
Zadie Smith
George Plimpton
Francine Prose
Andrea Barrett
David Mamet
ary Lecture Series 2002-2003
Seattle Arts & Lectures
15th anniversary season
four poetry readings
james tate | c.d. wright | louise glück | galway kinnell
presented by Seattle Arts & Lectures in collaboration with ACT Theatre
and Open Books: A Poem Emporium

The systematic brochure series for Seattle Arts & Lectures takes advantage of color, graphic shape, photography, and typography. Designer Karen Cheng sensitively exploits each element, making the most of a limited budget to keep the series diverse and unified.

The type treatment for the brochure series is classically composed. The sans serif typeface—Interstate—is clean and modern. A variety of font styles, including italic and multiple weights, is exploited advantageously to shape a legible, ordered sequence through each brochure. The organization of the information relies on "typographic differences (size, placement, value, texture) to establish hierarchy," explains Cheng. The typographic treatment fosters consistency without monotony. Though the cover designs change for each brochure, the interior text is consistently applied throughout the designs.

The effectiveness of the brochure series is demonstrated by its reception from the client and viewers. "Seattle Arts & Lectures has had a very positive response to this 'rebranding' and standardization of their materials," says Cheng. "Many of their long-term subscribers have been specifically quite complimentary about the change in their materials." The final design, which is elegant in its pure, modern simplicity, is a reflection of the designer, client, and viewer coming together successfully.

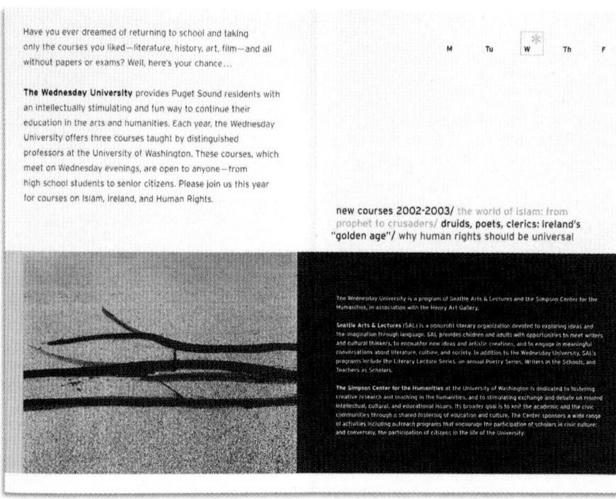

The Wednesday University brochure is divided into halves. Photography and color draw the eye down and across the spread because of their visual weight, while the horizontal design of the imagery flows seamlessly into a field of color.

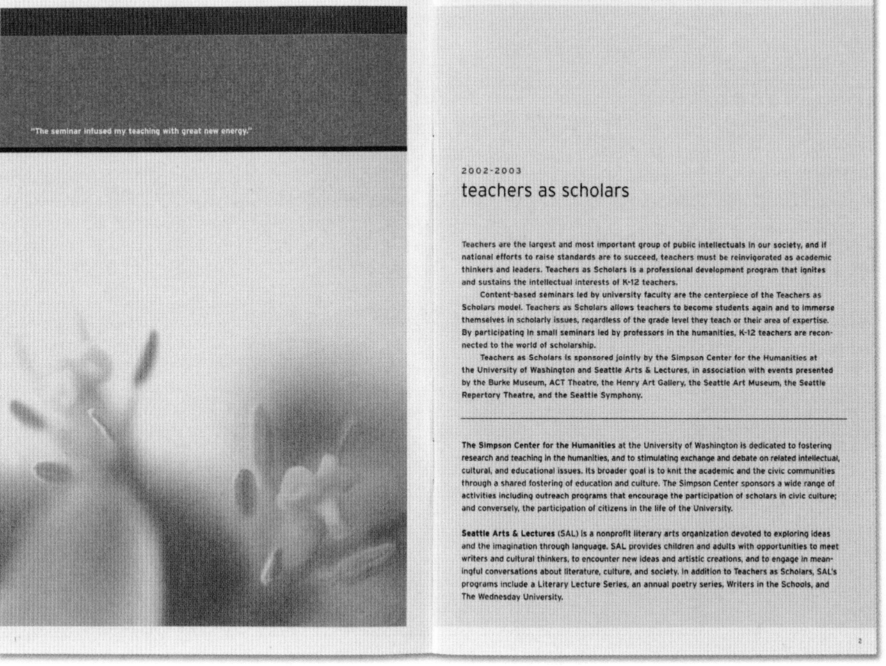

The *Literary Lecture Series* brochure uses typographic size, position, and space to achieve an elegant, fluid hierarchy of the visual elements. The title sits boldly in the top-left corner of the composition. It draws immediate attention because of the white space that surrounds it; its isolation creates activity and prominence.

Large photography commands attention to the *Teachers as Scholars* brochure (opposite). The photograph is contrasted by the dark field of color above it, which isolates a quotation. The quotation, set in a small point size, rests quietly, yet with a strong voice, in the rectangle. Type and image are complementary and provide visual impact and meaningful messages.

A colorful pattern of rules creates horizontal movement across the spread of the *Four Poetry Readings* brochure. The directional flow, which includes a set of photographs, leads to the typography that falls down the page in a flush-left alignment.

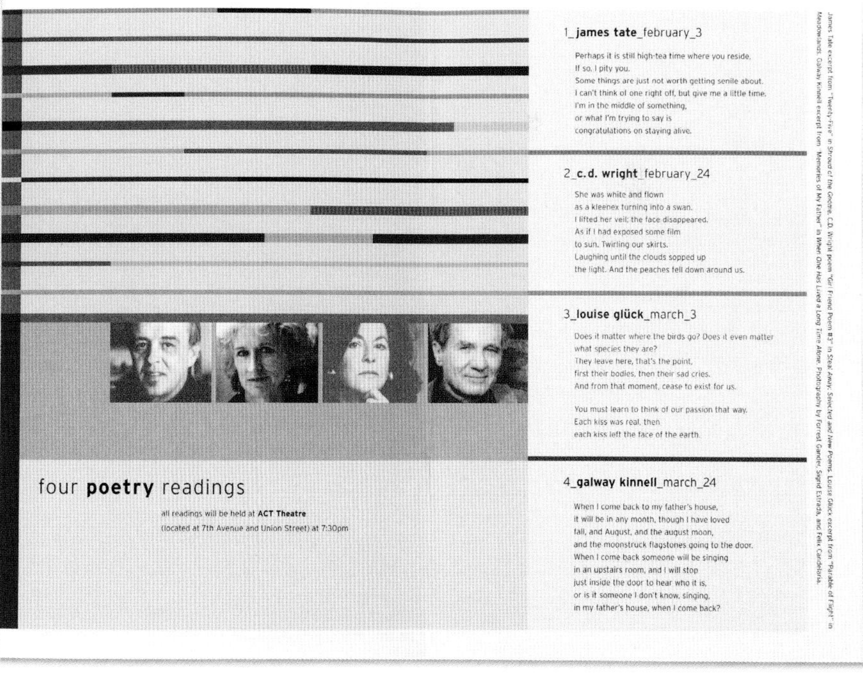

CI STUDIO

Broadcasting Commission of Ireland
Annual Review

***creative director* mel o'rourke**
***designer* katie quinn**

A subdued cover, featuring large embossed numerals, is a quiet start to the active design that lies inside. The title treatment—set in Converse DIN—in addition to the Broadcasting Commission of Ireland logo, accents the edge of the page. The elements mark the margins and establish the location of headings.

The Broadcasting Commission of Ireland is responsible for the activities of television and radio services, including developing standards for programming and advertising, as well as licensing independent broadcasting services. CI Studio was brought in to design the commission's annual review with the objective of communicating their range of services and many achievements throughout the year. The client also wanted the design to be visually unique and dynamic, as well as representative of the progressive attitude of the company.

The visual approach toward the annual review was inspired by design styles of the 1950s, including "the way black-and-white photography was treated with a wash of color, as well as the graphic treatment of sound waves," explains creative director Mel O'Rourke. With an aesthetic direction established, CI Studio developed multiple ideas that would best represent the commission. The concept of the design was "to take key milestones and achievements from the year, represent these milestones through photography, and link them with large, graphic sound waves," describes O'Rourke. "This created a very visual introduction to the annual review, which needed few words to communicate the range of activities the [Broadcasting Commission of Ireland] were involved in."

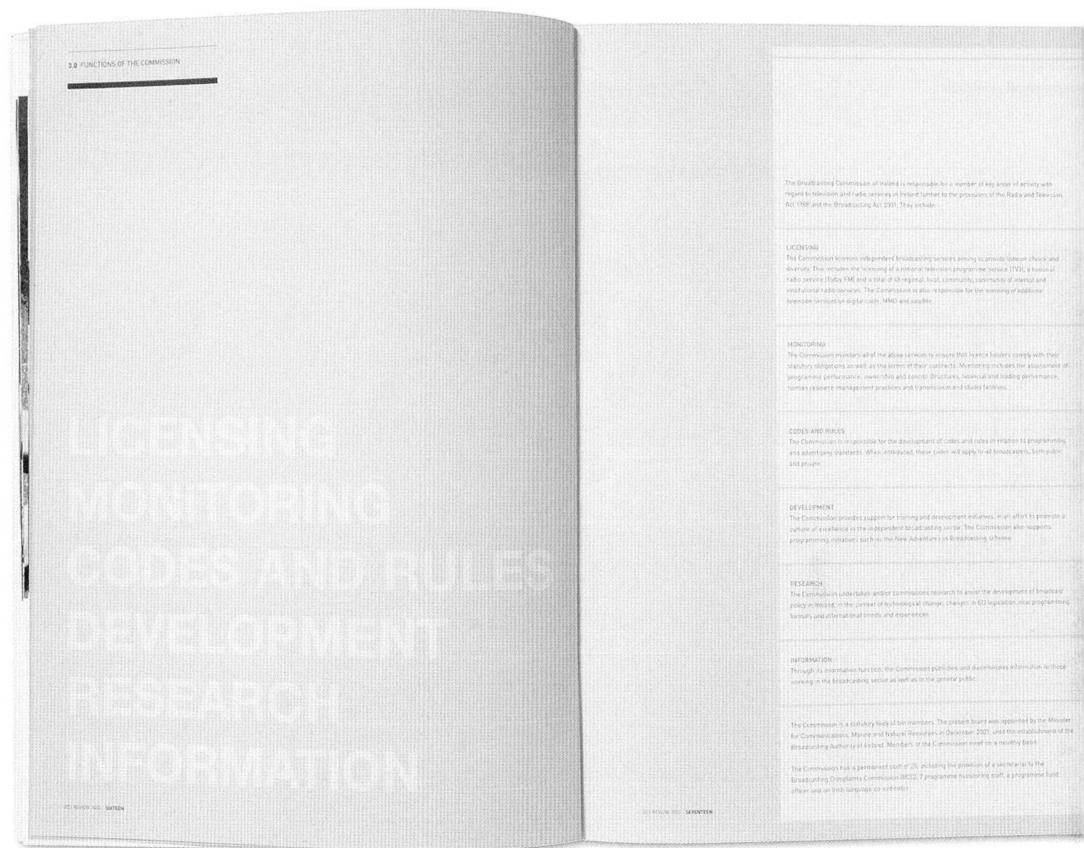

The scale of elements is dramatic and adds variety. A three-column grid divides the page into vertical divisions that accommodate the body text. Changes in type color and weight create hierarchy.

CONTENTS 1
CHAIRMAN'S STATEMENT 14
FUNCTIONS OF THE COMMISSION 16
BOARD MEMBERS & STAFF 18
LICENSING 20
COMPLIANCE 22
TRAINING & DEVELOPMENT 24
STANDARDS IN BROADCASTING 26
RESEARCH 28
IRISH LANGUAGE DEVELOPMENT 30
CORPORATE SERVICES 32
TRENDS 34
OTHER ACTIVITIES 36

The contents page is bold and dynamic. Large letterforms, set in Helvetica, clearly note each section of the review. The change in color between the type and numerals provides contrast to enable easy identification.

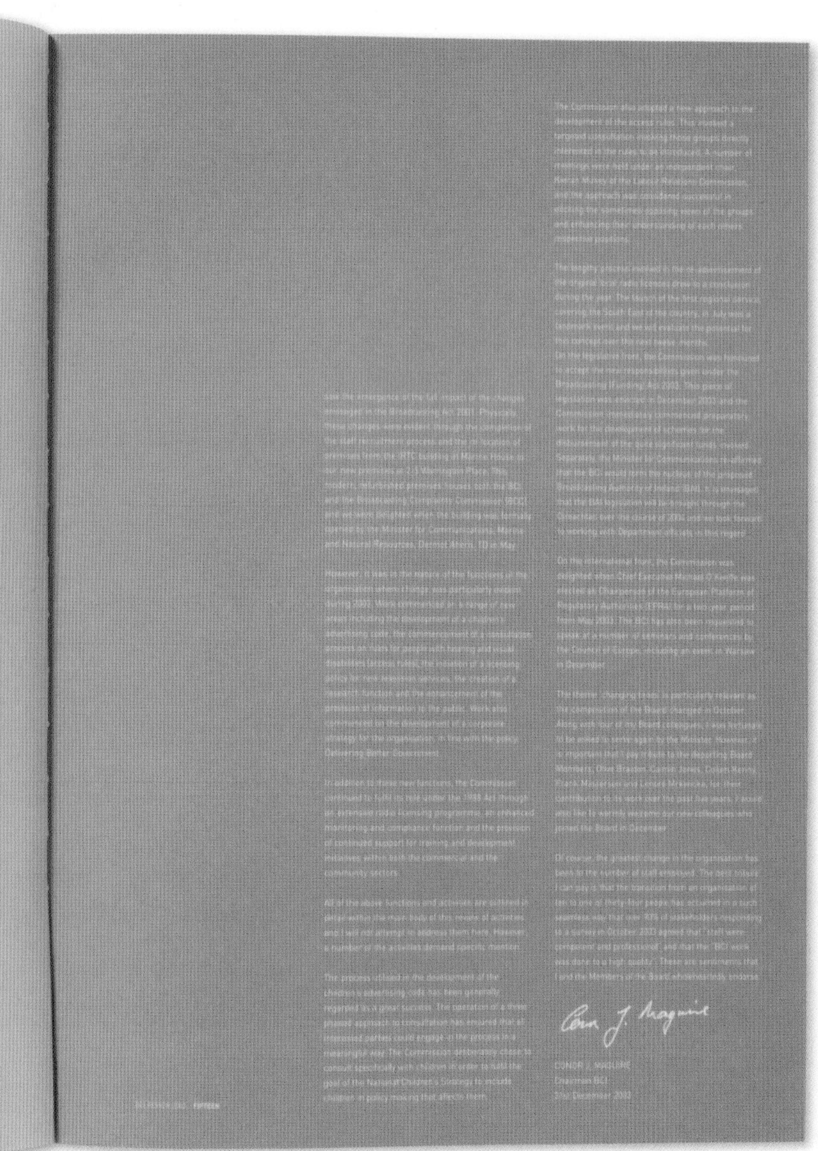

A color bleed provides a strong background field for the textual content. The page is divided into three columns, which provides an accommodating structure for the body text.

The oversized format of the annual review is commanding and presents a strong image of the company. In addition to the shape of the page, the soft and contemporary color palette is also distinctive. Large photography, graphic shapes, and fields of color provide depth within the compositional space. The scale of the visual elements is dramatic and adds variety throughout the design. A three-column grid divides the page into vertical divisions that accommodate the placement of the body copy, which is set in Converse DIN. Changes in type color and weight (from light to medium) create hierarchy within the primary text. In addition, large typographic elements, which are set in Helvetica, create a bold impression and clearly communicate the messages. O'Rourke comments, "We knew the kind of image the [Broadcasting Commission of Ireland] wanted from their original brief, but it was our intuition that carried us through when making decisions regarding layout, colors, and style. We had a gut feeling for what would work."

The Broadcasting Commission of Ireland review "visually represented their achievements throughout the year in a clear, easy-to-understand fashion, whereas the fresh, modern style of the layout, typography, and photography conveyed their forward thinking as an organization," concludes O'Rourke. "The piece was successful for us because it was a collaboration between us and the client. The client knew what they wanted and trusted us to deliver that message. These are the ingredients for the success of any project of this nature."

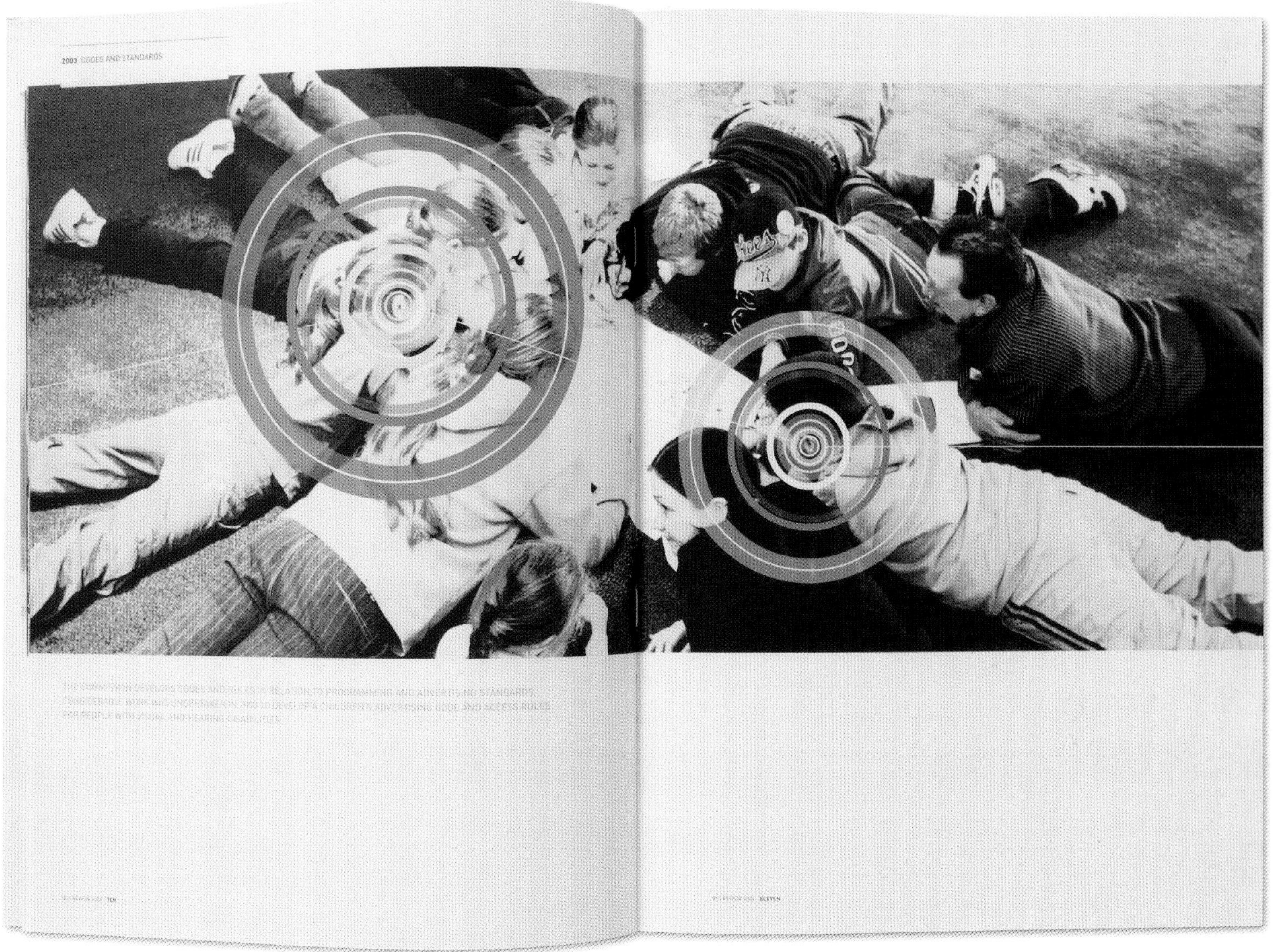

2003 CODES AND STANDARDS
THE COMMISSION DEVELOPS CODES AND RULES IN RELATION TO PROGRAMMING AND ADVERTISING STANDARDS. CONSIDERABLE WORK WAS UNDERTAKEN IN 2003 TO DEVELOP A CHILDREN'S ADVERTISING CODE AND ACCESS RULES FOR PEOPLE WITH VISUAL AND HEARING DISABILITIES.

Black-and-white photography runs across the spread. It is given a wash of color that provides a rich tone. The graphic elements add activity to the composition, while the type is set under the image and takes a secondary role.

CONCRETE [THE OFFICE OF JILLY SIMONS]

Washington University in St. Louis, School of Architecture, *Graduate Programs Bulletin*

designers **jilly simons, regan todd**
copywriter **peter mackeith**
photographers **various**

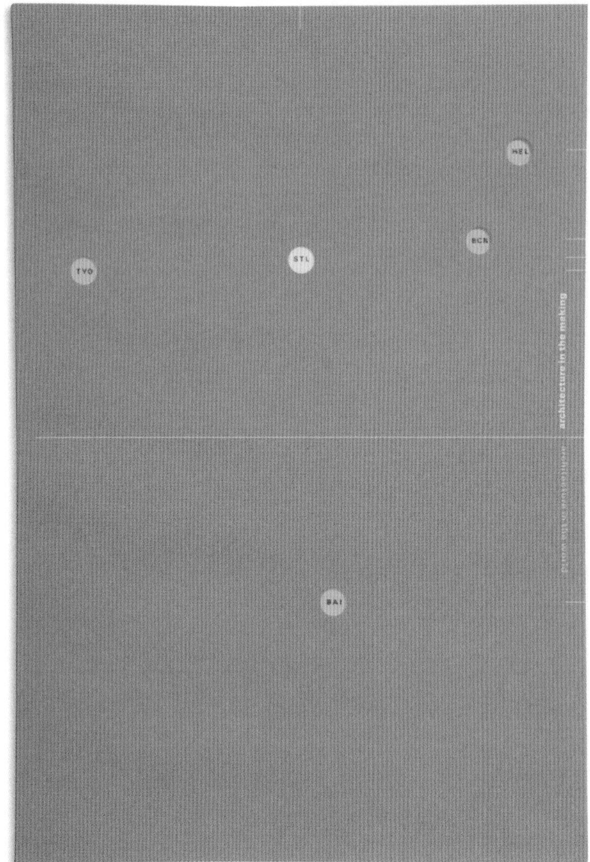

The *Graduate Programs Bulletin* is rich with details that solidify the design. On the cover, a thin white rule connotes the equator and divides the phrase *Architecture in the world. Architecture in the making.*, which is the theme of the design. Circular die cuts fall above or below the horizontal center and reveal typography that notes the locations of the international program.

Building on a five-year relationship, Concrete worked with the School of Architecture at Washington University in St. Louis to develop the *Graduate Programs Bulletin*. "Initially, I visited the school and had conversations with many of the faculty and students," explains designer Jilly Simons. "I spent a considerable amount of time working with our client developing concepts and exploring a variety of ways to introduce the idea of interactivity and 'making' into the piece."

The time spent in the research and information-gathering phases contributed to a concept "inspired by the school's identity, which resonates with the diverse realities of its multiple locations," says Simons. Reflecting internationality, the conceptual direction of the design and its structure is connected to the cover phrase, *Architecture in the world Architecture in the making*. The bulletin captures the duality of the phrase by being divided into two sections. "The two-color 'hardworking' front matter covers the information about the school—its curriculum, faculty, and admissions," states Simons. "In contrast to the uncoated front section, we introduced five full-color gate-folds, on a coated sheet, at the back of the piece. This back section serves as a travelogue through different international studios and student work."

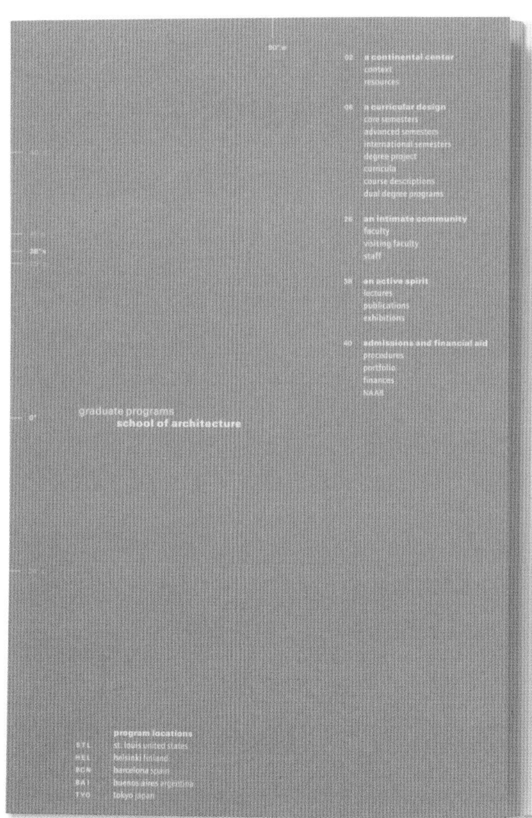

The School of Architecture at Washington University in St Louis cultivates the designer's identity as a leader: as both an expressive individual and a socially responsible citizen. The School's commitment to the ethical practice of architecture spans disciplines, contending cultural theories, and the range of representational media. The School's curriculum emphasizes the physicality of design through regard to site, purpose, material, technique and meaning. The School's identity resonates with the diverse realities of its multiple locations: St. Louis, situated at the virtual center of the United States, at the confluence of the Mississippi and Missouri river ecologies, possessing a rich architectural heritage and a complex urbanity; and international semesters in Barcelona, Spain, Buenos Aires, Argentina, Helsinki, Finland, and Tokyo, Japan—all cities of vibrant architectural cultures. The diversity of the Faculty, Visiting Faculty and the student community embodies this expansive intellectual territory. Intertwined with the School's character is the continuous thread of modernism's many-faceted, optimistic vision. This prospectus invites you to participate in the graduate programs of the School of Architecture at Washington University in St. Louis: **architecture in the making, architecture in the world.**

Interior spreads demonstrate the typographic system applied throughout the design. Quay Sans is the dominant typeface featured. It is paired with Univers and presents a contemporary image. The typefaces' application features subtle changes in color, size, style, and weight to organize the content hierarchically.

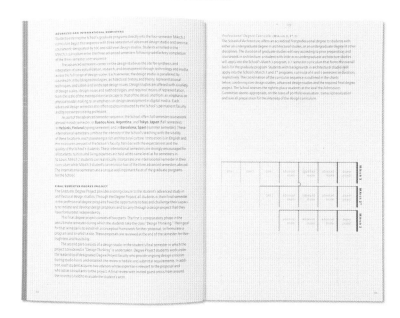

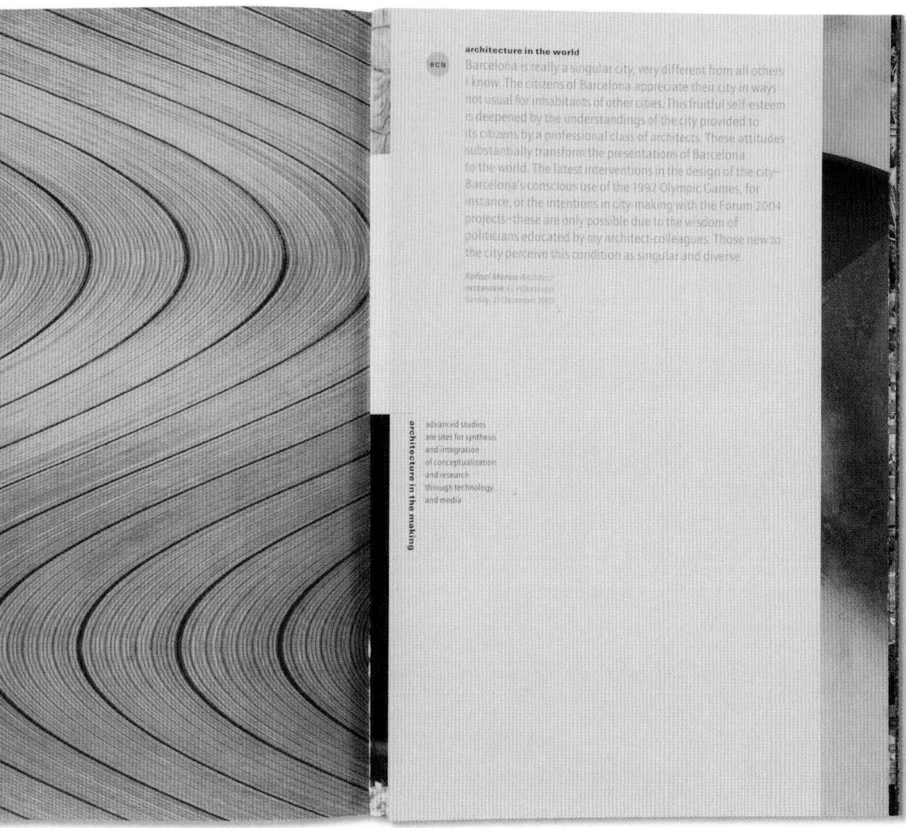

Both sections of the *Graduate Programs Bulletin* adhere to a consistent grid, color palette (blue and yellow), and typographic application. Variation within the primarily typographic layout, including the use of color, size, style, and weight, establishes hierarchy. The sudden appearance of color photography is the surprise element of the design. It is expansive and brings the viewer into new architectural environments that evoke the global opportunities the program provides.

The *Graduate Programs Bulletin* is designed with conceptual strength and aesthetic agility. It presents an intelligent and professional image of the School of Architecture. It also grabs the interest of potential students. "The client reported that the bulletin was extremely well received by faculty, students, and prospective students," says Simons. "Although the bulletin itself cannot claim full responsibility for the increase in enrollment inquiries, it can be attributed some of the success."

The back matter contains five gatefolds that highlight the international graduate studios. The recto page is typographic and contains insights from architects from the countries. The facing page is a full-bleed photograph. When the gatefold is opened, the spread hosts drawings and models. The final pages are intriguing and contrast the objectivity of the front of the bulletin.

HEL

A conventional, staid GRID would have killed THE PICTURES.

CART Magazine

COOK DESIGN

art director/designer **gary cook**
editor **marcus simmons**

Cook Design was approached by Racer Communications, Inc., to redesign *CART* magazine and "raise the profile of Champ Car racing, making it appear more glamorous, exciting, and closer to Formula One," explains art director/designer Gary Cook. The previous image of the magazine was a "very business-led look," adds Cook, which did not accurately portray the intensity of car racing. The client aspired to invigorate this impression with modernity and sophistication to entice advertisers to invest in the sport.

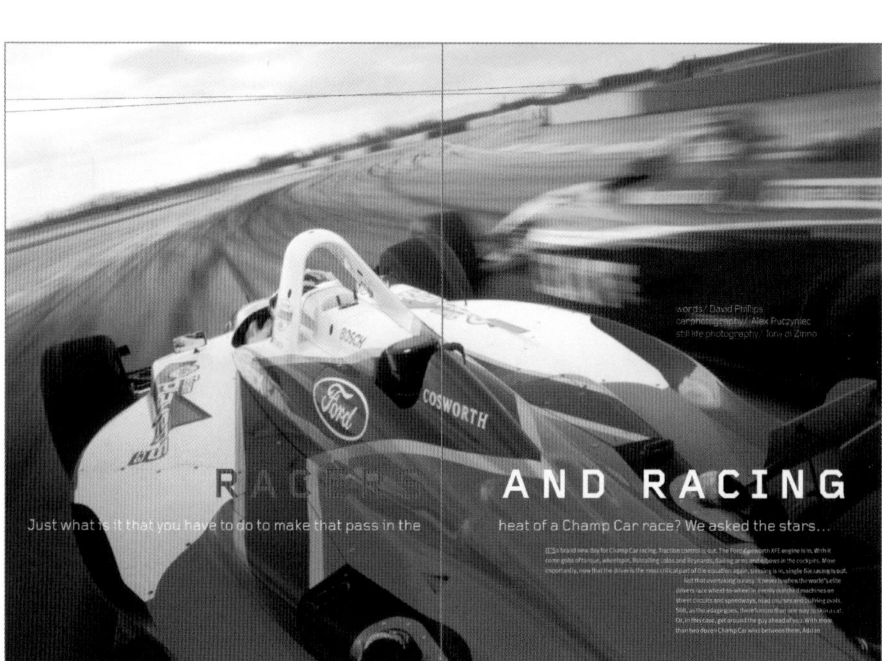

CART uses dynamic photography to activate its pages and glamorize car racing. The viewer feels like part of the action. The photography connotes speed; the sensation also influences the type, which appears to be in motion as it runs horizontally across the spread.

To begin the design process, Cook Design experienced the racing scene firsthand during numerous photo shoots that defined and inspired the rest of the process. The objective of the design was to capture the "energy of the shoots," states Cook. He wanted the viewer to "feel like someone walking around the track with an 'access all areas' pass. I felt the design had to be very raw."

Vivid color and black-and-white photographs (shot by fashion and specialist car photographers) are a strength of the design and connote drama, energy, motion, and speed. The images are rough and smooth, beautiful and jarring. They capture the allure and attitude of car racing, while adding insight into the personalities of the drivers. Featuring perspective and sharp angles, the photography brings dimension and dynamism to the spreads. In addition, the structure and organization of the layout is dictated by the photographic imagery. The designer composes "a minisequence of pages based on the best pictures," describes Cook, "to end up with a run of pages that work in both a visual and informative sense."

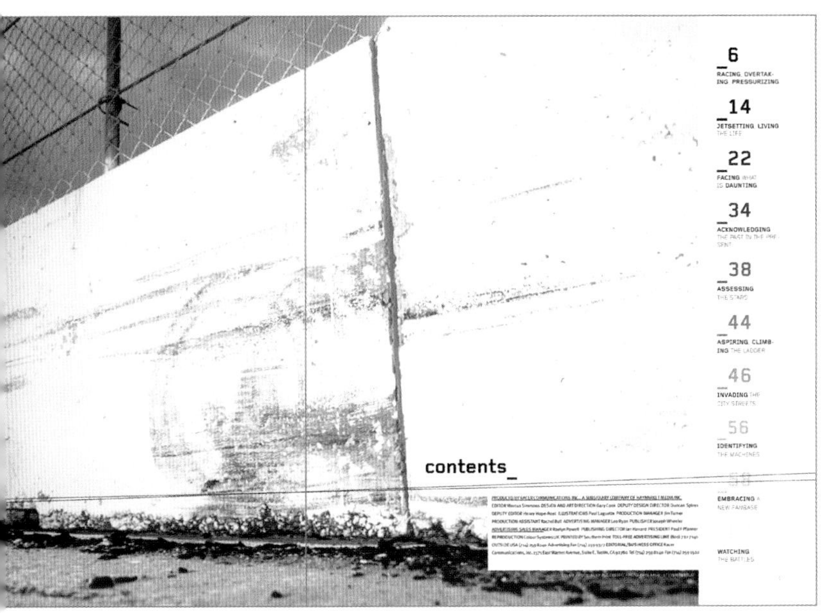

6
RACING OVERTAKING PRESSURIZING
14
JETSETTING LIVING THE LIFE
22
FACING WHAT IS DAUNTING
34
ACKNOWLEDGING THE PAST IN THE PRESENT
38
ASSESSING THE STARS
44
ASPIRING CLIMBING THE LADDER
46
INVADING THE CITY STREETS
56
IDENTIFYING THE MACHINES
EMBRACING A NEW FANBASE
WATCHING THE BATTLES
contents_

The contents spread sets the trend of large-scale photography seen throughout the magazine. The imagery is complemented by clean typography set along the right side of the spread.

Cook Design reinvented *CART* magazine and created a visual environment that is edgy and vibrant. The cover introduces the aesthetic of the design. Vivid photography is complemented by clean typography, whereas scale and perspective are used to achieve drama, tension, and variety.

CART is typographically spare, which contrasts with the active and bold photography and augments the character of the magazine. Gridnik, the dominant typeface used, has an industrial look that supports the objective of the design. Large numbers are applied as graphic shapes that create divisions of space on the page. Thin, oversized letterforms provide structural edges for the arrangement of body text. The photography and type work together to shape a flexible grid dependent on the needs of each spread. "A conventional, staid grid would have killed the pictures," says Cook.

awesome
challen-
ges
Champ Car drivers face a range of mountains to conquer. In the coming pages, past champs Cristiano da Matta and Juan Pablo Montoya reveal six of the absolute toughest
words/ Tom Clarkson, Mark Hughes & Niki Takeda

CART is energetic, fresh, polished, and infused with a refined design sensibility. "The client was very pleased, and the fans' message boards were alive for weeks when the magazine came out," comments Cook. "I think people were excited by how different it was—people found it very unexpected." According to Cook, the only downside of the design was "the fire ants that populate the Sebring circuit and how much it hurts when you lie on the floor to take a picture then realize they are biting your arm."

Interior spreads illuminate the personalities of the drivers, bringing their characters to life. The photography is dynamically composed to bring the viewer into the spatial environments. Large typographic elements, particularly the headings and large numbers, add a graphic texture and informative layer on top of the imagery.

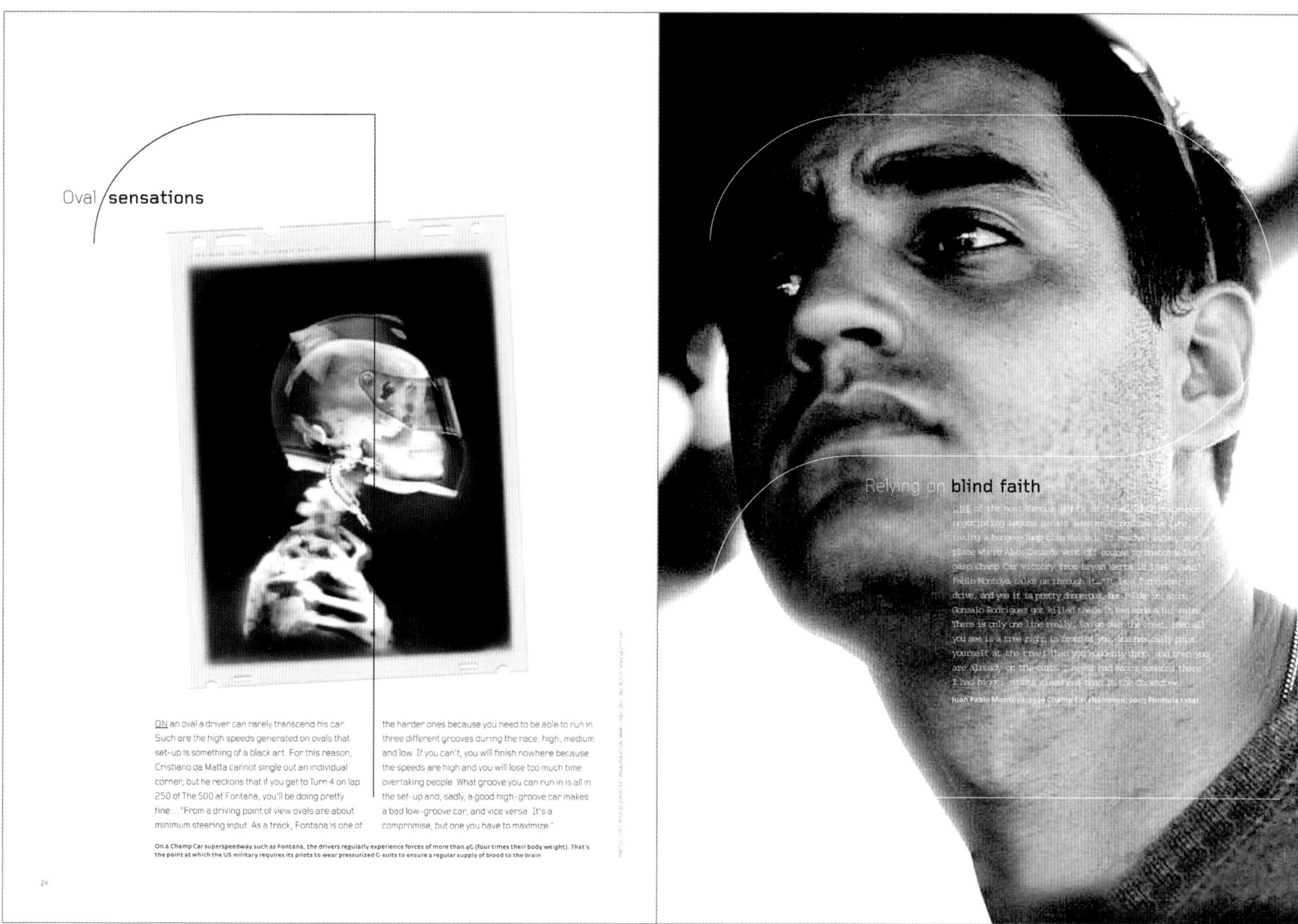

Oval sensations

ON an oval a driver can rarely transcend his car. Such are the high speeds generated on ovals that set-up is something of a black art. For this reason, Cristiano da Matta cannot single out an individual corner, but he reckons that if you get to Turn 4 on lap 250 of The 500 at Fontana, you'll be doing pretty fine... "From a driving point of view ovals are about minimum steering input. As a track, Fontana is one of the harder ones because you need to be able to run in three different grooves during the race: high, medium and low. If you can't, you will finish nowhere because the speeds are high and you will lose too much time overtaking people. What groove you can run in is all in the set-up and, sadly, a good high-groove car makes a bad low-groove car, and vice versa. It's a compromise, but one you have to maximize."

On a Champ Car superspeedway such as Fontana, the drivers regularly experience forces of more than 4G (four times their body weight). That's the point at which the US military requires its pilots to wear pressurized G-suits to ensure a regular supply of blood to the brain

24

Relying on **blind faith**

ONE of the most famous sights in the world of motorsport, negotiating Laguna Seca's awesome Corkscrew is like taking a bungee-jump blindfolded. It reached infamy as the place where Alex Zanardi went off course to snatch a last-gasp Champ Car victory from Bryan Herta in 1996. Juan Pablo Montoya talks us through it..."It is a fun corner to drive, and yes it is pretty dangerous, but [illegible] Since Gonzalo Rodriguez got killed there it was made a bit safer. There is only one line really. You go over the crest, then all you see is a tree right in front of you. You basically point yourself at the tree! Then you suddenly drop, and then you are already on the curb. I never had major moments there. I had bigger shunts elsewhere than in the Corkscrew."

Juan Pablo Montoya: 1999 Champ Car champion; 2003 Formula 1 star

EVELOCK DESIGN

The Collaborated Mind Brochure and Poster

designer, illustrator, copywriter **james evelock**

The Collaborated Mind is an inventive promotional piece that functions on two levels: it is a brochure that sequentially unfolds into a double-sided poster. Designed by James Evelock of Evelock Design [formerly Collaborated, Inc.], the design engages the viewer because of its intelligent content and visual presentation. "As a promotional item, the piece needed to capture attention immediately. I wanted the company to appear as serious thinkers, yet cool," says Evelock. Via the metaphorical use of the left and right brain, the design reveals insight into the methodology and thought processes of the company. It reads, "We're using both sides of the mind to develop smart and original solutions to our clients' creative problems."

The Collaborated Mind promotional piece is diagrammatic in presentation. Visually reflecting the relationship between art and science, the piece is inspired by "a medical school human anatomy textbook I found on the street and annual report charts," notes Evelock. To fine-tune the concept, "I began thinking about where art and commerce came from, and the idea of being right or left brain emerged. The idea seemed like a perfect fit for the company," states Evelock. "I really like the idea of pairing graphic design capabilities with a concept not regularly associated with graphic design—science." The design integrates charts, illustrations, and typography—all of which are kept to a minimum. "I felt if I explained too much about right and left brain activity, the readers would be turned off thinking it was a scientific direct-mail [piece]," comments Evelock.

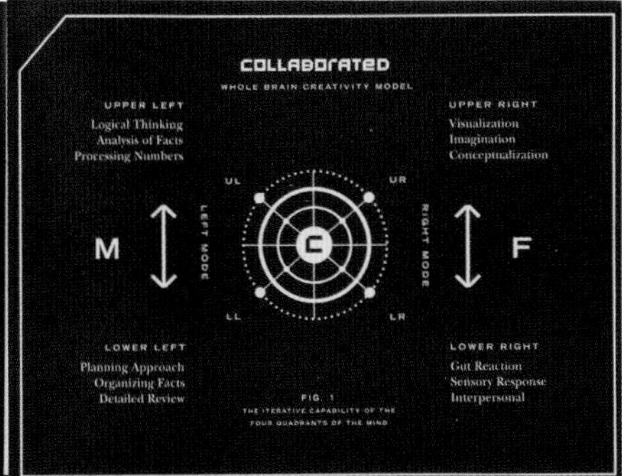

Opening the brochure on the side asking "Are you a righty?" leads the viewer through the multifunctional piece. The recto page contrasts the differences between the left and right brain. On the left side, a large arrow directs the viewer to the next fold, which opens to a long, narrow spread addressing female creative attributes. The presentation is cleanly composed. White text, illustrations, and graphic shapes are centered in the spacious, black field. Unfold again and find male attributes, as well as the first glance at the poster.

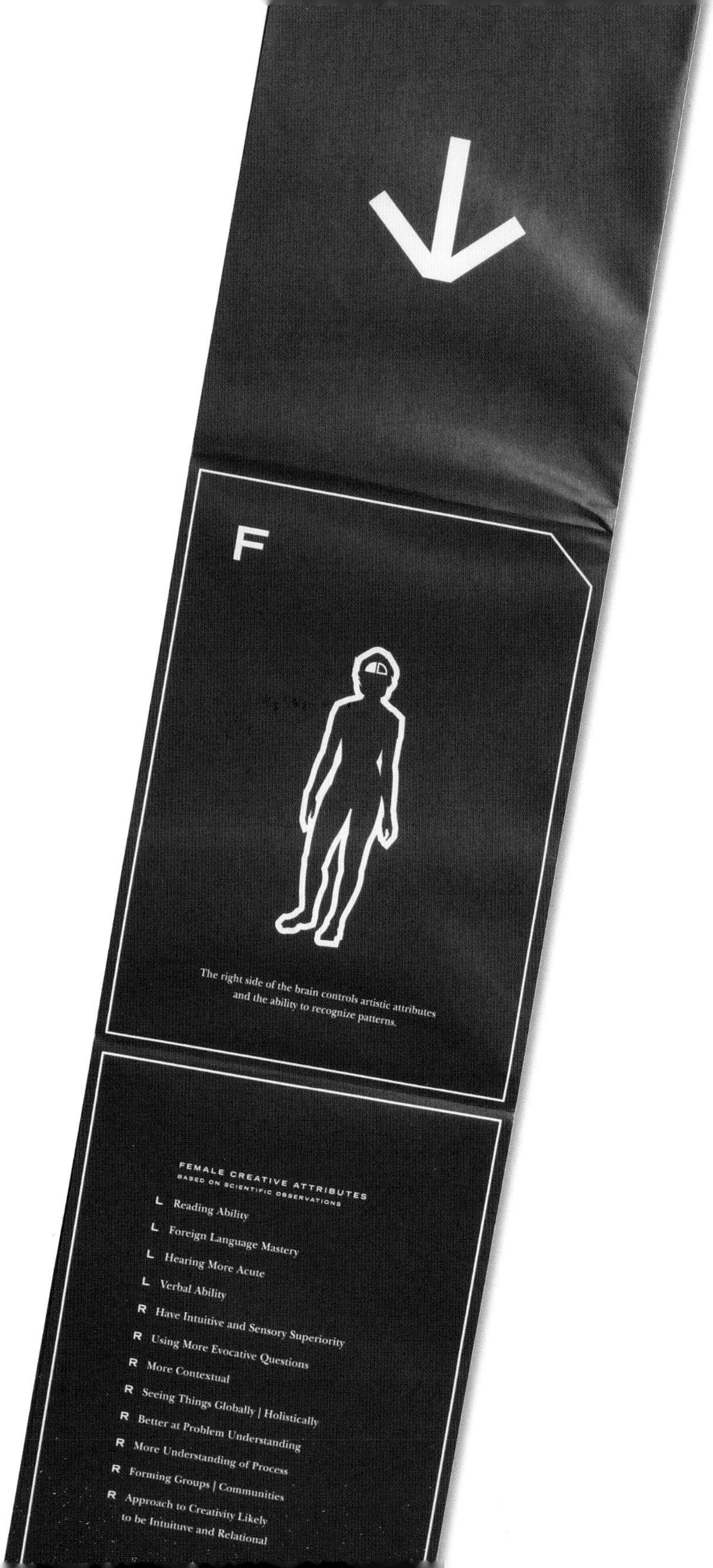

F

The right side of the brain controls artistic attributes and the ability to recognize patterns.

FEMALE CREATIVE ATTRIBUTES
BASED ON SCIENTIFIC OBSERVATIONS

- L Reading Ability
- L Foreign Language Mastery
- L Hearing More Acute
- L Verbal Ability
- R Have Intuitive and Sensory Superiority
- R Using More Evocative Questions
- R More Contextual
- R Seeing Things Globally | Holistically
- R Better at Problem Understanding
- R More Understanding of Process
- R Forming Groups | Communities
- R Approach to Creativity Likely to be Intuitive and Relational

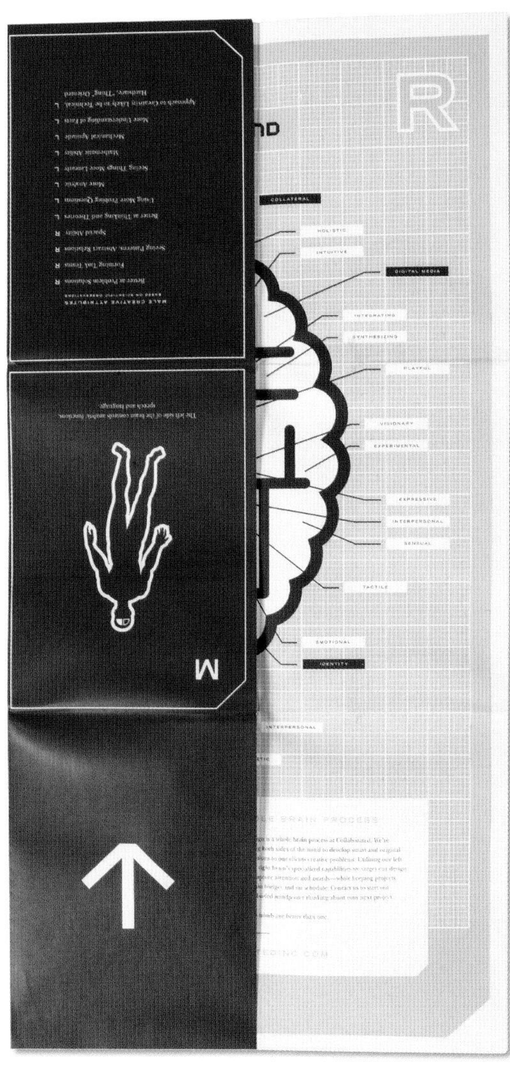

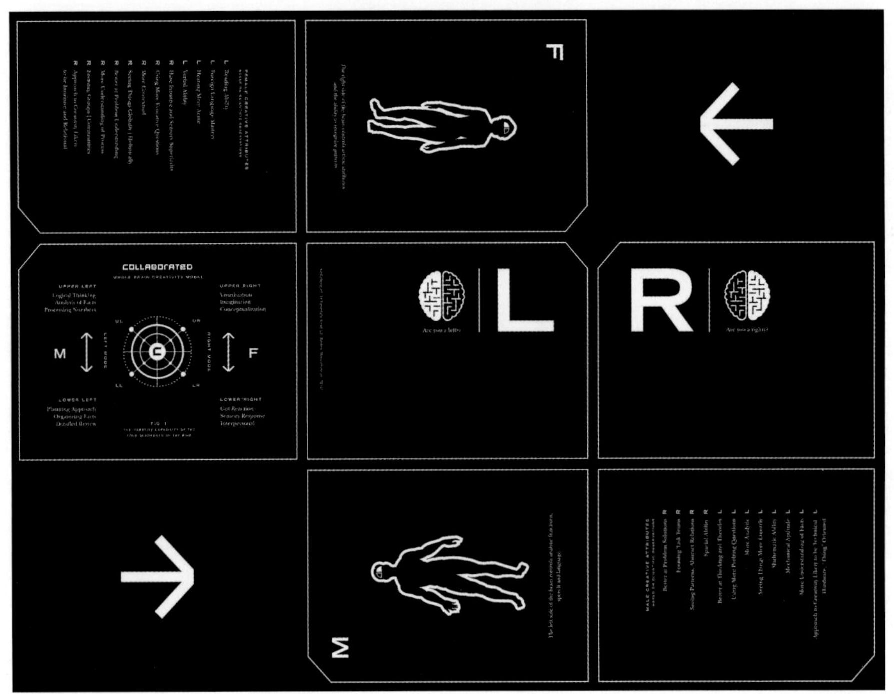

Large letterforms on a dense, black field provide an initial, mysterious impression and lead the viewer into the design. The folded piece presents the questions "Are you a righty?" or "Are you a lefty?" on opposing sides. From this point on, the viewer makes a decision, moves through the design, and learns about the left and right brain. When the piece is completely unfolded, a bright blue poster is revealed that further explains the function of the piece.

Intriguing and informative, *The Collaborated Mind* brochure and poster is a refreshing approach for a promotional piece. It educates the viewer about the thoughtful considerations that go into the design process in a creative presentation. Commenting on the function of posters, Evelock adds, "I consider the poster to be one of the most important media within the graphic design field and felt it would be one of the most attention-getting ways to communicate." The design supports this statement—it is visually strong and teaches the viewer about the science of the mind and the science of graphic design. "I knew *The Collaborated Mind* poster would work from the moment I thought of it," concludes Evelock.

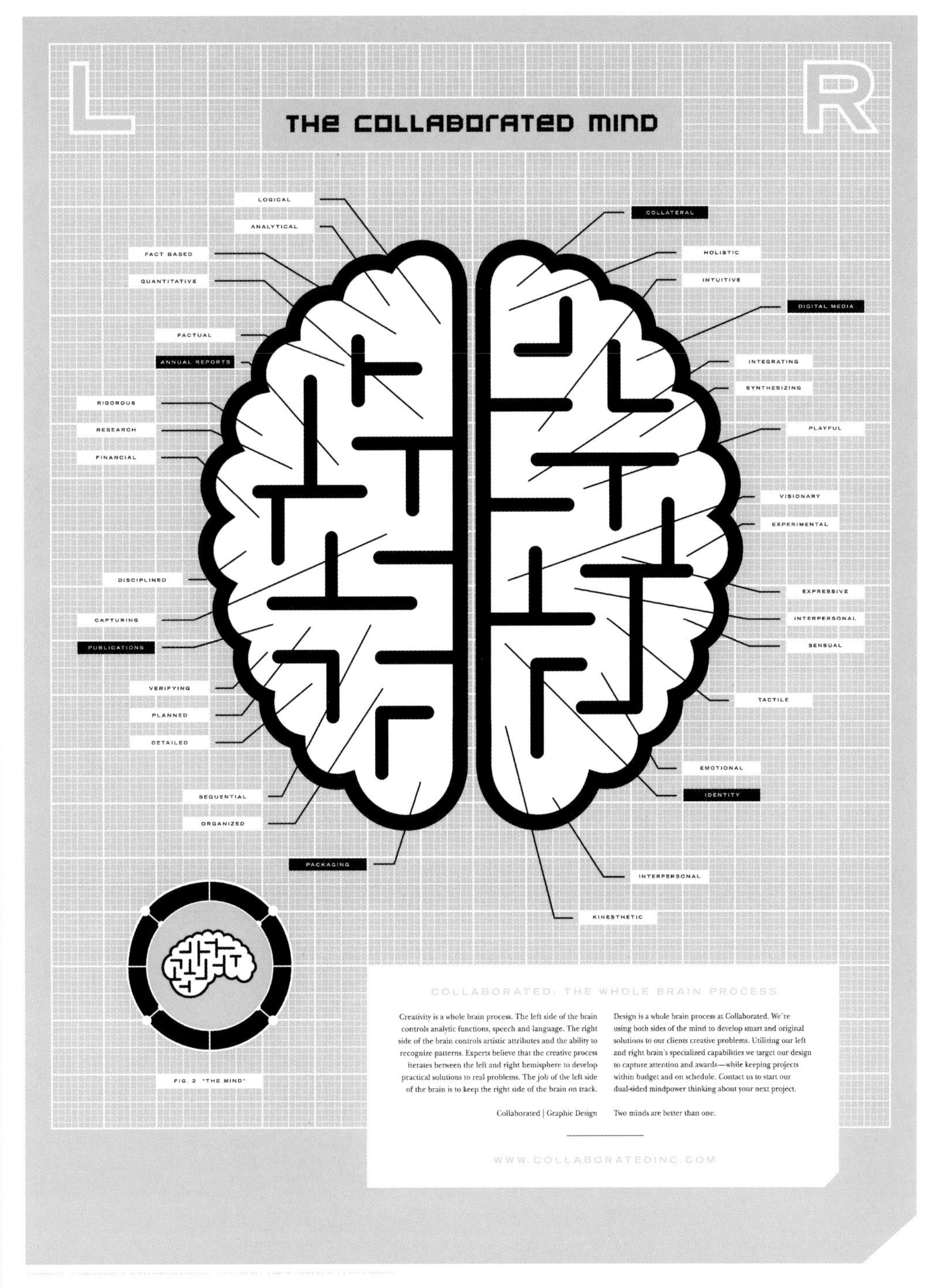

The Collaborated Mind piece is conceptually strong and visually engaging. Combining simple graphics and minimal text, the poster is readable and scientific in feel. To counter the text, which discusses the function of the left and right brain, the illustration is composed in the center of the page. The design expresses the complex subject of left- and right-brain activity in an intriguing and clever way.

RENATE GOKL

A View by Two: Contemporary Jewelry Exhibition Catalog

designer **renate gokl**
photographer **erik gould**

A View by Two: Contemporary Jewelry exhibition catalog was designed to support a contemporary jewelry exhibition at the Rhode Island School of Design, Museum of Art. Co-curator Louis Mueller describes: "I hope this exhibition provides an opportunity for people to appreciate what goes into [the artists'] struggles and their creative efforts." The catalog, designed by Renate Gokl, features the diverse work of fourteen international artists. "I was brought onto the project by the curator of the exhibition, a former jewelry professor of mine, who trusted that I could capture the spirit of the work," explains Gokl. "He had no specific direction for me but was hoping for something a bit unusual and nontraditional."

The jewelry was the primary inspiration for the design and influenced its development. "Even though [the jewelry] was varied in terms of concept, style, materials, and technique, there was an attention to detail and perfection about the work," comments Gokl. The attention to concept, style, and detail are evident in the design of the catalog. Its format is progressive, while it is also typographically sophisticated. Addressing the conceptual and formal development of the design, Gokl elaborates, "The concept, one of integration and formal means, became the way of expressing it. Looking at all the material (visual and textual), it became clear that I needed to develop a system that unified the parts instead of treating them as separate pieces of information. A traditional catalog sequence of front matter, essay, artists' works, biographies, and checklist seemed too disparate. To challenge that structure, I devised a system whereby the artists' plates and bios would group together but would also be interwoven with the essay/interview of the curator. This allowed the curator's perspective and voice to accompany the viewing of the work."

WHEN I DESIGN, I always put myself in the place of the reader and think about how **SEQUENCE**, **PACING**, and **PAUSES** might affect the experience.

CONTENTS

5 PREFACE
6 ACKNOWLEDGMENTS
8 LOUIS MUELLER ON CONTEMPORARY JEWELRY
10 GIAMPAOLO BABETTO
12 ALEXANDRA BAHLMANN
14 MANFRED BISCHOFF
16 HERMANN JÜNGER
18 DANIEL KRUGER
20 MYRA MIMLITSCH GRAY
22 MANFRED NISSLMÜLLER
24 TED NOTEN
26 RUUDT PETERS
28 DOROTHEA PRÜHL
30 GERD ROTHMANN
32 BERNHARD SCHOBINGER
34 SONDRA SHERMAN
36 IRMGARD ZEITLER
38 CHECKLIST OF THE EXHIBITION

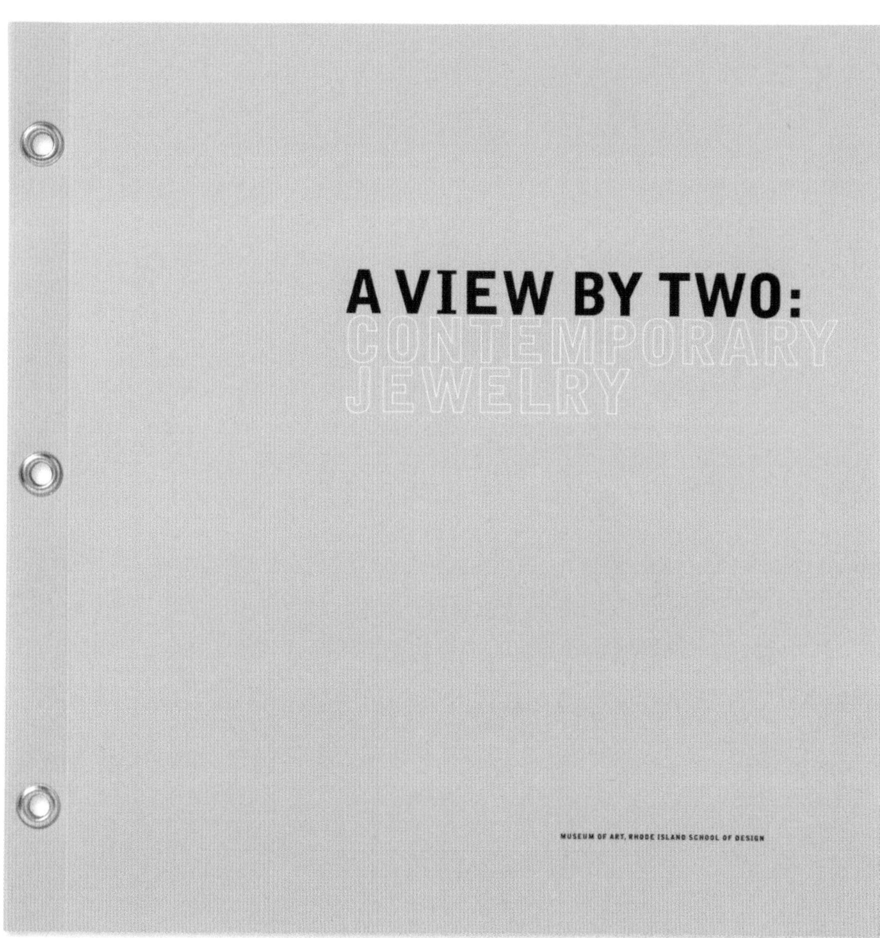

On the contents page, contrast between light and bold type weights, which are elegantly set in uppercase, creates a clear distinction between the front and back matter text, as well as the artists' names.

The asymmetric cover design commands attention through bold yet minimal typography. Well-spaced capitals align just above the cap height of the letterforms beneath them. Contrasting with the solid black letters, the words 'contemporary jewelry' are thinly outlined in white and suggest the delicate attention given to the jewelry presented inside.

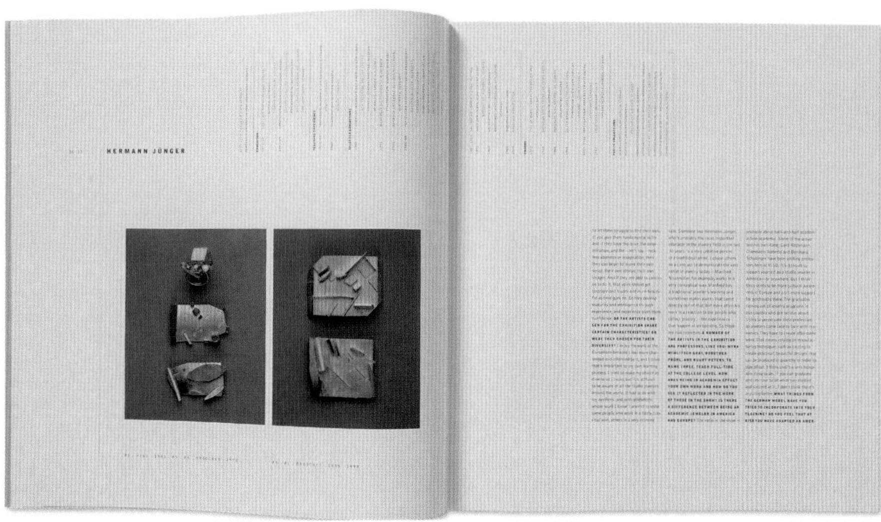

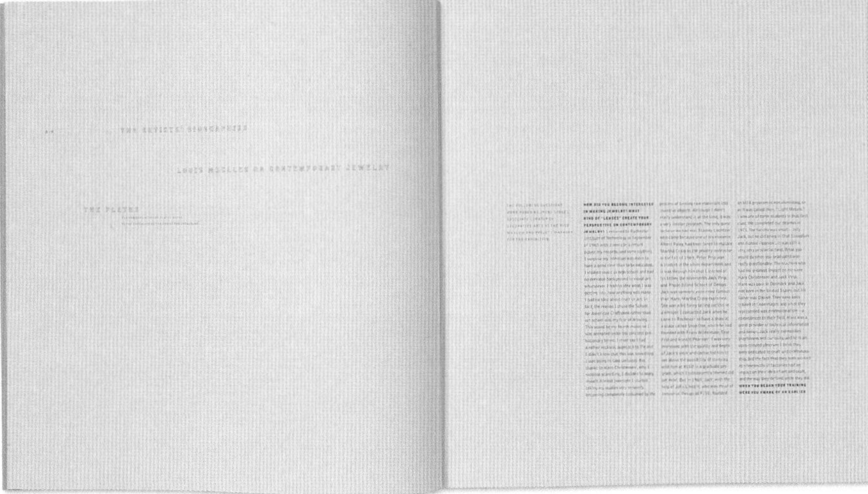

The design is built on a grid system that divides the page into several spatial intervals that flexibly accommodates the range of content. "A grid structure with several main horizontal alignments and five vertical columns per page helps reinforce the hierarchy," says Gokl. "The size, weight, and position of type are also keys in establishing dominant, subdominant, and subordinate relationships. Unifying the size of the images created a natural parallel between the various artists' work, whereas the formal grid structure became a scaffold upon which positive and negative space defined discrete areas of information. Also, the minimal use of a hairline rule helped articulate boundaries and groupings."

A View by Two: Contemporary Jewelry exhibition catalog is thoughtfully presented with aesthetic skill, while serving the interests of the artists and jewelry, as well as the viewer. "When I design, I always put myself in the place of the reader and think about how sequence, pacing, and pauses might affect the experience," adds Gokl. "So, formal decisions are usually tied to functional issues." The design is avant-garde. Its form appropriately reflects its function; it unifies a broad range of text and imagery in a dynamic, engaging, and artistic presentation. The sequence of the typography leads the viewer through each page, whereas the visuals of the jewelry captivate attention.

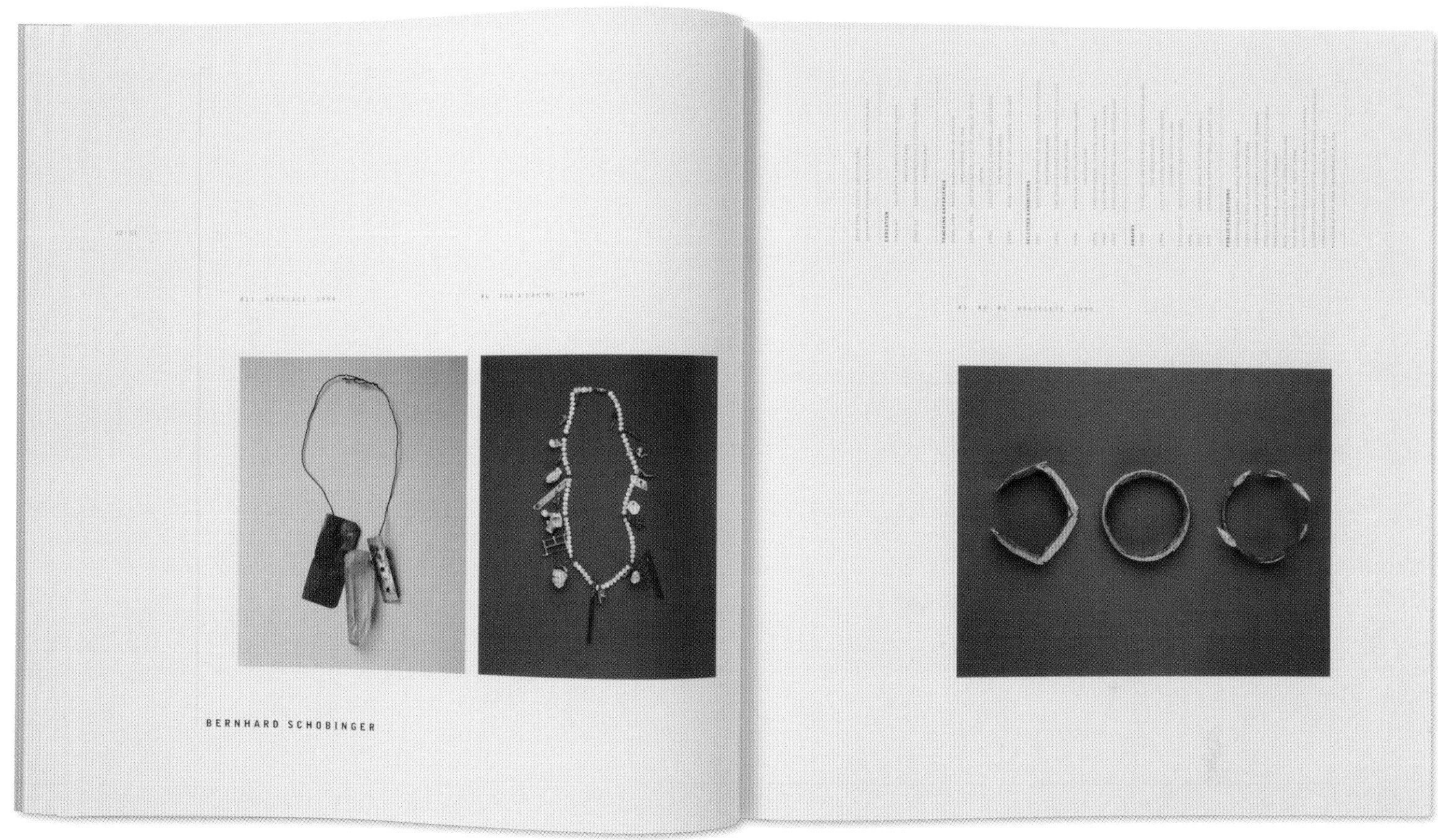

Horizontal flowlines define the starting and stopping points of visual elements. The body text and photography share the dominant top and bottom alignment points, which create consistency throughout the design. Vertical divisions of space allow the widths of images and the number of columns, to vary per spread.

HAMMERPRESS STUDIO

Rocket from the Crypt, Yeah Yeah Yeahs, and the New Pornographers Concert Posters

***designer* brady vest**

Hammerpress Studio is a letterpress and design studio in Kansas City, Missouri. Founded in 1995 by printmaker and designer Brady Vest, Hammerpress relies on traditional, handcrafted printing methods to create a diverse body of engaging work ranging in scope from postcards to invitations to book covers. Vest embraces the art of letterpress to create tactile and dynamic communication experiences. Though the letterpress is not a new technology, its aesthetic is an alternative to offset printing and today's design practice in which designers and clients often (and for practical reasons) rely on digital technology for production.

The primary objective of the concert posters is the promotion of live music performances at a variety of venues, so the designs must provide immediate impact and accessibility to quickly send pertinent information to the viewer. Describing the initiation of the design process, Vest states, "The sources of reference and inspiration are varied, and, usually, each new poster plays off the previous poster produced, as well as the anticipation of what we'll do for the next poster. For example, the Yeah Yeah Yeahs and New Pornographers posters, draw obvious references from Old World postage stamp graphics. There are also bits of ornamentation or imagery added that are a bit more absurd and playful."

Inspired by Old World postage stamp graphics, the Yeah Yeah Yeahs and New Pornographers posters command attention with iconic imagery. Changes in the orientation and position of the letterforms add variety and interest to the layout, while further enhancing the eclectic flavor of the designs.

The design process is expressive, often relying on chance and accidents to create unique, memorable pieces that, once printed, can never be re-created in the exact same way. Although the compositions are planned and systematically approached—which is evident in the horizontal and vertical alignment points on all the posters—the visual solutions are diverse, unpredictable, and always changing.

"Generally, the design process is 75 percent on the press," says Vest. "Many decisions are based entirely on accidents, such as misaligned registrations or even illegibility. The Rocket from the Crypt poster was actually the third in a series of three posters. The first poster led directly into the second poster, even though it was an entirely different concert and date. The type and ornamentation, as well as the gunfighter images, which were lifted from a collection of old pulp Westerns, shifted and evolved from the first print run to the final piece. Much of this process was based on performing subtle shifts in copy, layering the colors, and allowing the posters to evolve into something interesting." Like all design projects, trusting the process is inherent—the designer is able to anticipate an outcome but is willing to flexibly adapt to unexpected changes along the way.

The eclectic Rocket from the Crypt, Yeah Yeah Yeahs, and the New Pornographers posters are captivating. Capturing an aged aesthetic, each design contrasts old imagery with serif and sans serif metal and woodblock letterforms. In ordinary design applications, the diverse combinations of type and image, in addition to the decorative elements including stars, arrows, and flags, might not be as successful as they are here. The rich union of colors, graphic shapes, and type, as well as the handcrafted expression of the letterpress, defines the posters and makes a lasting impression.

Colors, patterns, letterforms, graphic shapes, and imagery establish the foreground, middle ground, and background of the poster. Visual elements are reprinted to add texture and dimension, while the amount of ink applied creates transparent effects. The scale of the cowboy image in juxtaposition with the Rocket from the Crypt title treatments creates a strong focal point amidst the layers.

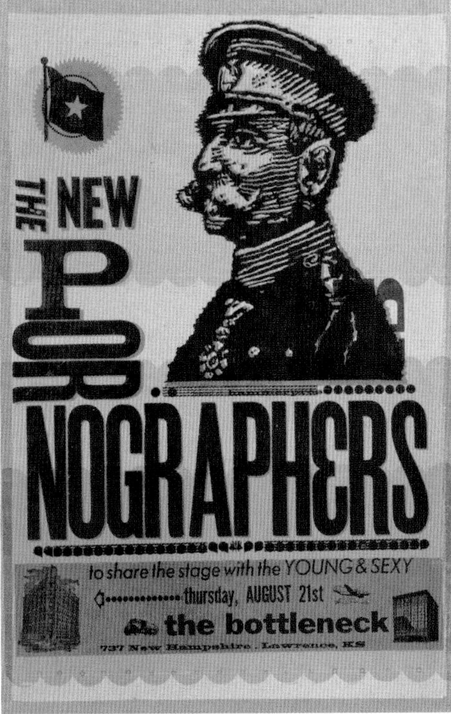

30 Gresham Street

HAT-TRICK DESIGN

creative directors gareth howat, david kimpton, jim sutherland
designers jamie ellul, adam giles, david kimpton, jim sutherland, ian mclean
photographers richard bryant, matt stewart
copywriter scott perry

WE HAVE A **BRAINSTORM** BETWEEN ALL OF US TO START **THE DESIGN PROCESS**.

30 Gresham Street is a marketing tool for Land Securities, the largest property developer in the United Kingdom. Designed by Hat-Trick Design, the objective was to promote the sale of a prominent building to one tenant. The building, 30 Gresham Street, is located in the financial center of London, also known as the Square Mile. Because the design would be distributed to a limited number of potential tenants (only 500 were produced), high production values were a component of the design process. "Our intuition told us that to market a property in an unconventional way would appeal to the bright-minded audience, [especially] when the property market is full of off-the-shelf solutions," states creative director David Kimpton.

The beginning of the process was marked by collaboration among the Hat-Trick Design team. "We have a brainstorm between all of us to start the design process," comments Kimpton. "We will have several of these as we progress through the initial designs. It is the most effective way of working for us and produces the best results." The results of the brainstorming sessions inspired the concept for 30 Gresham Street, which "was to communicate the message using thirty pictures in a purely photographic book, which would sum up the scheme without the need for words. [In addition], a thirty-word brochure said it all. We provided guidebooks, such as *30 Illustrious Neighbours*, which help sell the area. It was also important to create a sense of theater from the building itself, because a large proportion of the audience would walk past it." The dominantly photographic piece is visually exciting. Typographic content is limited, yet handled classically with a pairing of Helvetica Neue and Perpetua. '30,' set in Helvetica Neue, is used for several elements of the design—it is iconic and brands the address. "We used the famous address of 30 Gresham Street to take ownership of 30," notes Kimpton.

Classic serif letterforms, set in Perpetua, adorn the packaging of the marketing materials; the uppercase setting is clean and sophisticated. The '30' is iconic and embodies the building in its appearance throughout the materials. Blind embossing adds to the refined spirit of the overall design.

The format of the design is distinctive and thoughtfully orchestrated. It combines all the materials into one box, and the shapes of the pieces work together to form a cohesive whole. "The building being in the Square Mile led to the inspiration for the format," adds Kimpton. "All of the literature fit in a box, which was a square foot." When the box is opened, "joint importance was given to communicating the scheme via thirty words and thirty photographs. So, the two separate books were presented side by side on top of each other." Under the two primary books lie building specifications and guidebooks that include *30 Points of View* and *30 Minutes Around*. The format of the elements is based on the square.

30 Gresham Street is a refined design that promotes the property. It is informative and serves as a useful reference tool. It provides information about the property, as well as the surrounding area. The production techniques, which include embossing and engraving, are elegant. Kimpton concludes, "30 Gresham Street has set the standard for property marketing by Land Securities and positioned them as a leader in their field."

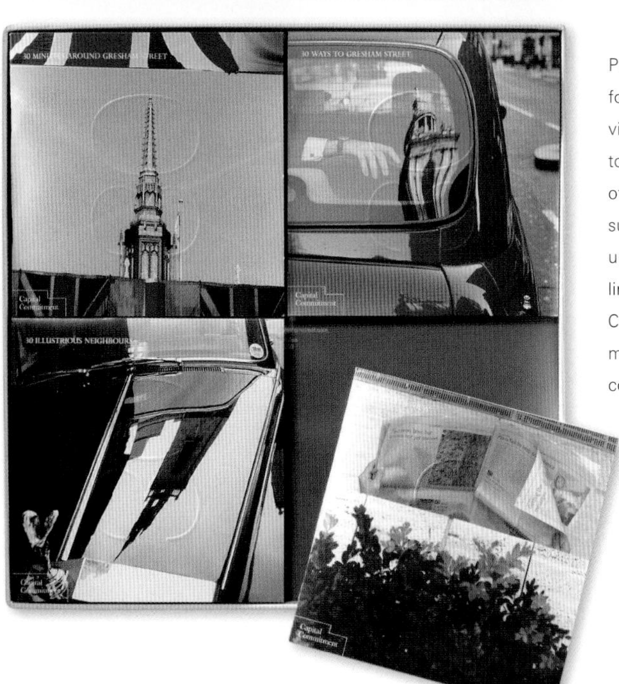

Photography is the primary force of the design. The imagery visually impacts and appeals to the emotions. Intimate details of the building, as well as its surrounding environment, provide unique views that feature strong lines and angular elements. Cropped photography creates movement within the square compositional fields.

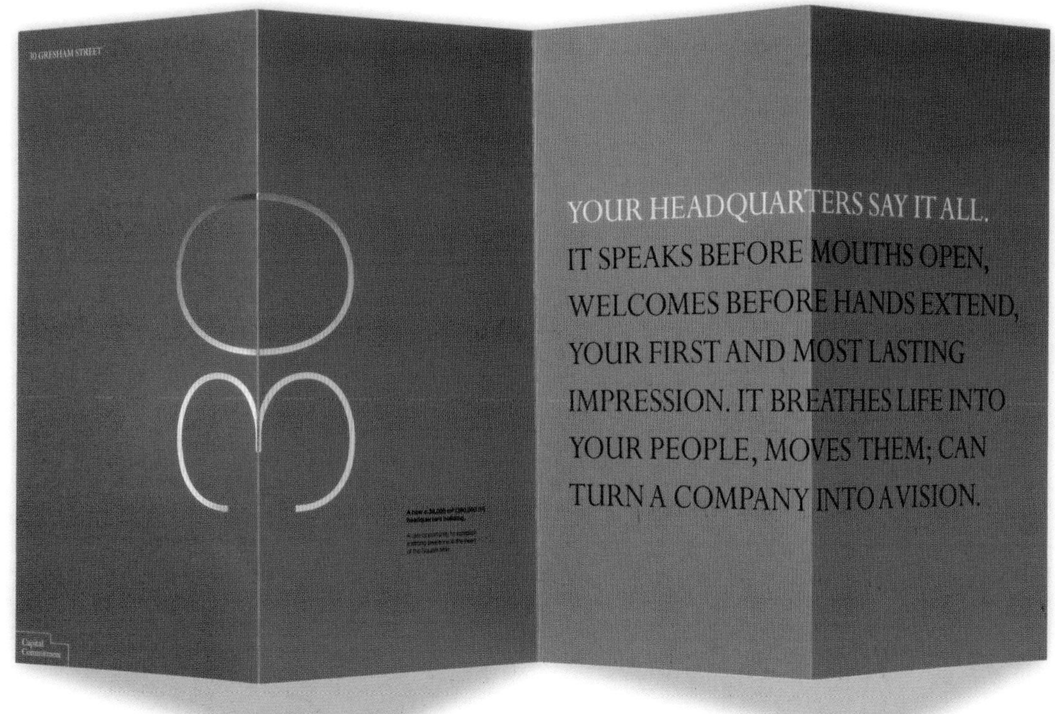

A thirty-word brochure simply states the message of the piece. The letterforms command attention and complement the contemporary, foil stamped '30' that opposes it. The positive areas also reflect the horizontal format of the page. Space is used generously to activate the design and lead navigation.

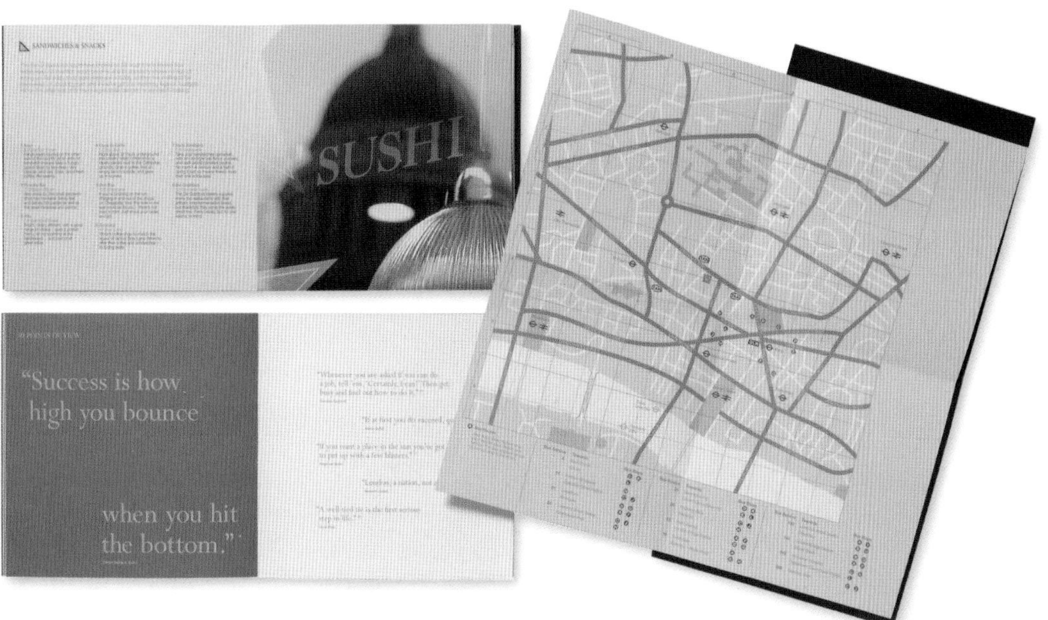

The format of the supplemental pieces is clear and simple. Equal margins define the active space of the page, which is primarily typographic. Contrasted by full-bleed photography or color, the text pages are composed within a three-column grid. Changes in typeface, as well as color and size, establish hierarchy.

Theater Faction *Oresteia* Poster/Program

HELICOPTER

designer **ethan trask**

According to their mission statement, "Theater Faction aims to set itself apart from mainstream theater practice, using unconventional and experimental methods to push theater in new directions. We will seek out the young, intelligent audience that has abandoned theater by crafting unpredictable performances in dangerous productions." *Oresteia* is the first production by Theater Faction, and the promotional materials needed to reflect an avant-garde, contemporary attitude, as well as the atypical approach taken toward *Oresteia*. Designer Ethan Trask of Helicopter explains, "Their concept for the play was [to] perform each section differently by having a different person direct each [of the three] sections." Initiating the design, which functions as a poster and program, Trask continues, "We wanted something different that spoke to a younger audience."

Inspired by "avant-garde posters and turn-of-the-century newspaper typography," the *Oresteia* poster combines graphic shapes, imagery, and typography within rich layers to communicate messages. The viewer needs to interact with the design to discern the meaning within the dense, typographic composition. Discussing the concept of the piece, Trask states, "*Oresteia* is about the loss of innocence of a prince in three acts. [Also], layered within the play were a tremendous amount of pop culture references. Our first idea was to do an exquisite corpse approach, but that satisfied only the three-act quotient. We wanted to have the idea of a Greek tragedy but in a street graphic way."

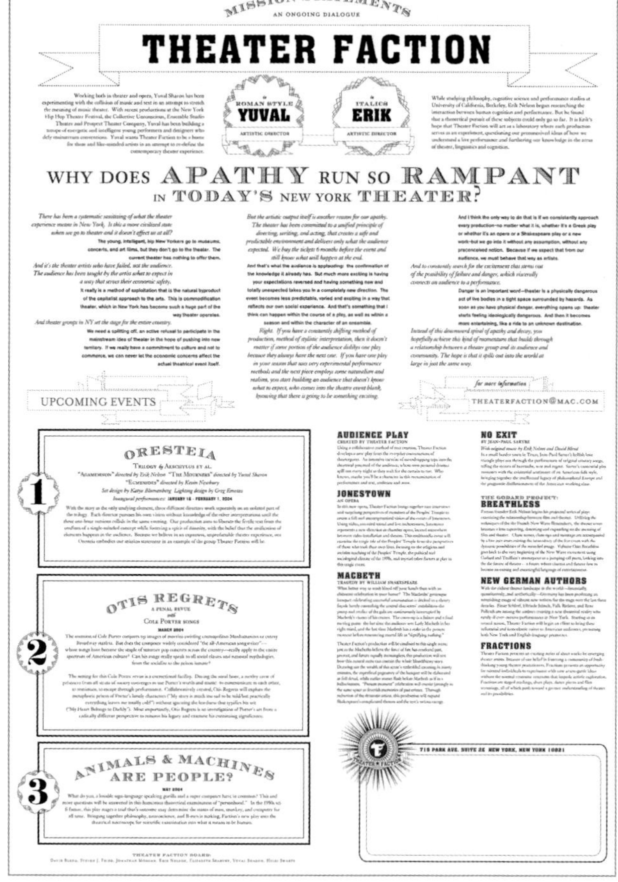

Black-and-white photography is an evocative background for the typographic elements. The image is a strong, central force and leads the eye into the title treatment, *Oresteia*, which is the compositional focal point. It features display letterforms turned in perspective, which add depth and dimension. The title floats on the page and moves toward the viewer. "The headline typography came from Las Vegas neon lights and the idea of wanting to be famous," notes Trask. It is flanked hierarchically by secondary typography, including the subtitle, theater name, and performance dates. Red numbers, encircled with a black stroke, label the three sections of the production and provide visual cues that guide the viewer from the top to the bottom of the layout. The poster features multiple typefaces, including Aachen, Birch, Chevalier, and Mrs Eaves. These typefaces add contrast, diversity, and texture to the design.

The *Oresteia* poster for Theater Faction is dynamic and engaging from a distance and informative and revealing up close. Intriguing photography is juxtaposed with distinctive typography that composes the title, *Oresteia*, and draws the eye into the design. On closer examination, the design is full of typographic subtleties that allow the viewer to navigate through the two-sided composition and glean its content. It is a unique solution that makes a strong first impression for a forward-thinking client.

Helicopter conceived the *Oresteia* poster and program in the innovative spirit of Theater Faction with intelligence and functionality. The hierarchically strong composition provides layers of information that are accessible and intriguing. The viewer must interact with the design to see its graceful details, which include the harmonious integration of multiple typefaces.

HENDERSONBROMSTEADARTCO.

AIGA Boom Exhibition Poster and Booklet

art director **hayes henderson**
designer/illustrator **billy hackley**

The American Institute of Graphic Arts (AIGA) *Boom* poster and booklet designs function as the marketing package and awards annual for the North and South Carolina chapters. Hendersonbromsteadartco. set out to create a meaningful, original design. "We chose to concentrate on the irony of the name and how it pertained to the bust economy as well as to the general climate of fear following in the wake of 9/11," explains art director Hayes Henderson. "Second, we merged this with the idea that, no matter the situation, creativity has to happen and that it can come forward even more powerfully in desperate times." The latter comment reflects the concept that ignited the style of the pieces.

The *Boom* materials are the results of a flexible process from start to finish. Finessing the concept along the way, Henderson details the approach: "After creating the illustration of the figure for the poster and mailer, Billy Hackley (senior designer and concept guy on the project) and I knew we wanted to keep the piece appropriately spontaneous to match the quality of his illustration. He then looked at typography that had a similar hand-drawn feel. This developed from the initial sketch phase (the thumbnail sketches prior to going to the computer). Billy's initial comps had a fun, offbeat feel, yet they were familiar to industry people in the way they resembled thumbnail noodlings. [It was] an unusual look for an awards annual but strangely complementary to the formal presentation of the work. As well, the illustrations of the judges and other renderings were created as doodles but ended up becoming the actual artwork used."

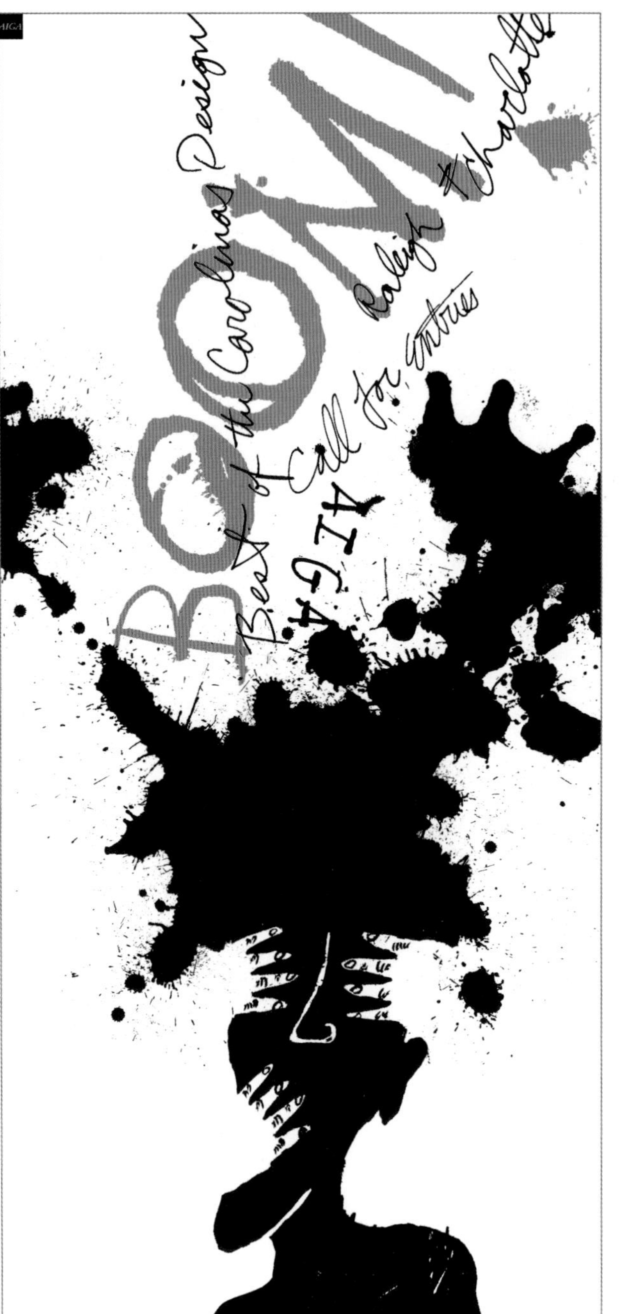

The *Boom* exhibition poster is an energetic display of illustration and hand-drawn letterforms. Both elements explode on the surface of the page and extend off its edges, while the textural quality emits a painterly expression.

The cover of the exhibition booklet is an extension of the poster. The illustrative 'boom' moves up the page, increasing in size as it rises off the top of the page. Combined with generous white space, the unconventional lettering is captivating and provides an impetus to look inside.

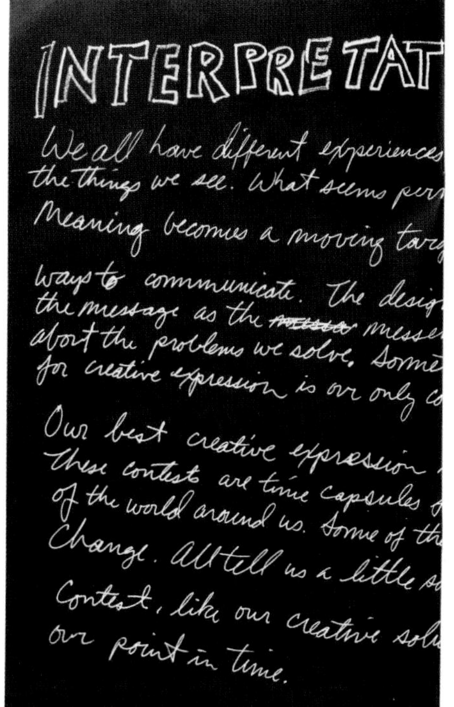

The inside front cover and title page spread provide dramatic visual contrast. Large black-and-white fields fill the composition. On the left side, a short statement, 'Interpretation Changes,' runs across the page and extends to the inside back cover. 'Boom,' in comparison to its application on the poster and cover, is diminutive, quietly sitting along the edge of the recto page.

Hendersonbromsteadartco. emphasized the winning design work in the *Boom* exhibition booklet. "From a layout standpoint," discusses Henderson, "we were inspired by recent design annuals that we felt had traded off proper representation of award-winning work for the designers' interest in turning the annual into a purely personal design opportunity." The oversized format is the perfect foundation for the booklet. It provides an open canvas for the spacious display of work. The limited number of examples per page is advantageous because the viewer can carefully examine each piece. Scale accentuates the details.

The *Boom* exhibition booklet and poster feature the use of space, scale, and handcraft—illustration and typography—as their dominant characteristics. The well-planned design is loose and improvisational, while its quirkiness leaves a lasting impression.

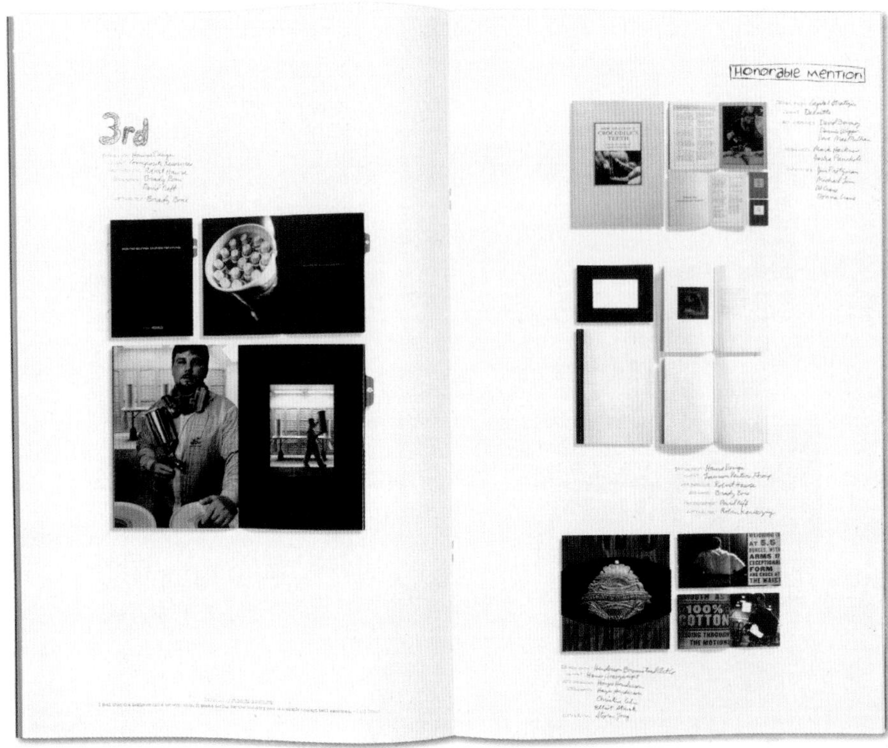

An interior spread demonstrates a clean and open composition. The visual emphasis on the winning design work, which is presented simply in the center of the page.

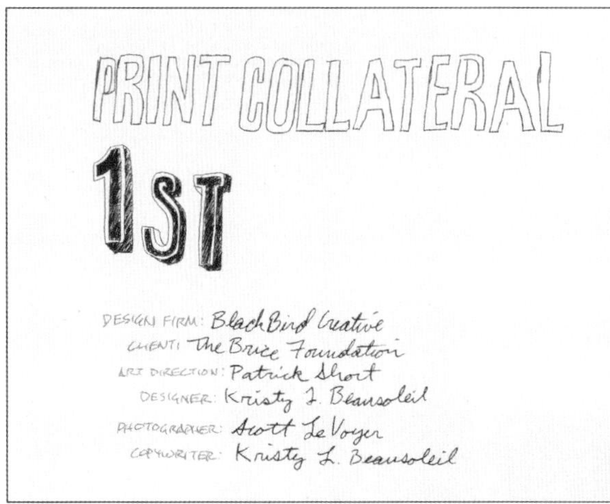

Using varying type sizes, color, and hand-drawn characters, the lettering hierarchically notes the headings, subheadings, and credit information without taking attention away from the featured work. Changing on each spread, the hand-drawn text is varied and includes scribbled, outlined, and dimensional letterforms.

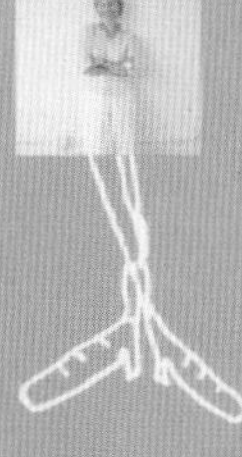

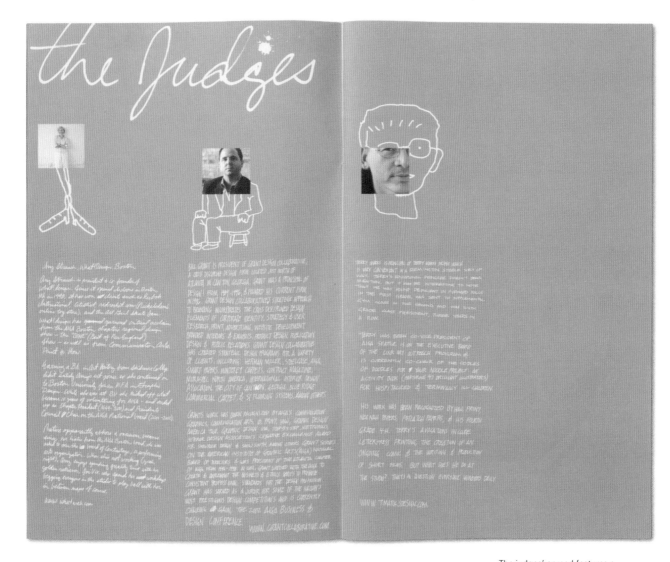

The judges' spread features a clever combination of illustration and photography. The imagery, which is framed in squares, is extended beyond its edges with the addition of illustrations that complete each picture.

HOET & HOET

The Skies Invitation and Greeting Card

***designer* véronique hoet**

The Skies is a self-promotional piece that functions as an invitation and a greeting card for the design firm Hoet & Hoet. The dual purpose of *The Skies* was to send best wishes to clients while inviting them to a festive celebration. The cards demonstrate an unusual format for an invitation and greeting card, which adds immediate interest to the design because it is an unexpected solution. The development of the piece was inspired by "beauty all around us. It was very important to show what we see each day," explains designer Véronique Hoet. "The sky surrounds us. If you turn 360 degrees, you see a different view or image of beauty with each step." The metaphor of the sky also communicates the hope for a prosperous future.

The imagery is evocative and carries the message of the design. The photography captures multiple views of the skies seen throughout the day—a total of fifty-five cards comprise *The Skies*. Each card is a picturesque view, while the combination of vantage points expresses a range of perspectives from the solid blue sky to the setting sun. The viewer is able to see everything at once, which provides a unique and memorable experience. "We forget to pay attention to the richness of the beauty around us sometimes," notes Hoet.

Typography is minimally composed on only six cards. The text communicates the spirit of the cards, while directing attention toward the dominant photography. In addition, the cards are bound with a custom-made elastic band that wraps around them. The fluorescent color is eye-catching and incites curiosity to see what it binds. The cards are also backed by bright colors that contain the Hoet & Hoet logo. The repetitive color and logo treatment unifies the cards as a set. In contrast, the card backs are always changing to provide new discoveries with every interaction. "Each time and moment is different. It changes. It is never the same. It is always unique," comments Hoet.

The Skies demands engagement to experience its beauty. It surpasses a practical function as an invitation and greeting card to provide a lasting impression. The design inspires the viewer to "go outside. Have a look. You will see wonderful things that are simple and beautiful," says Hoet.

YOU WILL SEE **WONDERFUL THINGS** THAT ARE SIMPLE AND BEAUTIFUL.

The invitation/greeting card uses photography as its driving force. It provides impact while delivering a message that beauty surrounds us from every vantage point. White borders frame each image and provide a distinctive edge for viewing. Each image is a snapshot that captures beauty and time.

FAITES VOS VŒUX
HOET & HOET WISHES YOU A CLEAR, SERENE, SHINY, PURE AND BLUE 2004 AND INVITES YOU UNDER ITS BRIGHT NEW SKY...
OP VRIJDAG 13 FEBRUARI 2004
VAN 16 U TOT...
PLEASE CONFIRM YOUR PRESENCE:
T 02 646 40 06
OR HELLEN@HOET-HOET.BE
E411 > BXL
CHSSÉE DE LASNE
ESSO
HOET & HOET

THE JONES GROUP

Show Your True Colors Brochure

art director **vicky jones**
designer **caroline mcalpine**

The brochure cover is divided by a horizontal flowline that creates an alignment point along which imagery and type rise and fall—it is the focused, active area of the design.

Geographics, a printer located in the southeastern United States, approached the Jones Group to conceptualize and design a promotional brochure that would feature their new ten-color press—one of only seventeen in the United States. "Their goal was to capture more business from the design and advertising agency community," explains art director Vicky Jones. "They wanted to position the press in a way that would dazzle designers." Inspired by the technology of the press, the Jones Group was determined to visually present the press's diverse range of capabilities to a broad group of designers. "The concept behind the brochure was to show how Geographics's new technology sets them apart in the printing business and how these advancements can directly increase the quality of work the designers create," comments Jones. "This concept shines in both the execution of the copy and graphics."

The visualization process of the brochure was led by strong writing, which outlines the overall theme of the design—The Geographics Difference—and articulates the functions and benefits of the ten-color press. Jones elaborates, "Our goal from a design perspective was to find imagery that would capitalize on all the benefits we defined [in the writing]. The basic command 'Show you how…' was applied in a way that outlined how the Geographics printing process helps designers set their work apart from the rest." Antique imagery—ranging from fishing lures to skeleton keys to clocks—was included. "Every image utilizes functions of the press that are unique to ten-color printing and not achievable by most presses," says Jones.

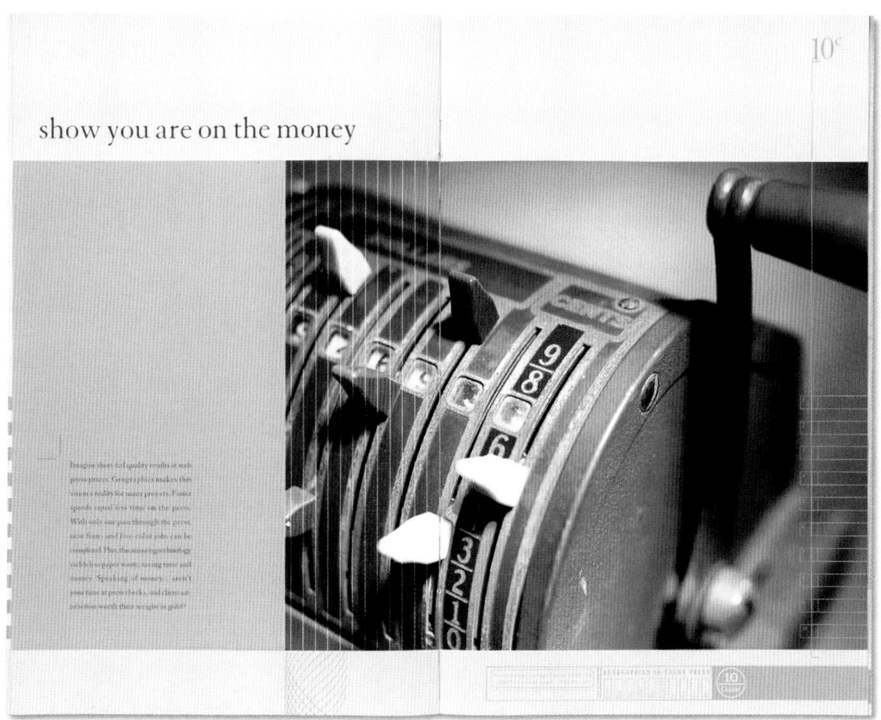

Photography dominates the brochure design and features the capabilities of the press. It fills single pages, as well as full spreads, with each image demonstrating different printing techniques. The imagery is complemented by a range of subordinate visual elements that creates a strong background of details that are noticeable on close inspection. Subtle linear elements run across the surface of the page, whereas tiny numerals knock out of the photography. Fields of colors, as well as small bars, accent several spreads and contrast with bright white paper. Controlled typographic elements interact with graphic shapes, linear elements, and photography. Crop marks accent the text and simply mark the locations of headings or body copy.

The *Show Your True Colors* brochure effectively exploits the unlimited printing options available using a ten-color press. The combination of strong, minimal copy and bold imagery clearly communicates the value and proficiency of the press. The language is focused and the design grabs attention. "The design was so effective that the brochure was reprinted a second time for client use," concludes Jones. "The Geographics sales team has come to rely on this piece to open new doors."

Composed within rectangular and square carriers, large photography is featured in the interior spreads of the brochure. Serif typography is set into levels of importance: headings, subheadings, and body text. Its position is activated by the edges of the photography and linear elements. Structured lines direct the eye through the compositional space.

KANGAROO PRESS

Songs: Ohia Concert Poster

***designer* ryan nole**

The screenprinting process of the *Songs: Ohia* poster features black, white, and red inks printed on gray stock. The technique is rough and textural, which adds a unique impression. In addition, the designer makes use of an unusual page size by complementing its shape through the vertical movement of the visual elements, such as raindrops falling down the page.

The design of concert posters encourages unlimited visual expression. Intuition and creative freedom are inherent to the design process. The results are emotive and engaging, interpretive and unusual. The aesthetic of the posters crosses the boundary between design and fine art. Yet, like all forms of visual communication, the purpose of concert posters is the delivery of information. They advertise and promote the music scene and announce events, locations, and times. The function is useless if they do not impress and inform the pedestrian viewer.

The process for *Songs: Ohia* began with an understanding of the client's needs. "In this particular case, I had worked with the artist and label enough to have a good idea of what they wanted," explains Kangaroo Press designer Ryan Nole. "On this particular occasion, I was asked to make a long, skinny poster, half the size of my normal show posters, and to print the posters two-up on the same stock that we are accustomed to using." The shape of the poster is a challenge; there is limited compositional space to create a memorable piece. "Because of the long, skinny format," adds Nole, "I knew it was going to be hard to get a good balance between type and image."

The inspiration for the design comes from "listening to the band for which I am creating a poster. If I don't like their music, chances are I'm not going to have an easy time designing. In turn, if I'm working for a band that I love, the poster seems to design itself," describes Nole. The next step of the process led Nole to refer to his collection of imagery. "Whenever I see an interesting image in an old magazine or book, I cut it out and store it in a cigar box," says Nole. "I started this design with an image of an owl that I had saved with *Songs: Ohia* in mind. The image was an old German trademark that really stuck out to me."

As the dominant element of the design, the owl is the focal point that draws the viewer into the composition. In support, a large rain cloud marks the top of the page. Raindrops fall downward onto a red umbrella, which adds a punch of color without taking attention away from the owl and its typographic perch. The vertical movement of the rain complements the shape of the page and leads the eye toward the bottom of the composition. White sans serif letters sit boldly within a black field that grounds the owl and contrasts the cloud. The band name, *Songs: Ohia*, is hierarchically strong and immediately accessible. Additional content falls below the name in a smaller, thinner type size and style. The *Songs: Ohia* concert poster presents a fresh approach toward design that is loose and instinctual. It serves as a reminder that design is full of expressive opportunities.

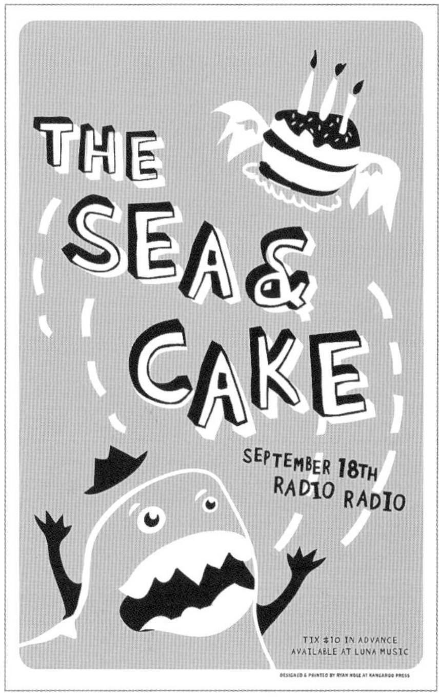

...IF I'M WORKING FOR a band that I love, **the poster seems to design itself...**

Other concert posters feature display typography in combination with unusual imagery. The richly colored pieces are actively composed to lead the eye around the page. The band names, *The Sea and Cake*, *Enon*, and *Bright Eyes*, are focal points. Their settings are integrated into hand-drawn and found illustrations, which add character to the designs. Each poster is distinct from the next, yet similar in their bold, visual appeal.

KEARNEYROCHOLL

KearneyRocholl Promotional Books

designer **frank rocholl**
copywriters **jesse kearney, frank rocholl**

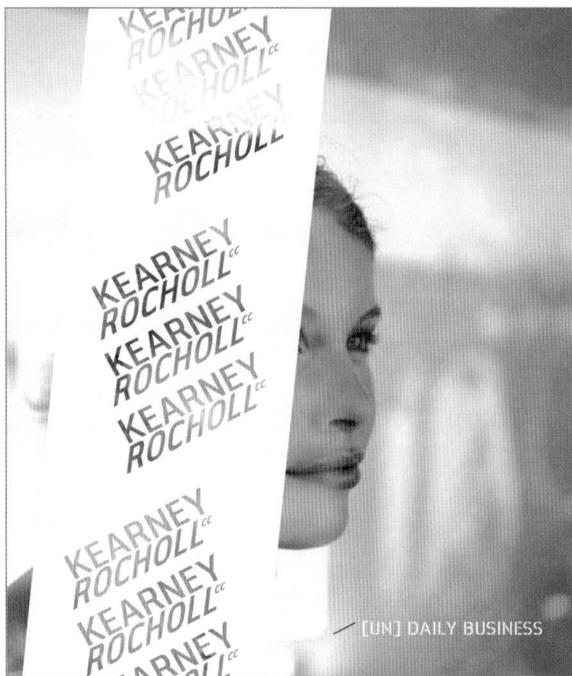

The covers allude to the visual system of the interior. Acting as a focal point, a vertical banner of KearneyRocholl logos overlays soft, alluring photography. The title of the pieces, *Daily Business* and [*Un*] *Daily Business*, is quietly positioned in the bottom-right corner and takes a subordinate role to the agency name.

The promotional books for KearneyRocholl—*Daily Business* and [*Un*] *Daily Business*—share a comprehensive, intelligent impression of the communications agency. The process began by determining the best method of communicating four elements: brand theory, the agency portfolio, founder interviews, and humor. The brand theory text explains the importance of branding. The portfolio section presents the work of the agency and shares examples of their diverse capabilities. An interview provides insight into Jesse Kearney and Frank Rocholl, founders of KearneyRocholl, creating a personal connection with the viewer. Humor communicates an additional perspective of the agency. It is most evident in *Daily Business*, which presents an unusual approach toward a fabricated case study. [*Un*] *Daily Business* features the theory component, as well as the portfolio of work and interviews. "All in all, our approach was to show different facets of KearneyRocholl in clever, portioned parts," says designer Frank Rocholl.

The conceptual approach is motivated by KearneyRocholl's desire to cultivate a "new, unorthodox agency profile," says Rocholl. As a result, the theme of "Design Seen through Art Glasses" was conceived. With this concept, "design was seen through an 'art' perspective. [The design] features funny, self-tinkered objects like Duchamp's readymades. Our logo is applied as some sort of Andy Warhol Campbell Soup assembly. A template font is used that gives [the pieces] a nondesigned charm. Sticky-tape-inspired layers run over pictures and personal statements," comments Rocholl. The design successfully combines all of the divergent elements into cohesive books. Both pieces employ the same format and structure, yet are differentiated by their content.
The typography is set in Nuri and Nuri Template, which are designed by Rocholl; it consistently hangs from the top margin. The amount of text is limited, which eases reading and allows for a generous amount of white space on the page. Typographic elements are juxtaposed with graphic shapes, photography, and type as texture, which adds dimension and interest.

HERE:
SOME OF KEARNEY AND ROCHOLL'S VIEWS ON ⁄ NOVELTY, THE DAY AFTER TOMORROW, IMAGES, BRANDS, BESTSELLERS, INITIATIVES AND THREESIXTYNOW (?)

PLUS:
AN INTERVIEW, SOME FAVORITE ITEMS AND MANY SAMPLES OF OUR WORK FOR WELL-KNOWN COMPANIES.

THE DAY AFTER TOMORROW WILL NOT BE MUCH DIFFERENT FROM TODAY. EVERYTHING WILL REMAIN THE SAME – EXCEPT FOR ITS APPEARANCE IN A MORE ACTUAL VERSION.

BUT THERE IS ONE THING TO BE STRICTLY AVOIDED IN YOUR FUTURE PLANS. DON'T LET YOUR BRAND BECOME AN OLD ACQUAINTANCE ⁄ TOO FAMILIAR TO STIR UP MUCH INTEREST ANY MORE.

KearneyRocholl analyzes what a brand stands for. We find ways into the future. Future compatibility: We initiate, mediate and implement communication that is clear and comprehensible. This is what we call brand activism.

Interior spreads demonstrate a consistent application of visual elements, including large headline text that anchors the page. The photography, which is placed in dynamic graphic shapes, adds dimension. In addition, strings of typography are used as textural elements. They are placed in color fields and atop the imagery to create surface depth.

XXXX CREATING IMAGES XXXX CREATING IDENTITY XXXX RECODING BRANDS XXXX

⁄ KEARNEYROCHOLL IS A COMMUNICATIONS AGENCY WITH A MARKED COMPETENCE FOR DESIGN.

IN OUR WORK WE SET NO ARTIFICIAL BOUNDARIES BETWEEN PUBLICITY, DESIGN, NEW MEDIA AND COMMUNICATIONS DESIGN FOR FAIRS.

OUR CORE ACTIVITIES ARE BRAND UPDATES, IMAGE AND COMPANY COMMUNICATIONS AND CI/CD DEVELOPMENT.

OUR WORK HAS REPEATEDLY FOUND GREAT INTEREST WITH THE MEDIA, AND WE HAVE RECEIVED A NUMBER OF INTERNATIONAL REWARDS.

Our references include various companies of international renown --- Audi AG, Deutsche Börse AG, Lufthansa, Toyota Europe, Guhl, Epson, Signum, Hugo Boss and smart (Daimler-Chrysler).

The promotional books for KearneyRocholl, *Daily Business* and [*Un*] *Daily Business*, effectively present the agency's mission and range of work, while alluding to its personality. The design is accessible, compact, and rich with content that is visually and verbally balanced. The books provide an opportunity for KearneyRocholl to redefine the agency and elevate the brand in an original way. Rocholl concludes, "We think it's always good for personal growth to torture yourself and find new ground, themes, and forms. Life is too short to be a copycat. It's interesting what happens if you have to find design solutions in an unfamiliar visual style. Anything goes these days, so let's push it."

A portfolio spread unfolds to share numerous examples—the diversity and skills of KearneyRocholl are evident. The combination of exciting work with strong text woven throughout the designs sends a powerful message. The strength of the books lies in the interaction of words and pictures.

ONE / WE FOUND THAT CLASSICAL MARKETING ENGINES OFTEN FAILED TO PRODUCE THE DESIRED RESULT.

A NEW LOGO DID NOT BRING ABOUT THE OVERALL CHANGE, SIMULTANEOUSLY EMPLOYING SEVEN AGENCIES CREATED A TOTAL VISUAL MESS, APPARENTLY IT COULD NOT BE AVOIDED THAT EVERYTHING HAD A DIFFERENT LOOK.

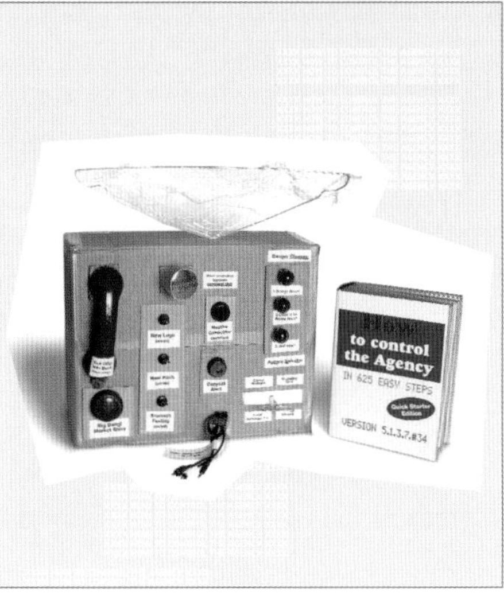

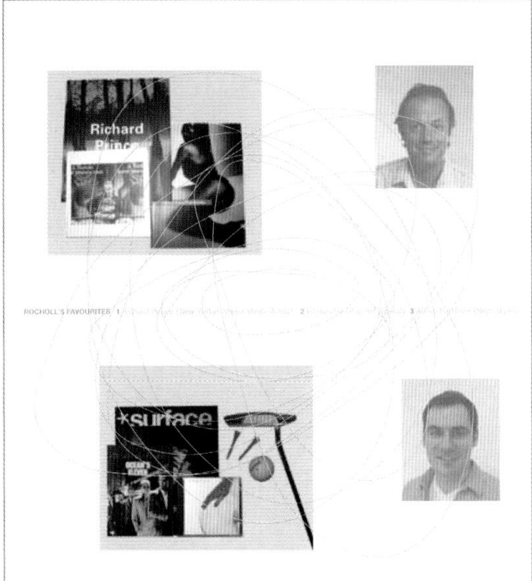

The opening spread of the interview section adapts the visual system and introduces a two-column structure used for the placement of body copy. Although the spread is heavy compared to the others, it is not visually overwhelming. Ample column intervals and spacing between paragraphs, lighten the impression of the text blocks.

THREE THE LONG STANDING IMAGE OF THE "ADVERTISING SUPER HERO" (SEE A PICTURE OF THE MALE SPECIMEN ON THE OPPOSITE PAGE) SEEMS TO WANE.
THERE IS A CLEAR TENDENCY TO CASH IN ON THE PROMISES MADE. THEREFORE EVEN SUCH PLEASANT EXTRAS AS INVITATIONS TO DINNER AT HIGH-TONED RESTAURANTS, INCENTIVE TRIPS TO FAR AWAY PLACES OR THAT FANCY SET OF INNOVATIVE COLORFUL CAPPUCCINO CUPS ARE INCREASINGLY REJECTED AS A SUBSTITUTE FOR MORE SUBSTANTIAL CONTRIBUTIONS.

Spreads from the *Daily Business* introduce humor. KearneyRocholl presents a mock case study about the value of branding and communication. Although the visual system and layout is the same in both books, stylized props designed by Rocholl, including The Advertising Superhero, distinguish the books and provide contrast to the photography and portfolio of [*Un*] *Daily Business*.

KINETIC SINGAPORE

The Observatory *Time of Rebirth*
CD Packaging

designers **leng soh, pann linn, roy poh**

The packaging design for The Observatory's debut CD, *Time of Rebirth*, captures their image and sound in print. The members of The Observatory assembled after leaving previous bands. As the album title suggests, designer Roy Poh comments, "they've left the past behind to come together to be reborn again." Briefed by The Observatory to design a "distinctive" package within a limited budget, Kinetic used the title, *Time of Rebirth*, as the conceptual foundation for the design. At the onset of the design process, "idea is always the king," says Poh.

Focusing on the theme of rebirth, the result of Kinetic's conceptualization process is the visual metaphor of a diary. Kinetic asked the singer of the band to scribble notes, lyrics, and drawings on paper to "provide an authentic look and feel" of a personal journal. With the exception of the serif typeface on the booklet cover that references an old-fashioned diary, the text treatment used consistently throughout the design is handwritten letterforms.

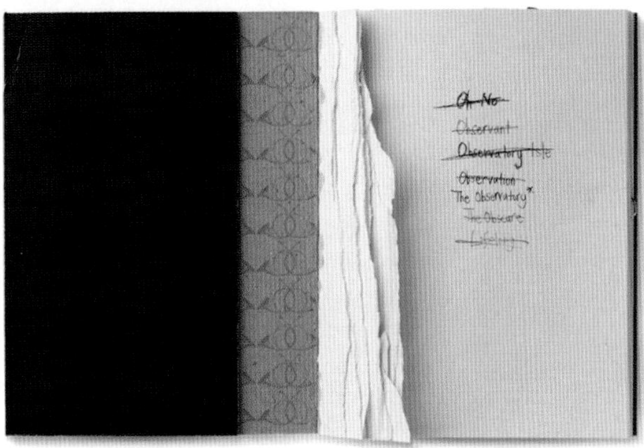

The packaging design for The Observatory's *Time of Rebirth* creates a link between the viewer and the band. Through the visual metaphor of a diary, the viewer is a voyeur to the album-recording process. Kinetic creates a package that is distinctive in its handmade, intimate quality. The torn and weathered pages of the album booklet are expressive. The design is given a human touch through the unique use of hand lettering.

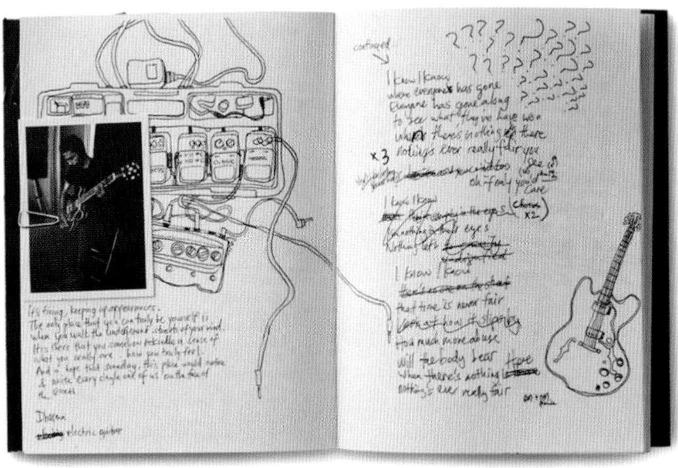

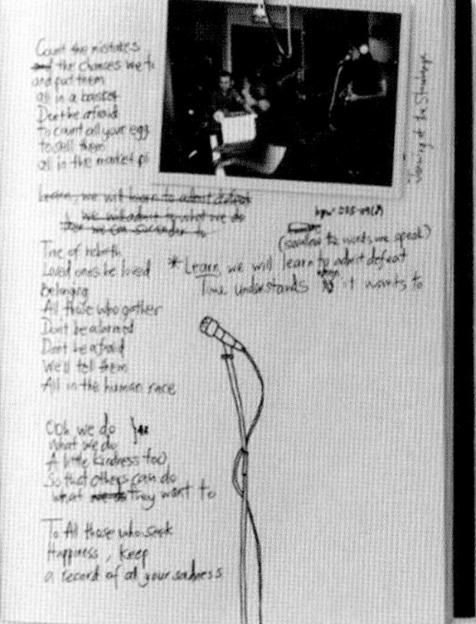

The lettering "completes the personal, honest touch," says Poh. The handwritten letterforms are imperfect, messy, and rough. As is standard in typographic application, weight is used to create emphasis. The scrawled words are written repetitively on top of each other to achieve a darker text color to define importance. An alternative to type, handwritten letterforms bring a human element into the design.

The tactile and tattered quality of the design is linked to the theme of rebirth and blends successfully with the gritty lettering. The torn pages of the booklet represent letting go of the past to embark on a new life chapter for each band member. The gray board and wood-free paper used for the cover and interior pages are thoughtfully considered. The stock will "age gracefully and provide a richly textured feel," adds Poh. The tactility of the album packaging is enhanced through the addition of paperclips that hold black-and-white snapshots of the band in the recording studio. Like a diary, the images are moments captured in time. Slightly askew, the photographs do not interfere with the text. The designers have composed the images to keep all the lyrics accessible. The photographs, as well as the line drawings, contrast with the letterforms and provide visual impact and further materiality to the design.

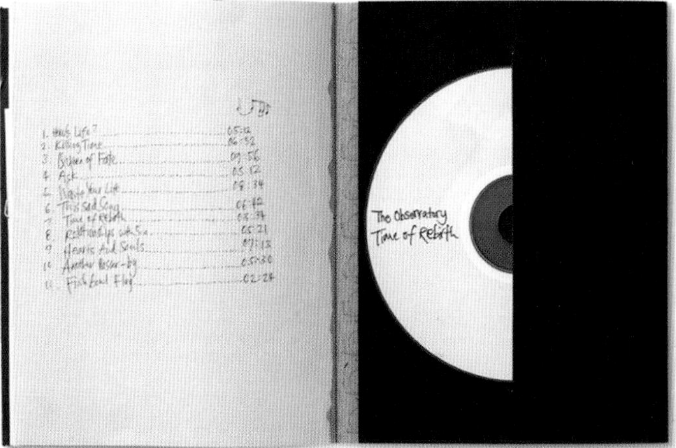

Interior spreads feature drawings, hand lettering, and photography. The elements add tactility to the design while communicating important content. Images of the band, as well as song lyrics, inform the viewer.

KOLÉGRAM

Opera Lyra Ottawa Brochure

***designer* gontran blais**

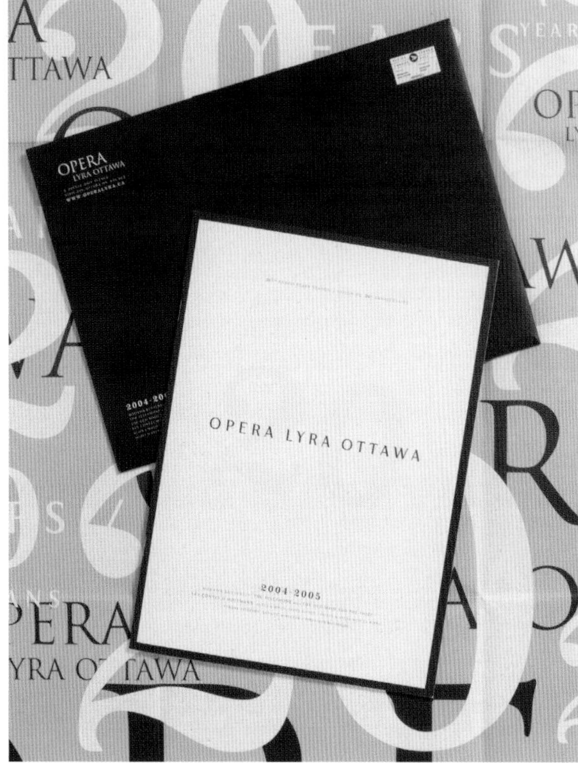

The Opera Lyra Ottawa brochure is wrapped in a black sheet that opens into a typographically ornate poster. The treatment is dynamic—large letterforms interact and create a rich texture. In contrast to this bold expression, the minimal cover is traditionally set in a centered arrangement. A subtly tinted '20' sits behind the title, and supplementary type falls to the bottom; a red subtitle accents the top of the page.

The Opera Lyra Ottawa brochure is an elegant presentation celebrating the company's twentieth season. Designed by Kolégram, the piece successfully captures the sophisticated, yet playful, character of the opera. The design is classically composed with a hint of novelty. The contrast of tradition and modernity is thematically woven throughout the design to support the directive of the piece, which "was to create a season brochure that would attract not only the existing opera crowd but also the young, hip crowd," says designer Gontran Blais.

The conceptually driven design features refined typography and unusual imagery. "I wanted to create a look that would stand out from the rest for the company's twentieth season," explains Blais. "I also did not want to use pictures of people. Instead, I used two-dollar plastic dolls to illustrate the two major operas [*Madama Butterfly* and *Les Contes d'Hoffmann*]. I thought that the mixture between fancy and contemporary would be a good balance. Basically, my concept was mixing old with new, creating something accessible to all."

The dominant content, *Madama Butterfly* and *Les Contes d'Hoffmann*, dictates the construction of the brochure's interior. Kolégram fashions a gatefold that calls attention to the operas and adds an element of surprise. "The two major operas were the most important information in the brochure," describes Blais. "They had to be the main event. I placed them in the middle of the brochure and worked around them." The inner page unfolds to reveal bright colors, quirky dolls, and a pair of small brochures lightly glued to the main page. The colors and dolls identify each opera, whereas the attached pieces provide an intimate focus.

Interior spreads are symmetrically composed to achieve balance. Ornamented, colorful pages add visual contrast to columns of centered and justified type on the facing pages. A two-column structure supports the bilingual requirement of the design.

The Opera Lyra Ottawa brochure is creatively packaged for mailing. An exterior wrapping that opens into a poster envelops the piece. Solid black on the exterior, the poster unfolds to expose a beautiful typographic texture that provides an expressive backdrop for the brochure. It is symmetrically composed along a central axis. A two-column structure, which features justified body text and centered, supplementary copy, accommodates the brochure's bilingual content. Changes in the type color and sizes in headings, subheadings, and callouts provide hierarchy.

A well-executed presentation, designer Gontran Blais of Kolégram transforms the Opera Lyra Ottawa brochure into a cosmopolitan design that integrates multiple levels of information into an interactive layout. Wonderment and drama begin as soon as the brochure is unwrapped to see what unfolds.

The middle spread of the brochure features a gatefold that opens to highlight *Madama Butterfly* and *Les Contes d'Hoffmann*. Showing curious imagery of plastic dolls stylized for each opera, the pages also contain smaller brochures that provide overviews of the main attractions. The gatefold is an unexpected, tactile solution that explodes with bright colors and original imagery.

Come Forward: Emerging Art in Texas
Exhibition Catalog

KONTOUR DESIGN

designer **sibylle hagmann**

The *Come Forward: Emerging Art in Texas* catalog and exhibition celebrates Texas artists "whose work is young but shows a conviction, clarity, and ambition that defy geographic borders, whose work history lies not behind but before them," describes John R. Lane, Dallas Museum of Art's Eugene McDermott Director. The exhibition catalogue, designed by Sibylle Hagmann of Kontour Design, features the artwork of a new generation of contemporary, forward-thinking artists, as well as accompanying essays by rising Texan writers. The catalog verbally and visually presents a broad scope of creative innovation. For the design of the exhibition catalog, the Dallas Art Museum "requested a fresh, young-looking, and, to a certain degree, experimental design—characteristics that are rather unusual for a Dallas Museum of Art publication," explains Hagmann. "Normally, the design of their books is conservative."

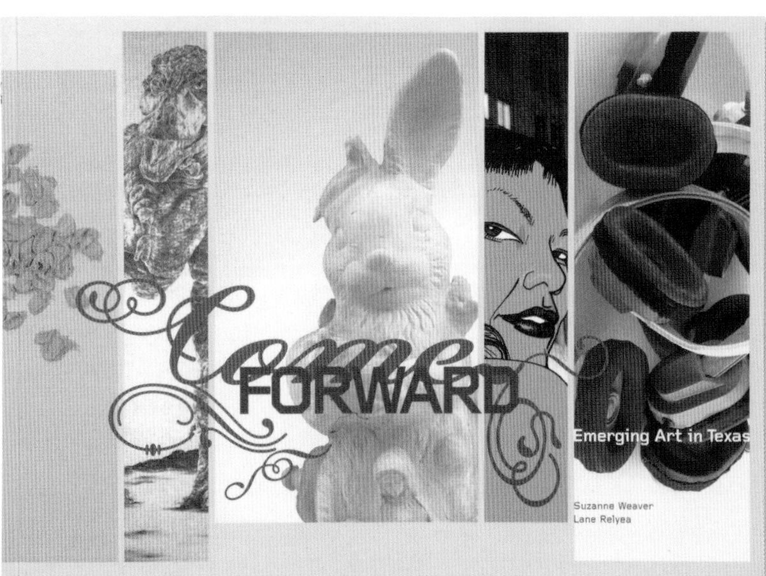

The cover sets the tone of the interior. Imagery is composed in vertical rectangles, which indicates the flexible grid used throughout the design. The type adopts a subordinate role on the cover, as the use of unique typefaces adds character to the progressive design.

I HAD AN INTEREST IN
MAKING THE BOOK AS

The diverse presentation of artists and writers is a driving force of *Come Forward*. "One of the goals was to present each artist's work appropriately and, at the same time, establish a visual consistency throughout the book," says Hagmann. "I had an interest in making the book as lively as possible." The catalog is structurally composed and adaptable to accommodate compositional expression and variety. Its horizontal format is divided into a number of spatial intervals to support generous amounts of text, which varies from limited front and back matter to long essays to artists' descriptions (the most expressive typographic spreads). The spatial intervals provide edges for artwork and fields of color that "harmonize with the widths of the text columns and sometimes don't—to create a livelier stage," describes Hagmann.

"The established layout, grid structure, and subentities allowed for great flexibility in terms of how text and images can be arranged. I was concerned with establishing an overall skeleton structure that had enough flexibility to keep a certain order and, at the same time, allow things to be placed where, intuitively, they felt best." In addition, the long, wide pages offer ample room for artwork featured in small and large sizes throughout the catalog. The effective use of white space allows for an ease of reading and the viewing of artwork. It also leads the eye toward important areas within the layout.

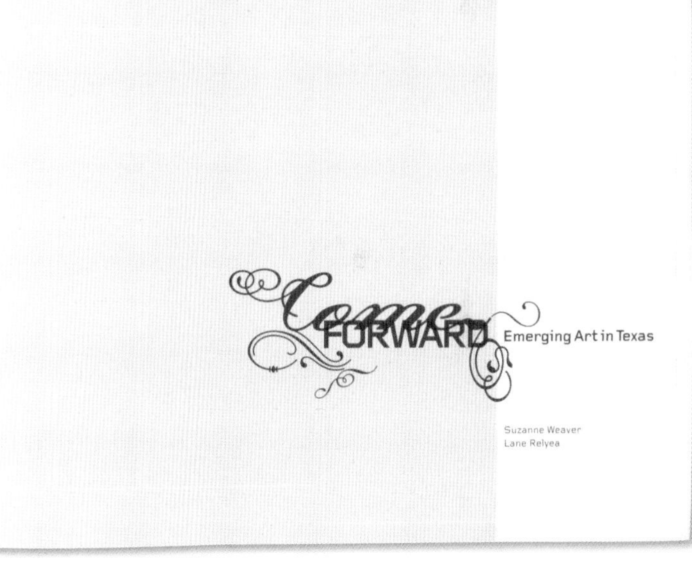

The opening spread introduces visual elements used throughout the design. Full-color imagery dominates. Subdued colors fill rectangular fields and linear elements outline the grid. White space provides an open field that draws attention to the title.

LIVELY AS POSSIBLE.

The *Come Forward: Emerging Art in Texas* catalog blends structure with poetic expression. The design is calculated and organized, yet it also relies on the strength of the designer's intuitive sense to elevate its final presentation. "To a certain degree, part of a design process and visual solution is based on intuition," says Hagmann. "Perhaps as a designer's experience grows, intuition becomes more and more part of the overall approach to establish the characteristics of a visual piece." Like the artwork and essays, the design of *Come Forward* is forward thinking and contemporary.

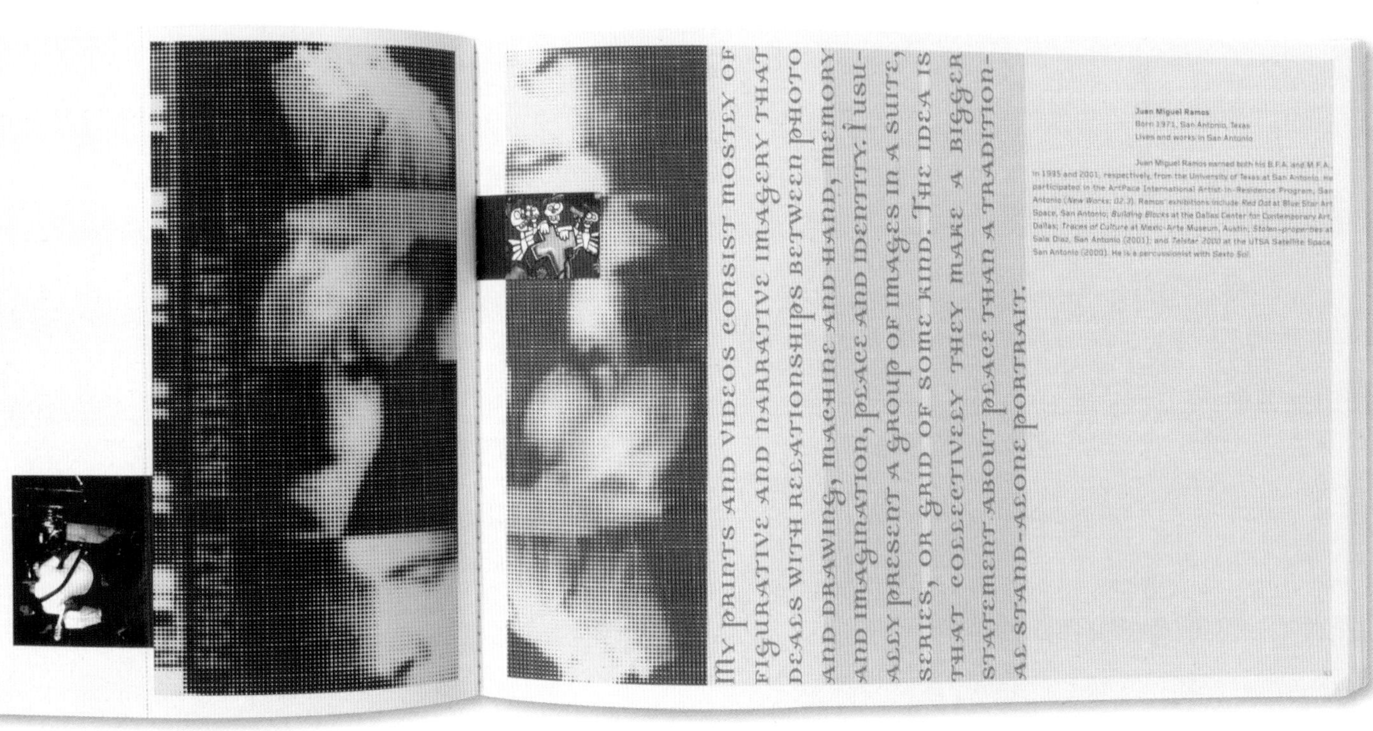

Display typefaces are used in the catalog and are most apparent in the artists' spreads. Such faces add personality to the design and reinforce the contemporary nature of the exhibition and the forward-thinking artwork.

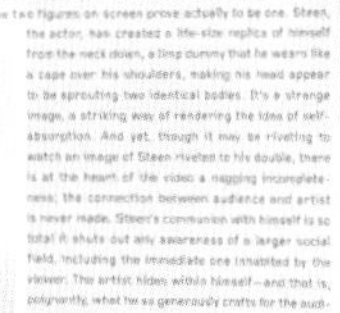

Wide spreads host large amounts of body copy. The grid provides strong edges for the placement of justified columns, where the relationship of type size and line lengths is well considered. Fields of color are used as background elements that change in width to contrast the column shapes.

LICHTWITZ

Europa, Hinterzimmer Logo and Flyer Series

***designers* kriso leinfellner, stefanie lichtwitz**

Lichtwitz was approached by Neubau Gastronomie GesmbH to design a logo and flyer series promoting the Vienna music club, Europa, Hinterzimmer. To begin projects, "we usually try to start an efficient design process with conceptual and strategic considerations," states designer Stefanie Lichtwitz. The design was influenced by a limited budget, as well as time restraints. "Flyers often must be produced on very short notice," states Lichtwitz. In addition, Lichtwitz would not be the sole designer for the flyer series. A logical, visual system needed to be established that would foster brand recognition and usability by different designers and nondesigners. "Some [events] are organized by external organizers who work with third-party designers of their own choice. If so, the club should be easily recognizable in each flyer, even when a completely different visual language is being used," notes Lichtwitz.

The visual direction of the Europa, Hinterzimmer logo and flyer series is inspired by the architectural details of the club, as well as "the lively, creative music and DJ scene." The circular logo "evokes [the shape of] a keyhole, because the name of the club, Hinterzimmer, literally means 'back room,'" adds Lichtwitz. The flyer series is shaped like a cassette tape. It is characterized by rounded corners, which soften the edges and relate to the shape of the logo. "We took the typical mix-tape produced by DJs as an analogy. They often come in packaging that is handcrafted in a personal and artistic way with the typical format of a cassette box [being] the only constant," says Lichtwitz. To standardize the flyer series, the logo is die cut into each piece. It is the focus of the flyers—a consistent brand identified with all club events. Though the logo size remains the same, its position changes on each card, which provides flexibility in the application of the visual elements.

The logo and rounded corners, which remain the constant elements, "built the framework for all the flyers," comments Lichtwitz. A flexible system "focused on a small set of fixed components" allowed others to work easily with the format. Lichtwitz elaborates, "We did not want to come up with too many rules [and] restrict third-party designers in their contributions." The changing styles of the flyers are dynamic, experimental, and interesting. "Some flyers are designed in our office and offset-printed in large quantities. Others are based on preproduced blanks that were customized by hand with stickers, rubber stamps, tags, stitching, or hand drawings by DJs or organizers," discusses Lichtwitz. "It was amazing to see the diversity of ideas and designs that these external 'design amateurs' came up with."

The Europa, Hinterzimmer logo and flyer series is fresh and innovative. It allows designers and nondesigners to create and share visual ideas. "The variety of flyer designs reflects the inventiveness and agility of the Viennese music scene well," states Lichtwitz. "We learned that many customers have started to collect the flyers."

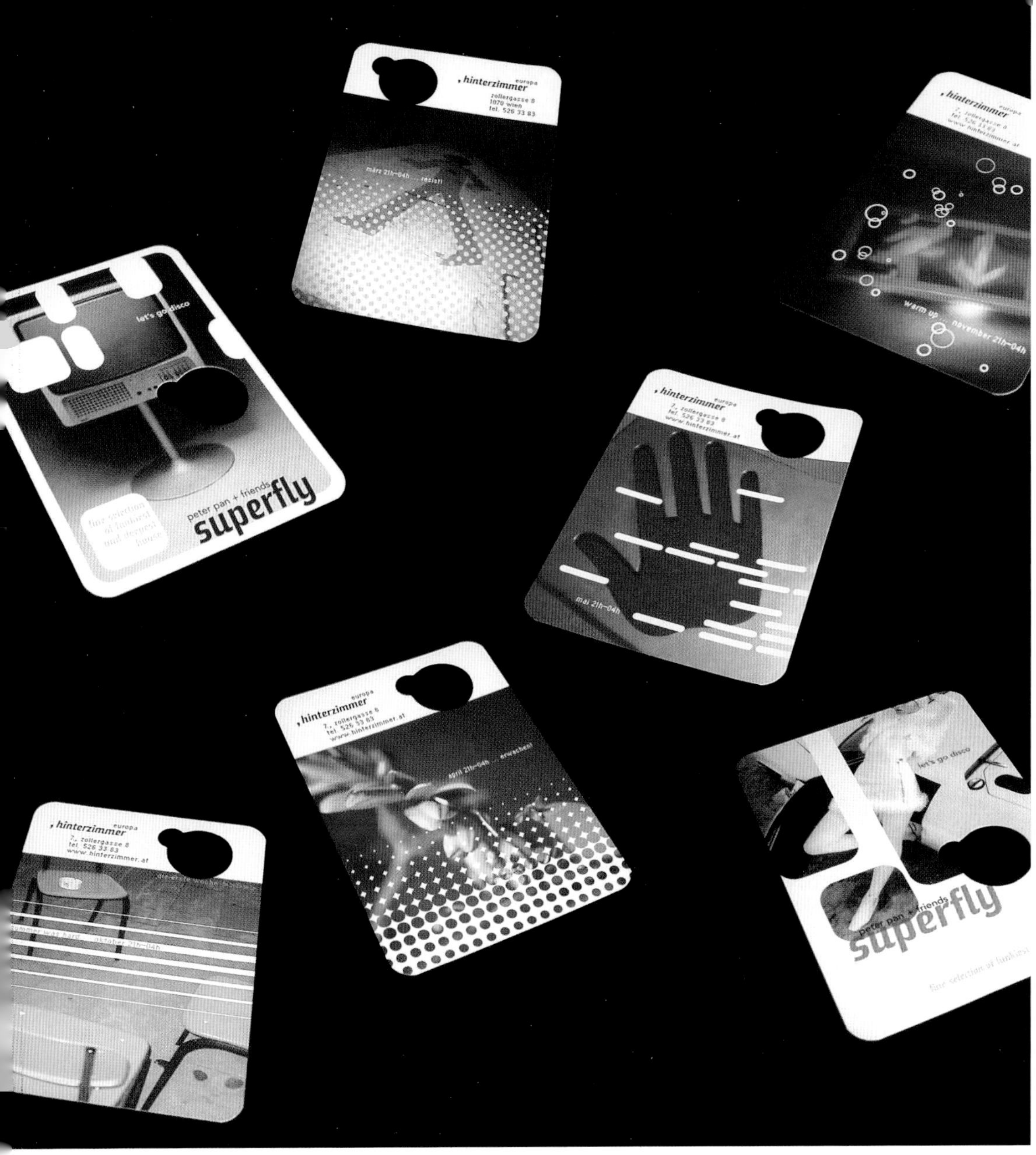

The consistent shape, as well as the die cut logo, defines the visual system for the flyer series. Each flyer is unique and customizable, demonstrating a range of designs that incorporate photography and texture. The range of examples is varied, yet remains connected because of the visual markers that tie them together.

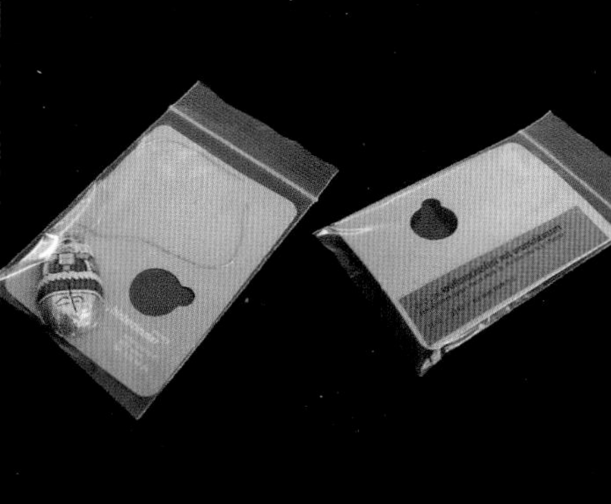

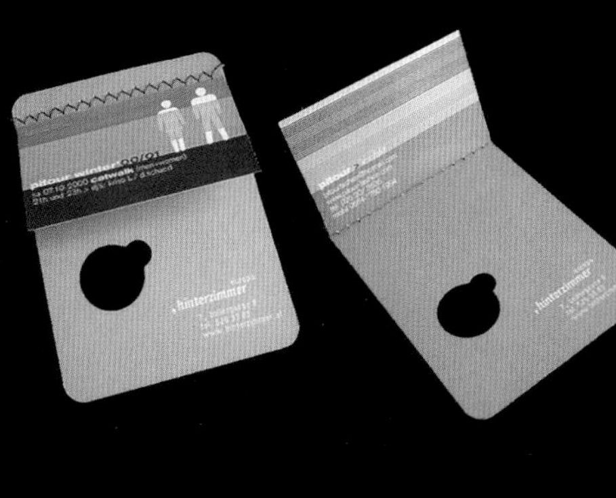

Additional handcrafted flyers feature the diversity of solutions available. They also serve as inspiration for club organizers to design their own flyers in the future. By keeping the system flexible, creative and expressive compositions are possible.

MITRE AGENCY

Make a Scene Poster

creative director troy tyner
designers john foust, kevin pojman, elliot strunk, troy tyner
copywriter julie curtis

The eclectic design of the poster is magnetic. Comprising four pieces, the poster is cohesive and demonstrates diverse solutions. A range of typographic treatments includes hand lettering contrasted with digital type. The surface textures are rough and smooth; the colors are bright and subdued. In addition to its visual impact, the function of the design is also a call to action—a positive campaign that supports the local community.

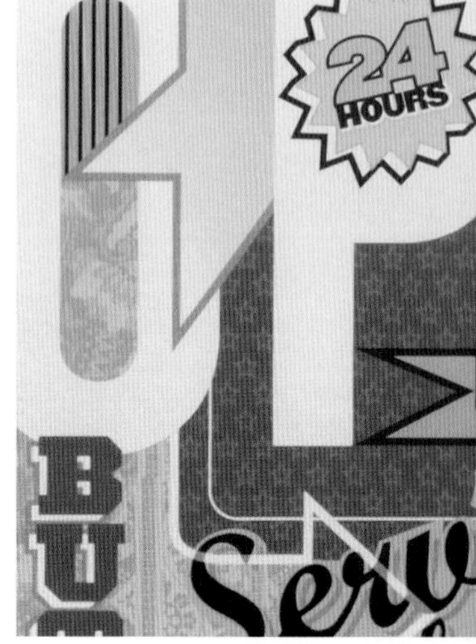

Classic Graphics, a printer in the southeastern United States, initiated a poster project with a number of regional firms. The content of the posters was to be determined by the participating designers; each firm became its own client. The opportunities for communication and visual expression were endless. Seeking inspiration in its "own backyard," Mitre Agency chose to maintain and cultivate local ties in the community "to help others understand that everyone plays a vital role in building a healthy, well-rounded 'hometown' by supporting the areas that form the unique fabric and culture of our local community—music, theater, art, and trade," explains creative director and designer Troy Tyner. The initiative developed by Mitre Agency, Make a Scene, is "a citizen call to action."

To reflect the areas of music, theater, art, and trade within one design, the poster was divided into four smaller pieces. Each quadrant focuses on one of the cultural areas. "The process was one of total collaboration by our designers," states Tyner. "Everyone worked independently to contribute ideas before we all came to agree on the best direction. Each designer had a specific view and emotional connection to what we were addressing." With the concept and format established, the designers sought visual inspiration. Tyner discusses, "Stylistically, our inspiration was drawn from many areas. Each mini-poster needed to speak in the visual vernacular specific to the cultural venue used to communicate the message (that is, music, theater, art, trade). So, our sources of inspiration were found in posters, bills, flyers, and so on, from similar venues—both historic and more current examples. The challenge was to create a look that was an immediate read without directly cribbing a style—or designing a cliché."

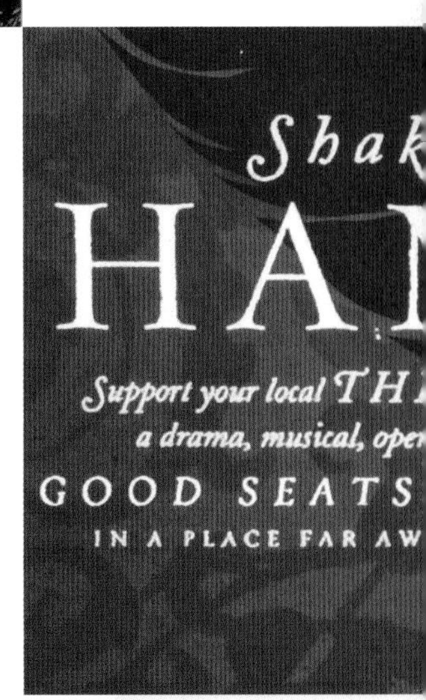

EACH POSTER IS DISTINCT, YET THE MESSAGE IS CONSISTENT.

The design of the poster is diverse, with its visual elements ranging from rough textures and hand lettering to ornate patterns and computer-generated type. The color palette is equally diverse yet balanced, which prevents any of the four pieces from dominating the others. (Although the poster works successfully as a single design, it contains perforated lines that allow the quadrants to be separated.) "Each poster is distinct, yet the message is consistent," notes Tyner. The viewer is provided with a dynamic visual impression that is immediately engaging and requires interaction with each section to understand its meaning. "At a glance, they read as they should and draw the viewer in. It's only when you read further that the true message is delivered," comments Tyner. "This is one of those cases where the look of the piece took a front seat."

Beyond the commanding aesthetics, the message of the poster is significant. The effectiveness of the Make a Scene poster has "expanded to additional offline marketing materials, special events, and a soon-to-launch community website," adds Tyner. The awareness brought to the local community, as well as the encouragement to participate within it, is the strength and success of the design.

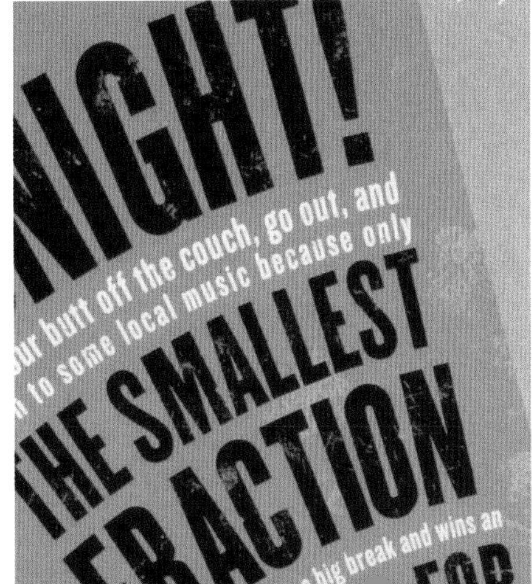

NB: STUDIO

Jerwood Applied Arts Prize: Glass
Marketing Materials

***photography* martin morrell**

The *Jerwood Applied Arts Prize: Glass* marketing materials demonstrate a consistent visual system that combines basic elements—color, photography, and typography—to create a unified series, including a poster, catalog, and invitation. Designed by NB: Studio, the materials promote an exhibition that features the work of glass designers. "We were looking for something that would talk about the interaction of glass and designer without showing a designer," explains NB: Studio's Alan Dye. "Usually, in an exhibition like this, the designer or curator chooses an iconic example that sums up the spirit of the show and becomes the marketing image. We knew that a prize was going to be awarded to one of the exhibitors later on, so we couldn't justifiably feature any single person's work in the material."

The inspiration for the design came from the work in the exhibition and the medium of glass. "Clearly, if you can see any of the work for real, this will provide the most inspiration," adds Dye. "[And], glass is so flexible a medium. It can be made to look painfully delicate or amazingly solid. It can be crystal clear or black as night." Experimentation was the key to a productive process. "We decided to do our own experiments, so we bought some glass from a local glazier and started to mess around with it, [including] layering, breaking, scratching, and shining light through it," comments Dye. "Inspiration came when we noticed a door in our studio had a window above it made from fluted glass. This stuff is great. It distorts what is behind it in a vertical, compound-eye way. We decided to order a large piece of this fluted, or readied, glass and photograph someone acting as a designer/craftsperson behind it. Now we had our image of material and human interaction."

The award-ceremony invitation introduces materials that connote the transparency of glass. The linear markings on translucent paper reflect the lines of the photograph used in the poster.

An abstract photograph activates the poster. Although abstract, the image is graphic. The impression of the glass creates long, vertical lines that define the alignment points for the typography.

With a dominant photograph established, the function of the imagery was enhanced with the addition of typography. Geometric, sans serif letterforms contrast with the abstract photograph. They provide a solid presence that commands attention throughout all the pieces and also serves as the leading edge for the alignment of typographic elements on the invitations. "We chose a stencil font based on Akzidenz Grotesk as our typeface for the job. It seemed appropriate as a display font. It was bold and easily legible," says Dye. "Taking the title of the show as our most important message, we used it huge on the poster in uppercase because it had to stand out of our complicated image." All of the pieces incorporate the title treatment to unify the system.

Striking photography is combined with strong typography to create an exciting visual impression of the *Jerwood Applied Arts Prize: Glass* materials. The final pieces "successfully capture the overall feeling of the exhibition," concludes Dye. They are the result of visually exploring and interpreting the quality of glass—experimentation yields powerful results.

The catalog introduces an additional abstraction of the primary image used on the poster. The compelling visual effect attracts the viewer. As a result, supplementary information is not needed—the photograph serves the communicative function of the design.

A bold, typographic title treatment on the exhibition invitation creates impact. An emphasis on the word 'glass' identifies the exhibition theme. The contrast of white on black is effective. The opposing side features a dynamically cropped abstraction of the poster image that establishes the color palette of the design.

NO.PARKING

Riadruck Product Catalog

designer **elisa dall'angelo**

Riadruck is a fabrication and production company whose work ranges from die-cut lettering to digital printing to sign manufacturing. No.parking was approached by Riadruck to design a catalog that would reflect the diversity of the company's services. Designer Elisa Dall'Angelo explains further: "[The catalog] should inspire new clients who work in the design business (graphic designers, architects, interior designers) and support them to get their ideas to work." A difficult challenge, the next step was to determine how to "show all [of the services] in a catalog, get a logical order into it, show real printing examples, and give the whole lot a strong image," adds Dall'Angelo. Another consideration was flexibility, which was essential to allow the materials to be updated without a complete redesign. According to Dall'Angelo, "the only important thing for the client was that the catalog had to offer the possibility to add or take out folders."

The design process began with the creation of an interesting metaphor. "We wanted to show the multiplicity of the company's products using fruits and vegetables to give a positive feeling," describes Dall'Angelo. For example, the tomato represents big prints; a melon signifies digital prints. Other fruits and vegetables incorporated into the design include lettuce, peppers, and strawberries. "They gave a fresh and colorful look to the company and are neutral objects that could be used to show different printing techniques," comments Dall'Angelo.

The exterior of the catalog introduces the viewer to the clever comparison of fruits and vegetables to fabrication and production services. The lettuce is a simple, eye-catching image that establishes the symbolism for the product information on the interior. The cover also establishes the visual system echoed inside the catalog.

The catalog features a bright, fresh color palette based on the fruits and vegetables featured. A diverse range of colors exists. Their vivacity ties the package together with a friendly and positive attitude.

No.parking established a straightforward visual system "by using the images of fruits and vegetables and strong colors combined with big numbers," says Dall'Angelo. The visual impact of the photography directs the viewer into the structured compositions. Large fields of color (determined by the hue of the fruit or vegetable) counter the imagery, dividing each of the individual pages into halves. The range of shades is also evocative and vivid when the catalog is viewed as a whole. Textual content is logically ordered throughout the design to achieve clarity. Large sans serif numbers create a typographic focal point that is followed hierarchically by a heading and tertiary descriptive text.

No.parking uses an inventive metaphor to establish the thematic foundation of the Riadruck product catalog. The playful symbolism of fruits and vegetables successfully parallels the diversity of services offered by Riadruck. The design combines clear communication with an energetic and stylish presentation.

Interior pages reveal the product samples and their specifications. The layout is composed in an orderly fashion to emphasize the swatches, yet it allows for product comparisons across the spread. The viewer can see everything and easily access information.

No.parking designed a systematic structure to compose the loose pages of the catalog. Although the fruits, vegetables, and color change on each cover, the basic method of spatial organization remains the same. Dividing the page in the horizontal center, imagery falls to the bottom of the composition as the type rises to the top.

NOON

ODC/San Francisco Dancing Downtown
Marketing Campaign and Collateral

creative director **cinthia wen**
designer **ellen malinowski**
photographer **rj muna**

The collateral materials for ODC/San Francisco, designed by Noon, bring dance alive. The presentation is dramatic and captures the expressiveness of dance throughout the range of pieces, which include a booklet, invitation, and postcard. "The campaign solution needed to visually represent the choreography, program, and company as a whole," explains creative director Cinthia Wen. "In addition, it had to be produced within a tight time line, with strict production parameters and a limited production budget." Understanding the needs of ODC/San Francisco was imperative. Noon met with them to discuss the project, as well as the objectives of the dance season. Wen continues, "We attended ODC's season performances in 2002, as well as work-in-progress performances and discussions throughout the year, to further our understanding of the company. We also attended performances of other dance companies to pinpoint ODC's uniqueness. Through the process, we learned what should be emphasized—the essence of ODC's choreography, stands, and poses to create a static composite that captures the energy of the live performance and represents the company as a whole."

The "energy, fluidity, and grace" of the dancers and the performances inspired the design. Dramatic photography provides a opportunity to observe the spirit and physicality of dance. "Respecting the work of the photographer was one of our main concerns," says Wen. "RJ Muna is a fantastic artist. The final piece is as much of a tribute to his talent as it is to our design." The collateral materials feature dancers on every page with their striking poses frozen in time. The photography heightens the strength of the dancers and vividly demonstrates the manipulation of the body. It intensifies every move and communicates the essence of ODC/San Francisco.

Emphasizing the motion of dance, the collateral materials exhibit "visual impact followed by information hierarchy," notes Wen. The arrangement of the photography on black-and-white surfaces elevates it as the dominant visual element. It is complemented by clean and sophisticated typography. Using the typefaces Mrs Eaves and Trade Gothic, the typography is composed around the active photography. It fosters clear communication of the content, including dates, locations, and performances. Changes in case, as well as color, position, and scale, add dimension and hierarchy. The contrast of the evocative imagery and type provides a spacious environment throughout the materials.

The collateral materials for ODC/San Francisco are strong, visual expressions. The design captures dance while effectively communicating content. Reflecting on the final design, Wen concludes, "Dance is a unique form of art. One can discuss the form of dance intellectually as much as one can, and it still would not compare to the real thing. As helpful as finding brand attributes and characteristics can be, the standard strategic analysis does not apply when it comes to performance art. The design for the final piece is ultimately from the gut, in response to the performances and to what was captured in the photography. It is incredibly visceral."

The ODC/San Francisco materials include a brochure, invitation, and postcard. The visual system features striking photography that activates the page and captures the intensity and beauty of dance. Imagery dominates the design—it is a focal point that attracts the viewer into the design.

ODC/SAN FRANCISCO'S
OPENING NIGHT CELEBRATION
Evocative, Magnetic, Explosive
March 6 — 23
Three weeks only!
ODC/SAN FRANCISCO
IN ASSOCIATION WITH YERBA BUENA ARTS PRESENTS
DANCING DOWNTOWN 2003
Artistic Director Brenda Way
ODC/SAN FRANCISCO 2003 HOME SEASON
3 award-winning
women choreographers
3 soul-stirring programs
ODC/SAN FRANCISCO
DANCING DOWNTOWN 2003
Artistic Director Brenda Way
Three weeks only!
March 6 – 23, 2003
Yerba Buena Center for the Arts Theater
700 Howard at Third Street, San Francisco
3 award-winning
women choreographers
3 programs of
soul-stirring dance
CHARGE BY PHONE
ORDER ONLINE

PETRICK DESIGN

Domtar Answer Packs

art director, copywriter **robert petrick**
designer **tracy west**
photographer **tom maday**
illustrators **tim tomkinson, friend and johnson**

Domtar approached Petrick Design to develop a paper promotion that would position them as an educator and become a reference tool for designers and printers. The results are the Domtar Answer Packs, a series of cards (collated and bound by subject) that explain and illustrate different printing techniques while promoting the range of Domtar papers. Some of the questions addressed in the Answer Packs—including the titles *On Color*, *On Dots*, and *On Texture*—are: What's the difference between varnish and coating? How do you get stunning effects using color ink on color paper? What happens when you emboss an embossed sheet? The approach began "with research, word mapping, and brainstorming," comments art director Robert Petrick. "We make sure we clearly understand the audience, the product we are selling, and the competitive landscape."

The Domtar Answer Packs were inspired by "old-fashioned flash cards that are used to teach children how to spell," describes Petrick. Taking the inspiration a step further, Petrick discusses the project's conceptual development: "[The Domtar Answer Packs are] a series of packs issued periodically and assembled over time to create a reference library of design, printing, and paper techniques. Each pack is limited to a precise and focused topic so that each one is covered in depth. The cards remain loose [unbound] so that comparisons between cards are easy and effective. The backsides of the cards have a narrative presented in storybook form, which is fun and fantasy-like and provides subject matter for the visuals on the front or demonstration side. The hero of each narrative is named in alphabetical order and alternating genders, the same way hurricanes are named. The models for each photo are actual Domtar employees."

With the idea thoroughly conceived, the size of the Answer Packs was determined based on the other products in the Domtar line. "The cards ended up being the same size as the Domtar swatch books so they could be kept, in theory, on the same shelf," says Petrick. Hierarchically, "because the image is the information in this context, it made sense to make the image dominate each card. The card number is also important, because we reference it constantly when discussing card comparisons," explains Petrick. "We ended up imposing further structure onto the content by separating it into sections, or chapters." The typography is logically ordered and consistently set in a flush-left alignment, while the imagery is evocative and informative.

The Domtar Answer Packs express a strong, harmonious union of writing and design. The design is educational and resourceful, while also aesthetically strong and classically composed. "The design, on a broad level, positions Domtar as a valuable resource for technical information and inspiration," says Petrick. "On a more practical level, it enables the Domtar sales force to present examples of how to use the wide variety of colors and textures available in the Domtar grade offering."

A visual system unifies a series of cards that features different paper grades and production techniques. Consistent margins, type settings, and position of the visual elements extend throughout the series and tie everything together. The design is approachable and accessible because of its simple elegance. The visual activity of the imagery is balanced by the simple and clear typographic presentation.

before assessing the damage.
He notices that large chunks
of the pile fell in unison, maintaining their numerical sequence.
With care, he might be able to
reassemble the entire pile in
relatively short order. But as
he reaches to retrieve the paper,
a shockwave races through his
rattled frame. He bends down
for a corroborative look and
determines that his expert fin-
are indeed telling his
07
B
A
C
17
on color
on dots

Process Letterhead System

RICK RAWLINS/WORK AND VISUAL DIALOGUE

designers rick rawlins, fritz klaetke, ian varrassi

Clements Horsky Creative Directions, a print production management firm, presented the design firms Rick Rawlins/Work and Visual Dialogue with a two-fold design problem. First, the name was confusing and required reconsideration; it was not clear what type of services Clements Horsky Creative Directions offered. Second, "their communications materials had an amateurish and haphazard look, which was inappropriate for a company that handles print production issues for designers," explains designer Fritz Klaetke. Rick Rawlins/Work and Visual Dialogue collaborated on the project, which began with the development of a new name for Clements Horsky. "Playing on the four-color process inks common in printing, as well as the process of design and print production, we gave the company a new name—Process," adds Klaetke. Once established, Rick Rawlins/Work and Visual Dialogue worked independently to explore visual solutions before coming together for the final concept. The inspiration for the Process letterhead system was "the production process itself—terminology, grids, specifications, colors, and so on," says Klaetke. The inspirational motifs would become the actual visual elements of the design—the grid and specifications are apparent in the end result.

Structurally, the system is innovative. "The entire stationery system—letterhead, window envelope, and business card—is constructed from a single sheet of 8½" × 14" (21.6 × 35.6 cm) paper. The complexity of these shared functions, as well as the array of production techniques used to accomplish them, becomes a Process case study that requires careful attention to detail—details that are revealed in the fabrication specifications imprinted on the reverse."

The inventive design of the Process letterhead is methodical. The color palette—cyan, magenta, yellow, and black—is used interchangeably throughout the system. The bold, simple company logotype, Process, is the dominant element of the design. Set in Helvetica Neue, it commands the top of the letterhead, as well as the back of the business card, which is perforated out of the 8½" × 14" (21.6 × 35.6 cm) sheet. The contact information, also set in Helvetica Neue, is treated in an uppercase, flush-left presentation. Color distinguishes information within the setting. Yellow text appears on the back of the letterhead and notes the specifications that describe the production of the design. For example, "10% screen of cyan for address field," and "process solid for security envelope." Klaetke elaborates, "This design was very systematic and rational because the process is very direct, factual, detail oriented, and precise."

Detailed views of the letterhead system feature the front and back of the business card. Uppercase settings in different weights of Helvetica Neue are consistently applied. The color palette is based on the primary printing colors: cyan, magenta, yellow, and black. It is used flexibly as color fields, while also calling attention to dominant textual content.

The Process letterhead system is clever and engaging. Rick Rawlins/Work and Visual Dialogue dramatically transformed Clements Horsky Creative Directions into Process. The system reflects their services in an appropriate and inventive format. "Bottom line: Sales increased 20 percent after the redesign/rebranding effort," concludes Klaetke.

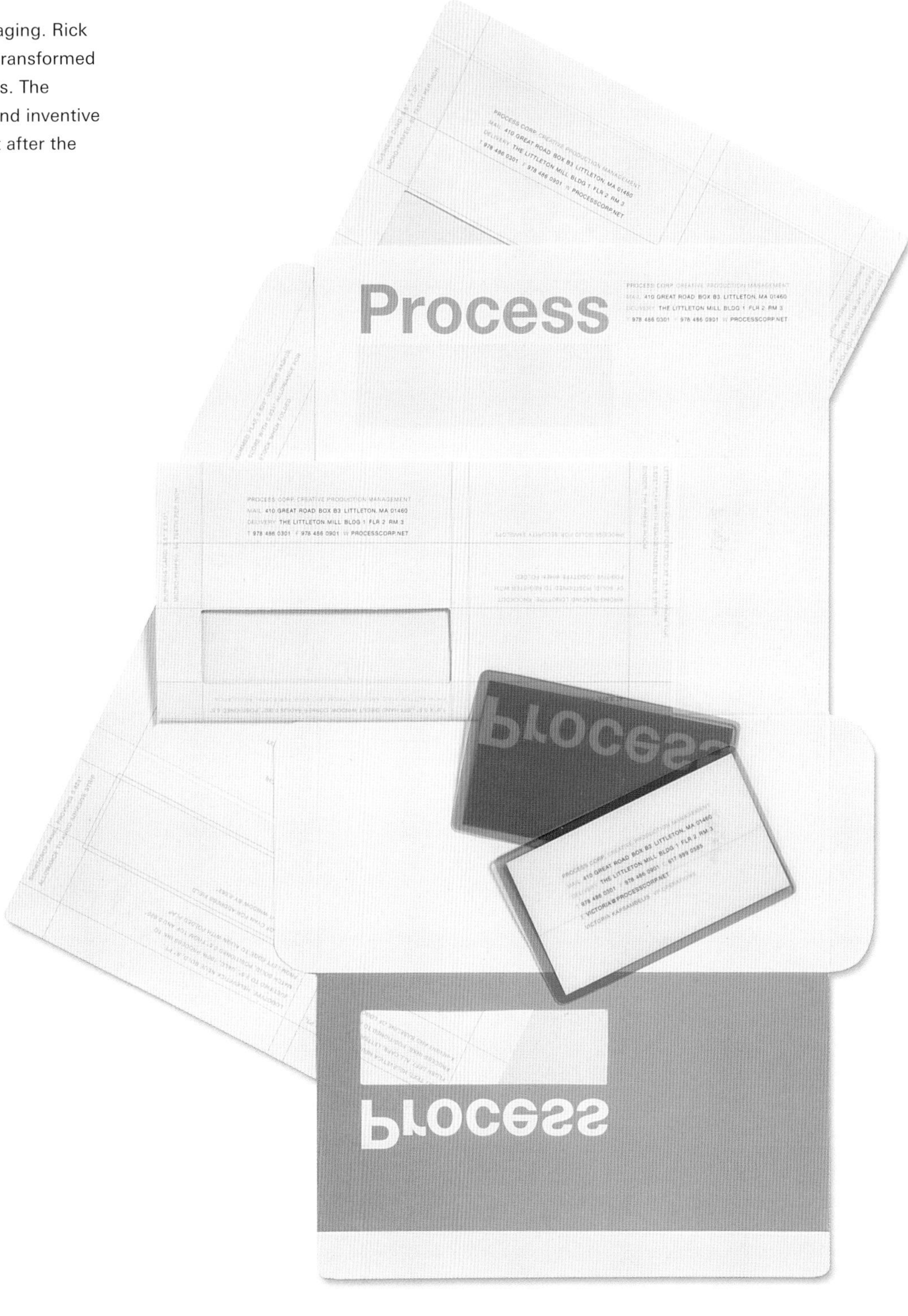

All of the pieces of the Process letterhead system are built out of an 8½" × 14" (21.6 × 35.6 cm) sheet. The design appropriately reflects a company dedicated to print and production issues. The business card, which is perforated out of the letterhead, folds onto itself to form the envelope. Typographic elements are thoughtfully composed within an evident grid structure that provides vertical and horizontal alignment points for the logo and contact information, as well as production specifications on the back of the letterhead.

Absolux Invitation

RMAC

***designers* ricardo mealha, ana cunha**

RMAC was invited by Lisbon's premier nightclub, LuxFrágil, to design a party invitation celebrating the launch of Absolut Vanilia in Portugal. "The challenge was to create a piece that mirrored the graphics and style of the Absolut Vanilia bottle without compromising the originality of the project," explains designer Ricardo Mealha. "We wanted to be original and not copy any previous ideas. So, we researched materials that would convey the message in an innovative way [and] reinterpreted the elements (bottle, textures, colors, flavor) of this particular type of vodka." The unique materials, which include acetate, fine papers, and vinyl, are tactile. The invitation engages the senses and aims to capture the essence of Absolut Vanilia.

Inspired by the Absolut Vanilia packaging, the conceptual direction of Absolux is related to the theme "transparency and ice." The aesthetic objective is "a graphic style that relates to the mood and spirit of the country of Sweden," states Mealha. Reflecting the themes, the distinctive feature of the invitation is the integration of materials. "We used different materials that conveyed the key elements of this particular vodka, [while] all related to the colors of the bottle," adds Mealha. Rich materials are introduced with the envelope, which is a cool, white tone with an unusual "velvety texture." A silver-foil LuxFrágil logo and address block rest on the left edge of the envelope. The metallic color reflects the design of the Absolut bottle, which is capped with a silver top.

The final piece of the invitation borrows the visual style of an Absolut bottle. The acetate sheet is screenprinted in white ink. The typography remains clear. Like the clear glass of a bottle, the viewer is able to see through the invitation.

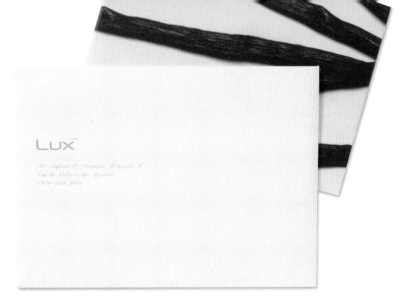

The envelope of the invitation connotes sophistication. Its smooth texture is imprinted with elegant, silver-foil typography. The contemporary sans serif LuxFrágil logo contrasts with the script typeface. The geometry of the logo's letterforms counters the fluidity of the linked script. The logo and address block rest quietly along the left edge, optically centered. The first impression of the invitation is a close-up view of vanilla pods. The image is abstract—its rough texture and angular composition counter the quiet tone of the envelope.

On the interior of the envelope, three pieces are folded inside of each other. The first piece is a large white sheet with an oversized photograph of vanilla pods that opens to reveal mirror paper printed with vanilla orchids. The reflective surface is glamorous and seductive, whereas the scale of the imagery provides a unique viewpoint. The photography of the vanilla pods and orchids is natural and refreshing, suggesting the purity of the vodka. Inside the mirror sheet lies a "giant, transparent vinyl sticker that is silkscreen printed in white with the name of the participants of the project, an illustration of the vanilla flower, and the Absolut Vanilia logotype," explains Mealha. The sticker unfolds and contains a third piece of the invitation—a single acetate card also printed in white. The typography imitates the graphic style of the Absolut Vanilia bottle by modifying the sans serif logotype and script body text.

The experience of opening the Absolux invitation is ethereal. It takes an existing object—the Absolut Vanilia bottle—and adopts its graphic style. The invitation is translated into a fresh design suited to its function. The interesting use of materials, as well as the process of unfolding the piece, is interactive and mysterious, while the tactile nature of the invitation dramatically affects its presentation.

The use of material is a dominant element of the design. A sheet of mirror paper is juxtaposed with a vinyl sticker; the tactility of each piece is unique. The invitation relies on illustration and photography. Rather than using words, the imagery effectively connotes nature and purity through its visual impression. A large image of vanilla orchids fills the mirrored sheet, whereas an illustration of the flower fills the background of the vinyl sticker.

SAMATAMASON

Seyle: Words Promotional Book

art director **greg samata**
designer **goretti kao**
copywriter **bill seyle**

Seyle: Words is a beautiful typographic design. The title is composed in the top-right corner. Its position near the edge of the page directs the viewer into interior spreads. The placement of text sets the consistent location of the headings in the book.

Seyle: Words is a promotional book for writer Bill Seyle that relies on the words and their typographic presentation to intrigue and gain clients. The design request given to SamataMason: "to create a book that presents a writer's work in the same way a photographer would present a portfolio of photographs," comments designer Goretti Kao. "We knew the writer well and wanted to design the book so that it represented his personality and style." The refined, letterpress book captures the spirit of the writing, which is given full attention. The typography commands interest and fosters a high level of readability within a spacious, compositional environment. Kao states, "We knew from the start that the book should be simple and elegant without being too flashy or corporate looking."

Inspired by the writings of Bill Seyle, SamataMason "wanted to create a piece that was typographically driven, like a book of poetry. The concept was to let the writer's work speak for itself, without explanation," describes Kao. "Each piece of writing became unique in its own way and depended on the typography for personality. Because each piece needed to work independently, as well as part of a whole, we designed the book using one typeface [Bembo] in various sizes and styles. We wanted the reader to react just by looking at the type design." Italic, small caps, and roman fonts, as well as slight changes in type size, are used to achieve typographic color, contrast, and variety.

TO EXPLAIN_

Fellow Shareholders,

Our business is simple.

Grass grows.
Bugs hatch.
Dust settles.
Pipes clog.
Carpets get dirty.
Furniture gets damaged.

It all just happens.

And today it's happening to more and more homeowners who just can't keep up with it the way they used to.

So they turn to us.

p_03

Dividing the page into numerous spatial intervals accommodates typography that cascades across the page in staggered flush-left alignments. The movement is quick and brings activity to the page. Breaking the text into short, thoughtful pieces enhances readability.

Seyle: Words is flexibly composed, demonstrating changes in flush-left, flush-right, and centered alignments throughout the design. Bodies of text change position on each spread; some fall onto the left page, whereas others rest on the right. Writings are balanced by pale green rectangles that contain titles of each piece and move along the top edges toward the gutter. None of the writings have dominance—the pacing through the design is fluid. "Each piece was treated equally, so that one could easily pick up the book and read any selection," says Kao. "However, from a writing standpoint, the pieces of work were selected and placed in a specific sequence to create a logical flow from start to finish."

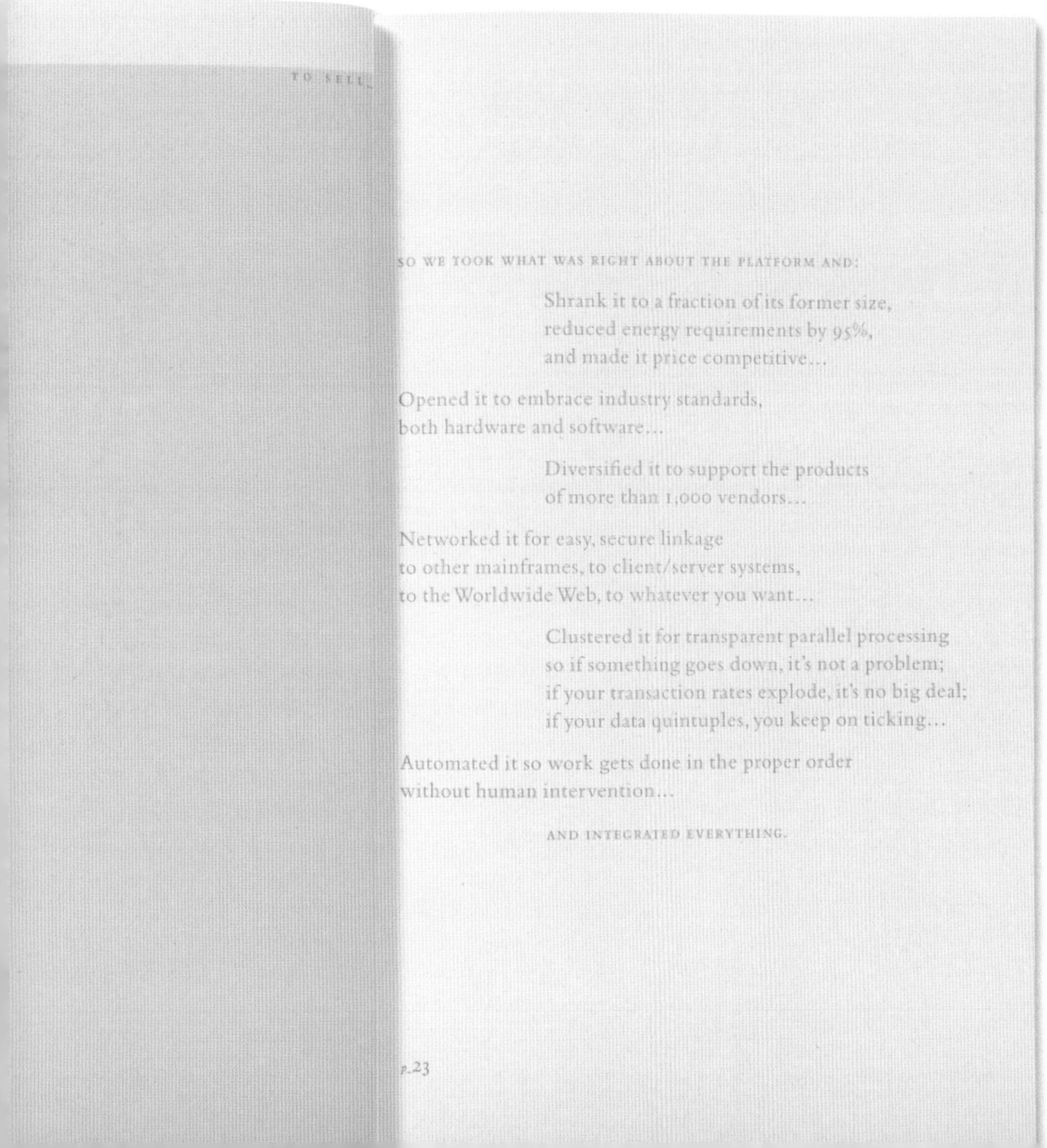

TO SELL

SO WE TOOK WHAT WAS RIGHT ABOUT THE PLATFORM AND:

Shrank it to a fraction of its former size,
reduced energy requirements by 95%,
and made it price competitive...

Opened it to embrace industry standards,
both hardware and software...

Diversified it to support the products
of more than 1,000 vendors...

Networked it for easy, secure linkage
to other mainframes, to client/server systems,
to the Worldwide Web, to whatever you want...

Clustered it for transparent parallel processing
so if something goes down, it's not a problem;
if your transaction rates explode, it's no big deal;
if your data quintuples, you keep on ticking...

Automated it so work gets done in the proper order
without human intervention...

AND INTEGRATED EVERYTHING.

p.23

Two alignment points create the structure needed to integrate flush-left paragraphs. The in-and-out motion separates the text into approachable pieces that are easily readable. The type size and leading is generous, which also increases readability. Small caps are used on the first and last lines for distinction.

The sophisticated design of *Seyle: Words* illuminates the writing, which is the primary function of the piece. The content of the book drives the design; its presentation makes the initial connection to the viewer. "The subtle use of color and simple typography that we chose made the book appear calming to the senses. We wanted to make sure that we allowed enough attention to detail so the book appeared valuable and worth keeping," concludes Kao. "So far, the response has been successful in gaining new clients for the writer. The investment has already paid for itself."

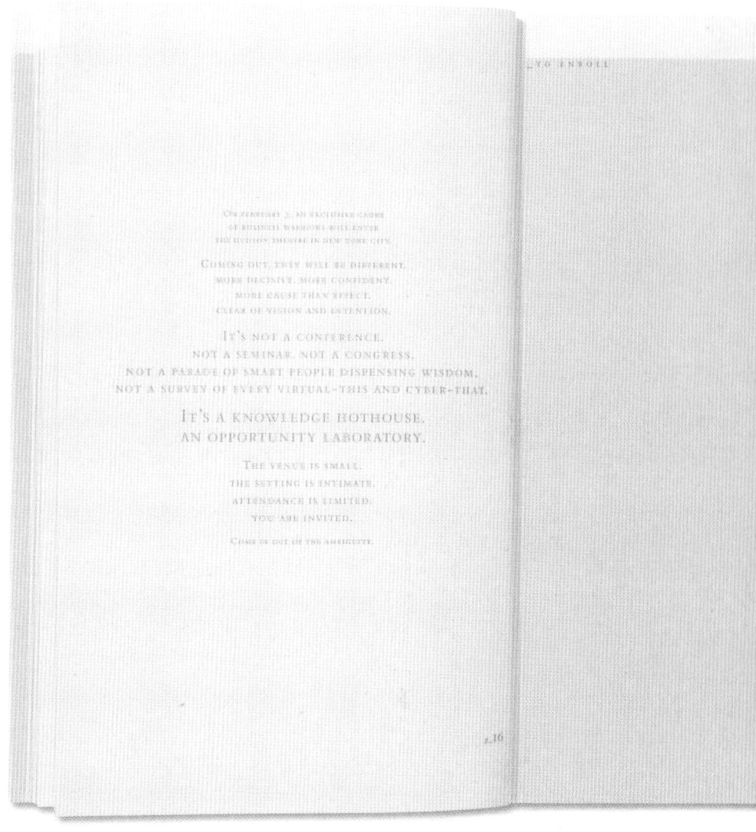

Typographic subtleties include the use of Bembo Italic, as well as small caps, which are used in limited quantities to create emphasis. Italic and small caps are distinct and provide a nice contrast to the roman font.

Caps set in a centered alignment show progressive changes in type size, which create distinction between the lines of text and add typographic color to the page. The caps are proficiently spaced, which is critical to this setting.

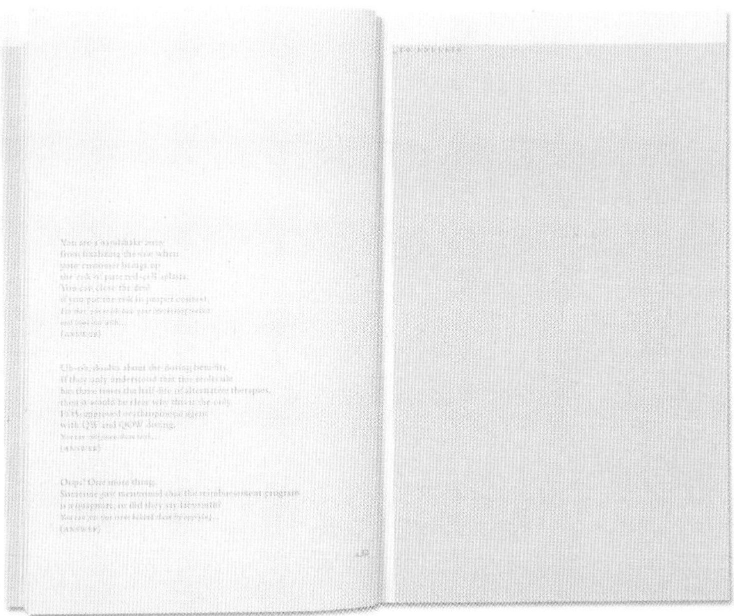

SHINNOSKE DESIGN

Yoshio Hayakawa: His Design, Times and Osaka

art director, designer **shinnoske sugisaki**
creative director **tomio sugaya**

A design project that honors another designer is a difficult challenge. Should the design mirror the style of the subject or adopt a neutral personality? Although imitation is the highest form of flattery, it is not a wholly inventive approach to design, which may be meaningless if it is a reproduction of existing aesthetics or trends. For all projects, visual solutions that accurately reflect content and function will best serve clients and viewers.

Shinnoske Design created *Yoshio Hayakawa: His Design, Times and Osaka* to honor Hayakawa, a pioneer of Japanese graphic design. Art director/designer Shinnoske Sugisaki faithfully presents Hayakawa's work as "timeless design," he says. "I wanted to make this book have [the same] feelings as the original work." Its presentation is formal, allowing the work of Hayakawa to rise to the foreground without the distraction of competing visual elements. It is an informative solution that presents the content objectively, without bias. "Accurate information design makes true impressions to people," states Sugisaki.

Working directly with the client, the Osaka City Museum of Modern Art, Sugisaki explains his methodology: "When I got this project, I first discussed [production] with the curator—the number of pages, size, binding, paper, and cover—because I thought that its concept could be found from [the] format of the book. The curator and I made a decision that the book should be created not to be a record of old work but to be an excellent, fresh book, especially for young designers and students." The project developed when Sugisaki examined the work of Hayakawa to gain an understanding of its scope. "I looked through all the work of Hayakawa," describes Sugisaka. "All his designs were made on paper, not electronic material, of course. I found, by touch, that a kind of aura comes from such old materials. So, I took some elements for [the] design motif of the book, [including] some graphic elements for printing systems, such as trim and crop marks, which had been seen on finished work before [the] age of desktop publishing." The research phase enhanced the concept and informed the final design. Though the presentation of Hayakawa's work is traditional, the crop and trim marks are subtly used to add modernity, bringing the design into the present.

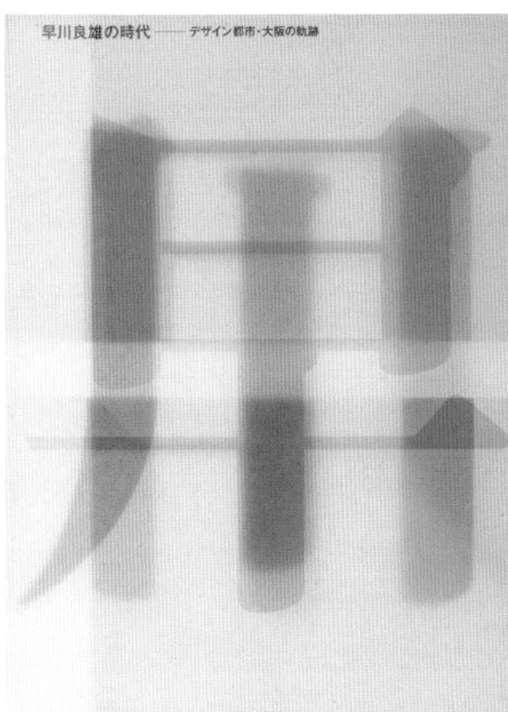

One of the remarkable features of Yoshio Hayakawa's work is the use of color. The cover reflects this characteristic by combining transparent layers of hues that mix to enhance the impression. Applied on a field of white, the effect is soft and poetic.

Yoshio Hayakawa: His Design, Times and Osaka is formatted to allow the work of Hayakawa to be respectfully featured. Each piece is composed in the center of the page to exalt its presentation. The alternating scheme of colored backgrounds adds variety without interference. The viewer enters into the design with ease. Shinnoske Design captures the essence of Yoshio Hayakawa in a straightforward, thoughtful design.

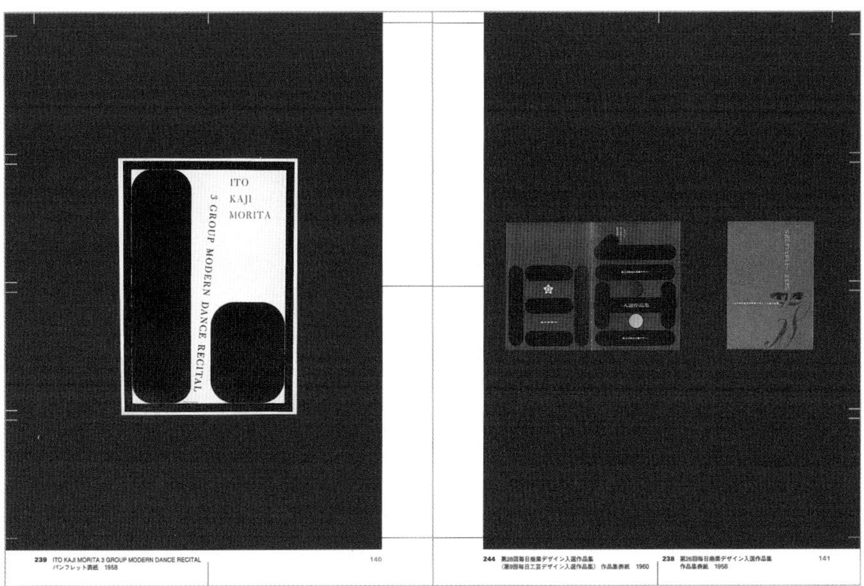

The work of Hayakawa dominates the interior spreads, which feature a flexible structure. The layout of each spread varies and is based on the size of Hayakawa's work and how each piece complements the shape of the page. Type supports the imagery, residing on the bottom of spreads as minimal, descriptive text.

Backgrounds of color provide the surface areas that contain Hayakawa's work. Connoting his distinctive use of color, the hue variations add interest and enliven the presentation. Thin lines in the form of intentionally applied crop and trim marks connect the spreads horizontally and add aesthetic details along the edges of the pages, giving it a more contemporary feel.

STUDIO NAJBRT

Daily Companion Exhibition Newspaper

***designer* ales najbrt**

Daily Companion, designed by Studio Najbrt, is a newspaper that accompanies an exhibition at the Municipal House in Prague. The newspaper and exhibition feature contemporary Czech design (industrial, graphic, furniture, glass, pottery, china, and textile). The goal of *Daily Companion* is to "introduce good-quality design available for everyone, not just for wealthier clients," explains designer Ales Najbrt. The design demands a utilitarian approach to reach the intended audience. Newspapers connote the everyday; they are affordable and readily available. Newspapers also provide quick, accessible information. *Daily Companion* provides an overview of Czech design in a format that is straightforward. The newspaper "was a new and exciting experience for us," states Najbrt.

The inspiration for *Daily Companion* is "the lifestyle of young people who live simply and cheaply," says Najbrt. "Quality does not have to be expensive." To reach the target audience, the aesthetic is bold and contemporary. "Black-and-white photography [is used], which is contradictory to a presentation of top design as we know it," adds Najbrt. Photography, typography, and a black, red, and blue color palette interact. Visual elements are distributed evenly across and down the strict columnar pages.

Prostor – architektura, interiér, design, o.p.s. Obecní dům Praha Municipal House in Prague
pořádají pod záštitou hlavního města Prahy výstavu hold an exhibition under the auspices of the Capital City od Prague
contemporary czech design
www.prostor.net
www.obecni-dum.cz
Lucite International,
Česká komora architektů

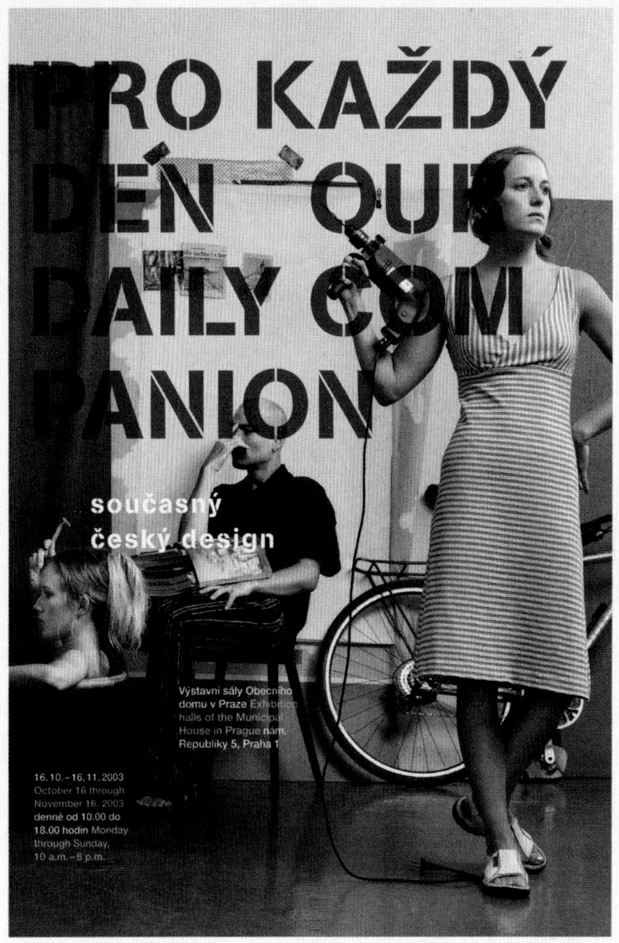
PRO KAŽDÝ DEN OUR DAILY COMPANION
současný český design
Výstavni sály Obecního domu v Praze Exhibition halls of the Municipal House in Prague nám. Republiky 5, Praha 1
16.10.–16.11.2003 October 16 through November 16, 2003 denně od 10.00 do 18.00 hodin Monday through Sunday, 10 a.m.–6 p.m.

The front page of *Daily Companion* integrates unusual photography and simple typography. The title sits boldly on top of the image. Subordinate typographic information, set in Helvetica Neue CE, provides information about the exhibition. This text enables flow around the layout and highlights the playful characteristics of the photograph.

grafický design
graphic design
nábytkový design
furniture design

The typography of *Daily Companion* is characterized by large, red letterforms that rise to the foreground of the composition. They are dynamic indexes that lead the viewer into specific sections of the newspaper. Though the letterforms dominate and cover the photographs and text, they are decisively transparent. The design is readable without sacrificing visual impact. Color is applied to the body text to separate content into usable segments. Black text marks the Czech language, whereas blue specifies English. The bilingual presentation increases the functionality of the design.

The practicality of *Daily Companion* shifts the perception of design and makes it accessible to the public. By using a format that is approachable and recognizable, the design challenges the stereotypical image that design is reserved for the elite. As the title of the newspaper references, design is for everyone on a daily basis.

Oversized letterforms, set in AG Book Stencil, are applied in the design as visual markers. 'G' notes the location of graphic design, whereas 'T' leads the eye to textile design. It is a hierarchically forward method that provides emphasis and counters the even rhythm of the long columns of text.

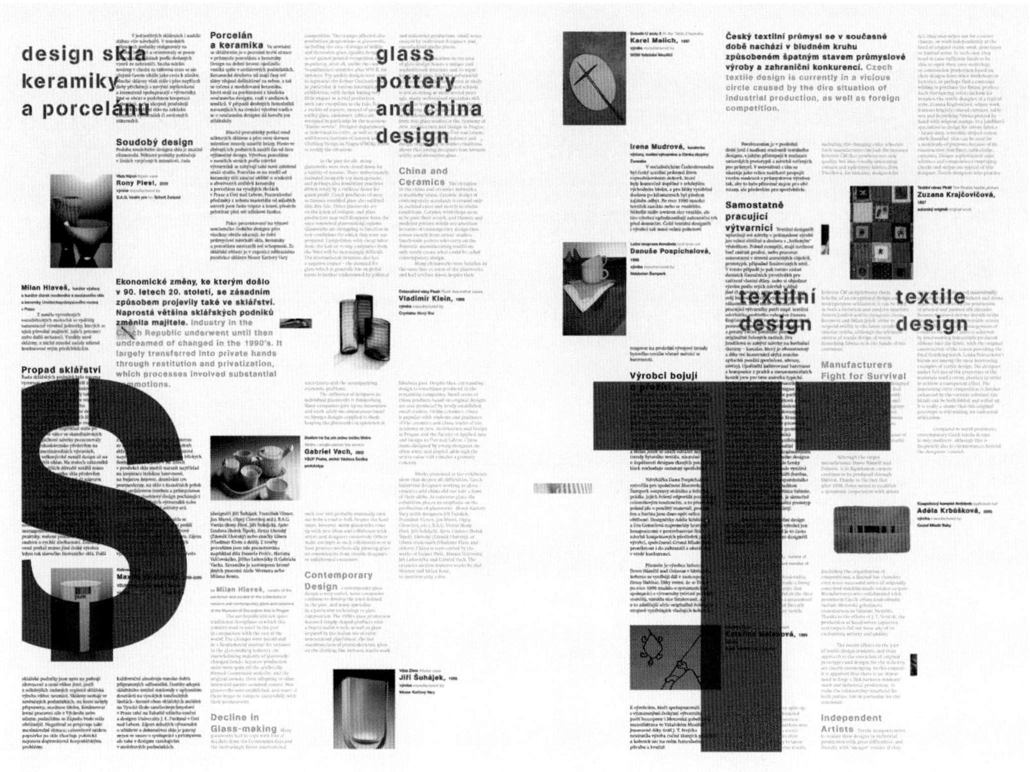
design skla keramiky a porcelánu
glass pottery and china design
textilní design
textile design

PRO KAŽDÝ DEN OUR DAILY COM PANION

Vývojové trendy průmyslového designu v Evropě nebyly ve druhé polovině 20. století nikdy určovány československými designéry a výjimku netvořila ani léta devadesátá. Naopak se radikální změna politického systému a následných ekonomických poměrů odrazila negativně především v činnosti designérů působících ve strojírenství.

Czechoslovak designers never set development trends in industrial design in the second half of the 20th century in Europe; the 1990's were no exception to this rule. On the contrary, the radical change of political system and the ensuing economic changes had a negative impact in particular on the activities of designers working in the engineering industry.

průmyslový design

industrial design

The design employs a multiple-column grid that accommodates large amounts of content. Like a typical newspaper, the text is set in long, narrow columns that support short line lengths. The setting promotes readability and movement from one section of the design to the next.

700

SUPERBÜRO

designer **barbara ehrbar**

The booklet, *700*, documents the conception, development, and completion of the Pavilion Art Place in Magglingen, Switzerland. The pavilion, which was designed by :mlzd architects for an annual exposition, was constructed of 700 plastic storage boxes. Superbüro was approached by :mlzd architects to design a piece to celebrate the innovative structure. "The booklet is basically a souvenir of the pavilion and functions like a set of postcards that wake the memories," explains designer Barbara Ehrbar.

The primary goal of *700* was to create "a small, compact, easily sellable and producible publication." Unfortunately, the design needed to be completed within one week—and with a limited budget—which truncated the design process considerably. "There was not much time for big concepts," adds Ehrbar. Although there was no sketching involved, there was "a lot of research and talking to architects and trying to understand the concept of the building," notes Ehrbar. The information-gathering process, which included collecting and organizing large amounts of imagery and text, accounted for much of the design process.

The cover of *700*, composed of 700 rectangles (the same number of plastic storage boxes were used to build the Pavilion Art Place), is light and airy. The presentation is combined with one typographic element, '700,' in the bottom-right corner. The cover is sparse; its lack of content visually compelling.

700
artplace

VERGÄNGLICHE HÜLLE FÜR EIN BEFRISTETES DASEIN Es ist nicht übertrieben zu behaupten, dass die Eidgenössische Turn- und Sportschule in Magglingen zu den besten architektonischen Zeugen zählt, die die Erinnerung an die Landesausstellung von 1939 in Zürich wachrufen. Zwar hatte die berühmte Landi ihre Tore schon geschlossen, als 1941 die ersten Vorprojekte für die Sportanlage in Angriff genommen wurden und einige Jahre werden noch verstreichen bis zum endgültigen Entwurf und dessen Ausführung im Jahre 1947. Doch alles, sowohl was die architektonische wie auch die landschaftliche Gestaltung der Bauten betrifft, bekundet dieses sensible Gleichgewicht zwischen Heimatgebundenheit und Moderne, das die Zürcher Landesausstellung erfolgreich hatte unter Beweis stellen wollen.

003

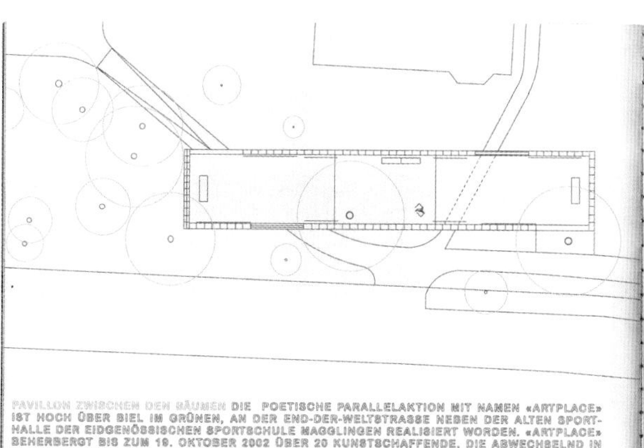

PAVILLON ZWISCHEN DEN BÄUMEN DIE POETISCHE PARALLELAKTION MIT NAMEN «ARTPLACE» IST HOCH ÜBER BIEL IM GRÜNEN, AN DER END-DER-WELTSTRASSE NEBEN DER ALTEN SPORTHALLE DER EIDGENÖSSISCHEN SPORTSCHULE MAGGLINGEN REALISIERT WORDEN. «ARTPLACE» BEHERBERGT BIS ZUM 19. OKTOBER 2002 ÜBER 20 KUNSTSCHAFFENDE, DIE ABWECHSELND IN ZWEIERBESETZUNG ZUM THEMA «BEWEGUNG UND SPORT» ARBEITEN. DER ELEGANTE PAVILLON KAM AUF EINER WIESE MIT BÄUMEN ZU STEHEN. SEIN OFFENER INNENHOF INTEGRIERT EINE BUCHE SOWIE EINE BRONZEPLASTIK.

Ein allgegenwärtiges Thema der Expo.02 ist die schwebende Plattform, die aus der Höhe ihrer Pfähle die unwahrscheinlichsten Baugründe höhnisch herausfordert. Es wäre nicht genug, in dieser Art die Bauten vom Boden loszulösen, allein die Umsetzung eines der Grundprinzipien moderner Architektur zu sehen: Je mehr man sich von lokalen Bedingungen des Geländes loslöst, umsomehr lässt sich ein Ideal der rationalen Vollkommenheit erreichen. Was bei Expo.02 auf dem Spiel steht, ist etwas Anderes: es geht um die maximale Einschränkung der Bodenbeanspruchung bei vergänglichen Ausstellungsbauten; es geht darum, die Orte vorübergehend fast unbemerkt auszunützen, ohne Spuren zu hinterlassen. Gleichzeitig und paradoxerweise geht die Minimierung der Stützpunkte auf dem Boden mit der Suche nach einem engen Kontakt mit den Naturelementen einher: lustvoll streicheln die Plattformen das Wasser; spielerisch ragen die Strukturen in den Himmel und bezähmen die Wolken; liebevoll werden die Bäume in die Architektur eingeschlossen samt den Licht- und Schattenspielen ihrer Blätter. Unter diesem Gesichtspunkt und trotz einer teilweisen Bejahung gewisser Themen der Moderne hatten damals die Architektur der Landi und diejenige, die später von ihr beeinflusst wurde, die Werte der Verwurzelung und einer im wörtlichen Sinne verstandenen Bodenständigkeit nie ganz aufgegeben.

The interior flows horizontally, with each spread spilling over to the next. Type spans the length of the page and reflects the shape of the pavilion. Spatially composed along the edges of the page, the type objectively informs and relies on the photography to tell the full story.

Inspired by the building and its architects, Superbüro designed the format of *700* based on the proportions of the pavilion. Relying heavily on photography to explain the narrative, typographic content is limited. Its use, like the size of the booklet, is connected to the rectangular shape of the building. "The outline type emphasizes the light, open structure of the building," discusses Ehrbar. "The text stretched over the whole page is a synonym for the long shape of the pavilion." The type works with the active and communicative photography and graphic shapes. It is generally isolated near the bottom or top of the pages as a secondary or tertiary element.

Color, graphic shape, photography, and type unite to record a unique, architectural experience. *700* adheres to architect Louis Sullivan's dictum, "Form follows function." The design decisions honor the content from the format to the layout. "Functionality in design is important," expands Ehrbar. "But function alone is mostly boring. In my view, the right combination of functionality and 'sex appeal' is what makes good design."

FLIESSENDER RAUM
GROSSE FLÜGELTÜREN
SOWIE SCHIEBEWÄNDE
ERMÖGLICHEN EINE
MOBILE RAUMAUFTEI-
LUNG DES "ARTPLACE".
DIE TRANSLUZENTEN
KUNSTSTOFFBEHÄLTER
KOMMUNIZIEREN EIN
FARBLICHES WECHSEL-
SPIEL DER ÄUSSEREN
LICHTVERHÄLTNISSE INS
INNERE, WAS NEBEN DEM
JEWEILIGEN SONNEN-
STAND VOM SCHATTEN
DER BEWÖLKUNG ODER
DEM GRÜN VON IM WIND
SCHAUKELNDEN ÄSTEN
BEEINFLUSST WIRD.

Die flexible Ausstattung des Pavillons gestattet es, sowohl den Bedürfnissen einzelner Kunstschaffenden nachzukommen, die hier im Turnus einige Tage schöpferischer Zurückgezogenheit geniessen dürfen, wie auch den Anforderungen punktueller festlicher Anlässe zu entsprechen. Diese Alternanz von verschiedenen Nutzungen im gleichen Raum ist besonders klug. Sie verdeutlicht nämlich die für die Reifung und den Austausch von kulturellen Werten notwendige Wechselwirkung von Rückzugs- und Begegnungsmöglichkeiten, von Zeiten der Ruhe und reger Geselligkeit, von Orten der Besinnung in unmittelbarer Nähe der Naturelemente und Orten der feierlichen Anerkennung jener schöpferischen Leistungen, die eine dynamische Gesellschaft in sich zu wecken vermag. Artplace macht all dies möglich, und zwar mit bescheidenen Mitteln. Dieser Kunstgriff freut insbesondere diejenigen, die hinter die Kulissen schauen. Wer auch immer hierher kommt, stellt fest, dass er hier nur vorübergehend zu Gast ist, dass andere zeitweilige Präsenzen ihm vorausgegangen sind und ihm mit anderen Vorhaben folgen werden. Der Raum ist für die unerwartetsten Nutzungen frei, unter der einzigen Bedingung, dass das, was entlehnt wurde, auch wieder zurückgegeben wird. Die Mehrzweckkiste aus Kunststoff, die den modularen Grundstein des Pavillons ausmacht, ist ein Symbol für sich: aufgestapelt und mit Spannbändern befestigt definiert sie einen Ort des Verweilens; für den normalen Gebrauch wieder freigegeben wird die Kiste zu einem Transportmittel, das von Hand zu Hand weitergereicht wird.

020/021

Interior spreads narrate the materialization of the pavilion from beginning to end. Color photographs are given priority. Handled in numerous ways, imagery fills the pages. Images are contained in circles and rectangles and silhouetted in space. Layered with graphic shapes, like lines and arrows, the photography is alive.

VISOCKY O'GRADY

S.A.W., Incorporated Annual Report

designers **jenn visocky o'grady, ken visocky o'grady, paul perchinske**

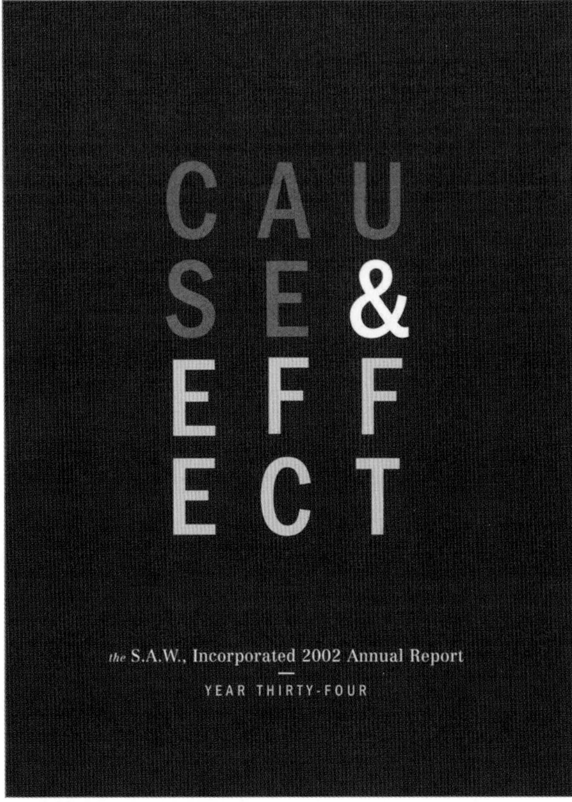

CAU
SE&
EFF
ECT
the S.A.W., Incorporated 2002 Annual Report
YEAR THIRTY-FOUR

The typographic settings on the cover of the annual report unite the words 'cause' and 'effect.' The proportion mirrors the shape of the page. The cover's hues are dominantly cool, yet 'effect,' in a strong, warm color, rises to the foreground.

The annual reports for S.A.W., Incorporated, are important marketing pieces for Solutions at Work—a company that creates opportunities for individuals with mental and developmental disabilities. Visocky O'Grady had worked previously with S.A.W. and was familiar with the organization and their need to "project a viable image and the year's accomplishments to different audiences: businesses and the MRDD (mental retardation and developmentally disabled) community," explains designer Jenn Visocky O'Grady. The challenge was to create a design that appropriately balanced the corporate requirements of S.A.W. with the unique and uplifting employee stories.

Visocky O'Grady and S.A.W. worked in collaboration with the beginning of their process marked by inspiration. "The people at S.A.W. are our biggest inspiration—whether individuals with mental or developmental disabilities who strive to make positive changes in their lives, or the folks who create opportunities for those individuals to thrive in a business setting," says O'Grady. With each designer contributing to development, the conceptual direction of the annual report is two-fold: thematic and visual. "Thematically, the concept was "Cause & Effect"—a play on words that illustrated both the human services and corporate focuses of S.A.W.'s mission," elaborates O'Grady. "Visually, we wanted to produce an annual that was more booklike, something small that created a more intimate and memorable viewing experience." She continues, "Once you have the concept established, you can juggle any number of aesthetic options to deliver the message."

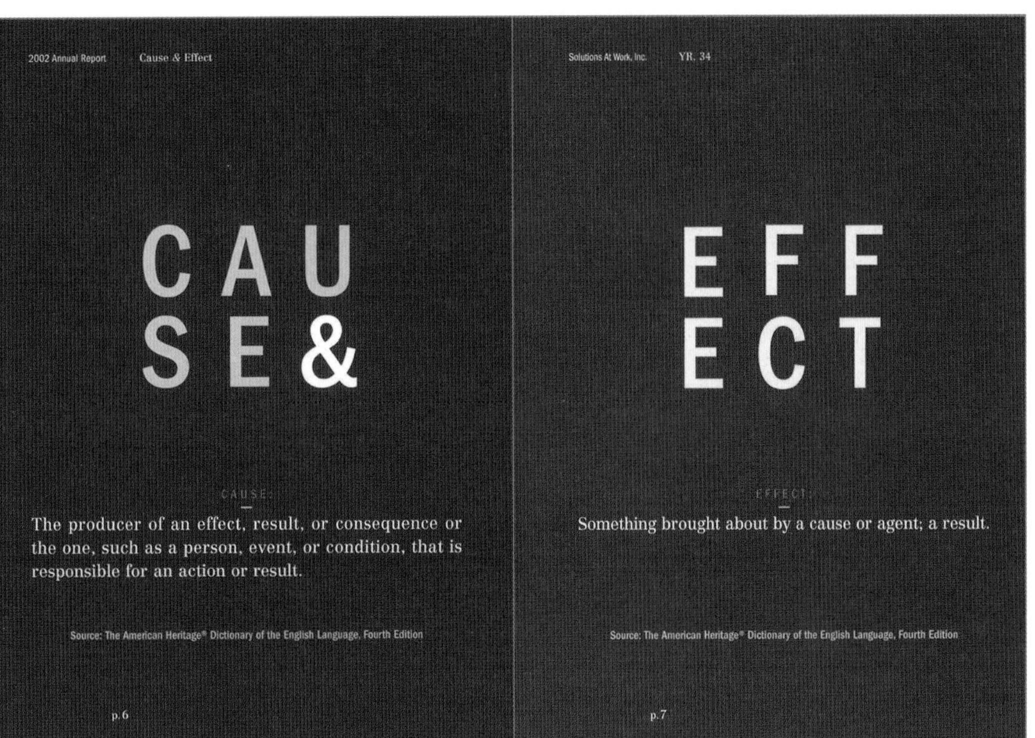

Interior spreads are cleanly composed. Changes in color and scale provide contrast and variation within a slightly more conservative, centered composition. This spread establishes the format of the subsequent pages, which distinguishes causes and effects on the facing pages of each spread.

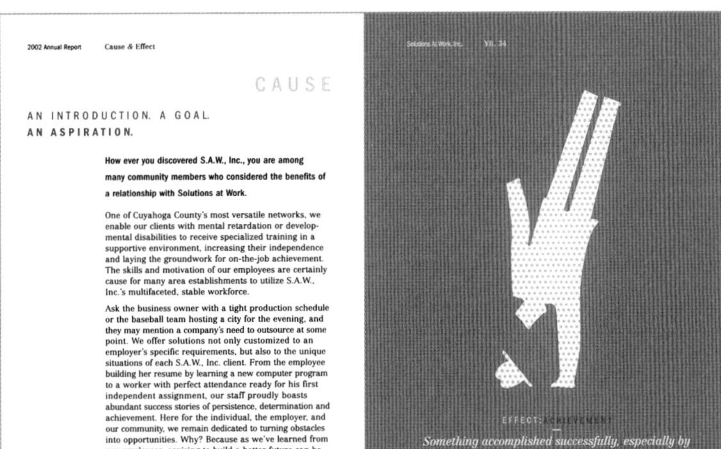

Color and scale are used to order the text, which enables clear navigation through the design. A bright red hue is introduced and effectively draws the eyes toward the dominant head on the page.

After experimentation, development, and analysis, the final design is diminutive in format and spaciously composed to easily access the content, which combines text, imagery, and information graphics. The goal to produce an intimate book is achieved "by using a loose chapter system, dividing the different sections with title pages; adding little typographic details like chapter headings, the year of the annual, and page numbers; utilizing a consistent type system; and perfect binding the piece," describes O'Grady.

The combination of a subdued color palette, accented by a sharp red hue, and classic typography, creates links to the corporate environment. Serif and sans serif typefaces (Centennial and Franklin Gothic) provide consistency in the structured design. O'Grady continues, "Hierarchy was controlled with size contrast, color contrast (brights with dulls, lights with darks), and an underlying grid structure that provided for consistent placement and alignment, to direct the viewer's eye toward important information." Photography juxtaposes type and serves as a visual pause to effectively portray the diverse personnel of S.A.W.

The S.A.W., Incorporated, 2002 Annual Report competently features yearly accomplishments, while adding a human perspective that reveals the strength of the organization's success. Visocky O'Grady delivered its positive message in an approachable, thoughtful design.

2002 Annual Report Cause & Effect

Solutions At Work, Inc. YR. 34

S.A.W., INC. IS PLEASED TO RECOGNIZE THE COUNTLESS ACCOMPLISHMENTS OF OUR CLIENTS OVER THE LAST 12 MONTHS. THEIR SUCCESS IS THE ULTIMATE REASON, MOTIVATION AND CAUSE FOR BUILDING OUR ORGANIZATION. IN THE SPOTLIGHT ARE OUR EMPLOYEES OF THE YEAR FOR 2002. WE CONGRATULATE THEM FOR GOING THE EXTRA MILE ON AND OFF THE JOB. **DISCOVER HOW UNIQUE EXPERIENCES LIKE THEIRS EFFECT US ALL.**

p.12 p.13

An interior spread provides a dramatic change from the more conservative approach taken throughout the piece. The contrast is appealing. The spread interrupts the repetitive rhythm of the design with a bold expression. The text introduces the employee spreads that follow with a loud typographic voice that commands the attention of the viewer.

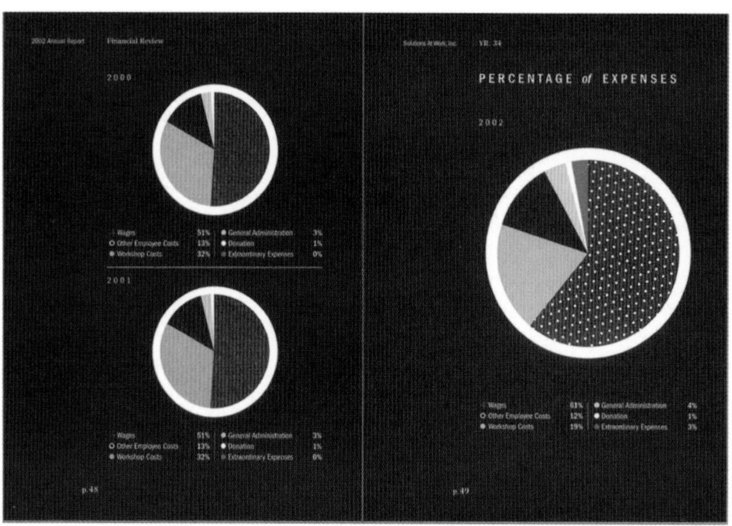

Financial spreads feature simple pie charts and tables. The financial information is clear and accessible—imperative functions of an annual report.

2002 Annual Report Cause & Effect

CAUSE:

ROBERT "BOBBY" MATT

Parma Center

Assembly Worker

4.5 Years

Outstanding employees usually possess admirable traits like punctuality and dependability.

We also cite employees like Robert "Bobby" Matt, who chooses enrichment over subsistence with earnest commitment to realizing his potential. We are fortunate to have seen Bobby's progress at the Parma Center since transition there in 1998. Taking great pride in his accomplishments and success at work, the love of his job is reflected by Bobby's positive attitude and exceptional attendance. We recognize Bobby for being a role model with enthusiasm to try new jobs and activities and natural willingness to give it all. The success of our organization directly results from the motivation of employees like Bobby to grow, and the progress that follows.

p. 22

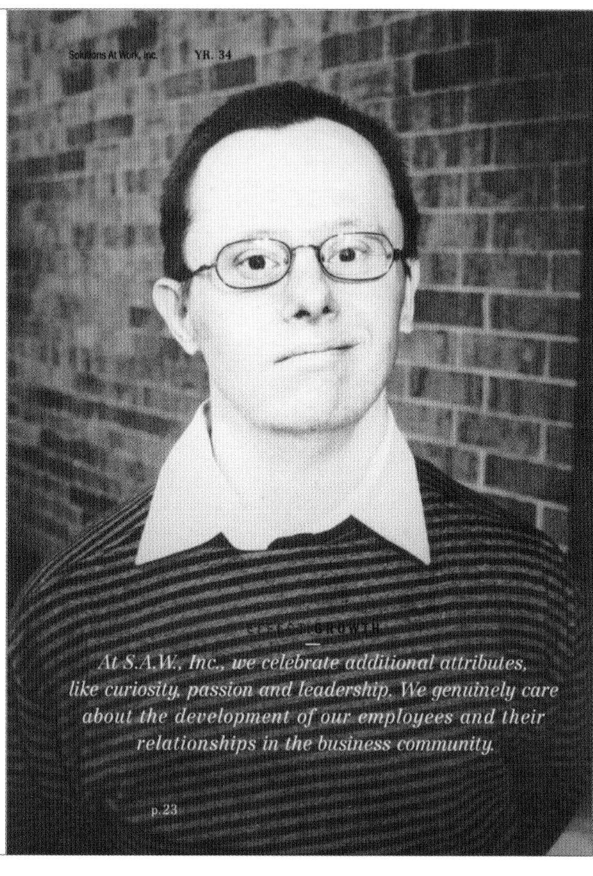

Solutions At Work, Inc. YR. 34
GROWTH
At S.A.W., Inc., we celebrate additional attributes, like curiosity, passion and leadership. We genuinely care about the development of our employees and their relationships in the business community.
p.23

2002 Annual Report Financial Review

FINANCIAL STATEMENT

Preliminary statement of activities and changes in net income, years ending December 31, 2001 to 2002

p.50

Solutions At Work, Inc. YR. 34

	2001	2002
REVENUE		
Sales	6,450,227	5,166,730
Respite Program	1,688,298	1,703,447
Other	135,629	115,336
Total Revenue:	**$ 8,274,154**	**$ 6,985,513**
EXPENSES		
Cost of Revenues		
Wages	4,949,834	4,565,465
Other Employee Costs	1,064,730	929,408
Workshop Costs	1,811,600	1,398,652
Total Cost of Revenues	**$ 7,826,164**	**$ 6,893,525**
General and Administrative	296,349	294,274
Total Expense Before Donation	**$ 8,122,513**	**$ 7,187,799**
Donation Expense	60,424	52,529
Extraordinary Expense	0	191,693
Total Expenses	**$ 8,182,937**	**$ 7,432,021**
ASSETS		
Current Assets—December 31, 2002		2,746,345
Net Fixed Assets		490,147
Other Assets		3,300
Total Assets		**$ 3,239,792**

The above is a preliminary summary from the financial statements that is subject to audit.

p.51

Spreads dedicated to employees maintain a cohesive visual system throughout the design. The text on the verso page aligns on the second spatial interval of the grid. The consistency allows the viewer to recognize the ordering system from one page to the next.

WILSONHARVEY/LOEWY

James Martin Institute for Science and Civilization Brochure

designer **paul burgess**

The James Martin Institute for Science and Civilization can be described by the phrase Shaping the Future. Excerpted from their mission statement: "The James Martin Institute for Science and Civilization will identify science and technology issues critical in shaping the future of world civilization. It will conduct research to help humanity to shape a brighter future for itself and the natural environment on which it depends." WilsonHarvey/Loewy approached their design of the James Martin Institute brochure with the purpose of "attracting funding for the world's most leading-edge think tank, as well as to convey a sense of the future and mankind's gradual path toward self-destruction," states designer Paul Burgess. "[The brochure] shows the [investors] and potential researchers where the studies may lead."

The inspiration and conceptual direction for the brochure "came from the studies [and] underlying issues currently facing us: global warming, nanotechnology, cloning, and corporate abuse," adds Burgess. The minimal design is inviting, while the quantity of textual and visual information is succinct and visually dynamic. "We used space as our greatest asset. The whiteness of the pages gives a clinical, scientific feel, whereas the graphic devices add a technological slant," says Burgess. Short, narrow columns of black typography move along the top and bottom of the spreads. They are readable and allow the viewer to easily absorb the information. Blue textual elements slightly larger in size and shorter in length than the black type move around the compositional space calling attention to key points. Burgess elaborates, "You can connect with the blue type and read the brochure on one level, or the black type and read it in more depth. This is a classic case of using the information to lead the visual, and it's been extremely successful."

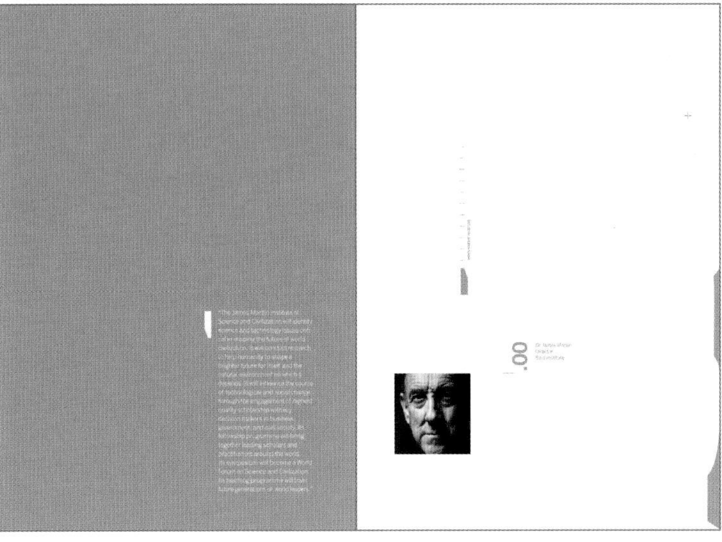

The use of space is the key element of the brochure. The openness of the design is evident on the cover, which introduces the dominant visual elements: clean, minimal typography and photography, and lines and graphic shapes that lead the eye through the composition and define the edges of the page.

In addition to the typographic system, white space draws attention toward full-color photography, which is also quietly composed. "The use of space was always the basis of the brochure and, consequently, we had room to work visually interesting page dynamics around that space," says Burgess. Delicate linear elements, as well as graphic shapes and plus signs, enhance the visual field and connote precision, science, and technology. "The space, color, and graphics allow the eye to be thrown around the page in different ways," notes Burgess.

The subtlety and spaciousness of the James Martin Institute for Science and Civilization brochure draws quick attention. It communicates efficiently with aesthetic strength. White space activates the positive areas of the design and leads the eye directly to the visual and typographic content. "We were very experimental, and luckily, the client loved our exploratory routes. The greatest challenge is always the communication of information: By letting the information do the work, the result is always very satisfying," concludes Burgess. "£10 million of funding was secured for the project once the brochure was produced."

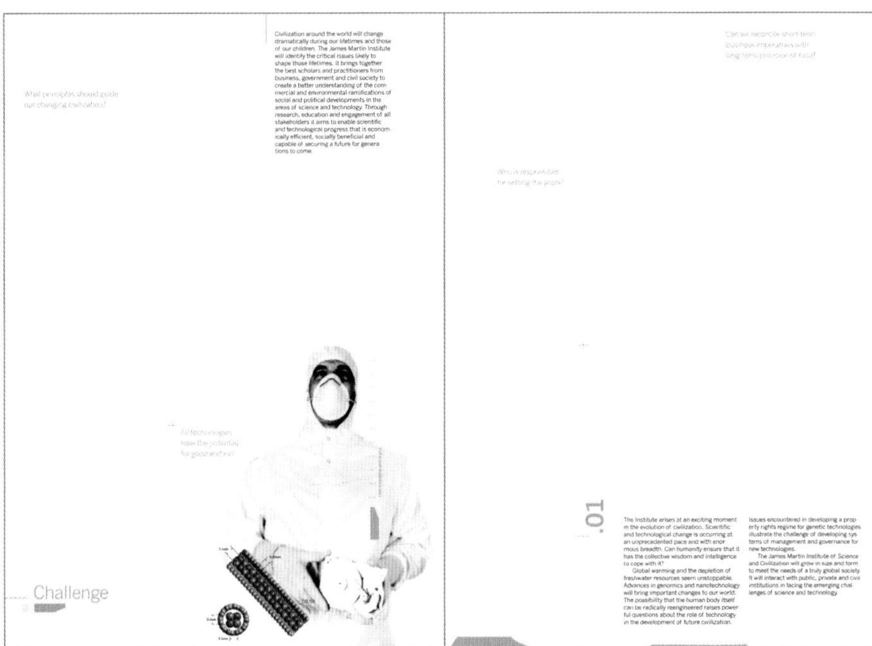

The asymmetric composition of the visual elements activates the page. Typography fluidly shifts position on each spread. Numbers are used to note sections (they are also the largest typographic element), and sans serif columns of body copy are composed along the top and bottom margins. Type size, column width, and length facilitate readability.

Headings, such as Mapping and Engaging, clearly define each spread. They are surrounded by linear elements and graphic shapes, which enhance their visual presence. The typography is visually stronger with the added elements. The combination of line, shape, and type creates horizontal motion that leads the viewer into the compositions.

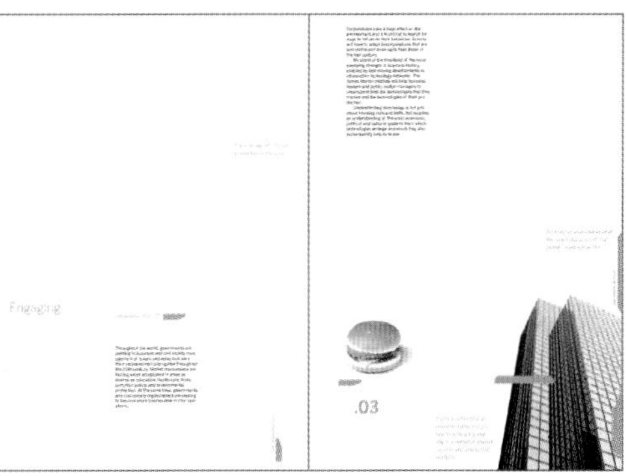

BASIC GLOSSARY

alignment The horizontal and vertical positioning of visual elements within the compositional space.

ascender The stroke of a lowercase letter that rises up from the baseline above the x-height to the cap height or higher.

baseline The horizontal line on which letters sit.

cap height The height of the capital letters measured from the baseline to capline.

capline The horizontal line along the top edge of the uppercase letters.

centered (c) An alignment setting in which text is ragged along the right and left edges and centered on the text block width.

character A mark, symbol, or sign, including letterforms and numbers, in language systems.

classification Systems that organize typefaces into groupings that allow for identification based on unifying characteristics.

color space A color model. The most common color models are RGB (red, green, and blue); RYB (red, yellow, and blue); and CMYK (cyan, magenta, yellow, and black).

column A vertical division of space on a grid that is used to align the visual elements.

column interval An inactive, negative space, also known as gutter width that separates one column from the next and prevents textual and visual elements from colliding.

counterforms Also counters, counterforms are enclosed white spaces located inside of, and partially enclosed within, characters that affect legibility, readability, and the density of forms.

descender The stroke of a lowercase letter that falls below the baseline.

em dash Em dashes (—) separate thoughts in sentences. No spaces are needed before and after, though kerning may be needed.

en dash En dashes (–) link items such as dates (2000–2018), times (6:00–8:00), page numbers (25–63), and other spans of numbers. Extra space does not need to be applied before and after en dashes. The designer may need to kern around en dashes to avoid accidental collisions.

flowline An element of basic grids that divides the page into horizontal intervals to provide additional alignment points throughout the grid.

flush left/ragged right (fl, fl/rr) An alignment setting in which text is evenly aligned along the left side, and the right side of the text is ragged.

flush right/ragged left (fr, fr/rl) An alignment setting in which text is set solid along its right edge with a ragged left.

folio Page number.

font A set of characters from a specific typeface in one size, style, weight, and width.

grid A series of intersecting axes that creates horizontal and vertical spatial divisions.

grid module An element of basic grids, grid modules are spatial areas that support the textual and visual content of the design.

indent A spatial interval used to signal a change from the paragraph preceding it.

justified (j, fl&r) An alignment setting in which text is flush along both right and left edges.

kerning Also known as letterspacing, kerning is a form of spacing used to adjust the slight distances between characters to avoid collisions and irregular, unwanted spaces.

leading Measured in points, leading refers to the vertical distance from one baseline to the next baseline. Leading is positive, negative, or solid.

legibility The recognition of letterforms and their relative position to other letters in word formation. The design of the typeface affects legibility.

letterspace The space between letters.

ligature A character produced by combining two or three characters into a unified form.

line length Refers to the width of a text line, measured in picas.

lining figure Also known as title figures, lining figures share the same height as full capitals.

margins Defines the active area of the composition and lead the viewer toward visual elements.

negative leading Leading that is less than the type size used (9 point type, 6 point leading).

non-lining figures Also known as old style or text figures, non-lining figures share an x-height with lowercase letters. They feature ascenders, descenders, and variable widths.

numerals Refers to lining, non-lining, proportional, and tabular numbers.

orphan One or two words from the previous spread that start on a new page, which should be corrected to avoid drawing attention to the isolated elements.

pica (p) A unit of measure used for line length and column width. 1 pica = 12 points; 6 picas = 1 inch.

point (pt) A unit of measure used for type size and leading. 72 points = 1 inch; 12 points = 1 pica.

positive leading Leading that is greater than the type size used (8 point type size, 12 point leading).

posture The angle of characters relative to the baseline.

prime marks Punctuation marks (' and ") that denote feet and inches, not apostrophes and quotation marks.

proportional figures Numerals with a variable width or body size. They may be lining or non-lining.

recto The right page in publication design.

readability The recognition of typography to the viewer as words, lines, and paragraphs. Readability is influenced by typographic settings, including factors such as line length, leading, and spacing.

rivers A series of inconsistent word spaces, which creates distracting holes running vertically through the justified paragraph.

sans serif A typeface without serifs.

serif A finishing stroke added to the main stems of letterforms.

small capitals Specially designed capital letters that share the same weight (and approximate height) as lowercase letters. Used often when acronyms or abbreviations appear in body text.

style The style of a typeface indicates its posture, weight, and width.

solid leading Leading that equals the type size that is being used (8 point type size, 8 point leading).

tabular figures Monospaced numerals. Numerals share the same fixed character width.

tracking A form of spacing concerned with overall spacing of words, lines, and paragraphs.

typeface The specific design of a full character set (alphabet, numerals, punctuation, diacritics) that is unified by consistent visual properties.

typographic alignment Refers to type settings that are centered (c), flush left/ragged right (fl, fl/rr), flush right/ragged left (fr, fr/rl), or justified (j, fl&r).

typographic color Refers to the density of the typographic elements and their perceived gray value. It is the overall feeling of lightness and darkness.

verso The left page in publication design.

weight Refers to stroke thickness and defines the lightness or darkness of characters.

width Refers to how wide characters sit. Variations include condensed, compressed, or extended.

widow One or two unwanted words left over on the last line of a paragraph that require attention to fix.

word space The space between words.

x-height The height of the lowercase letters without ascenders and descenders. X-height is determined by looking at the height of the lowercase x.

INDEX OF CONTRIBUTORS

| 344 design, llc |
Los Angeles, California, USA
www.344lovesyou.com
14, 33, 48–49, 109

| andrio abero |
Portland, Oregon, USA
www.andrioabero.com
51, 84–85

| aufuldish & warinner |
San Anselmo, California, USA
www.aufwar.com
61, 72, 118–119, 127, 132–135

| tommo brickner |
San Francisco, California, USA
26

| capsule |
Minneapolis, Minnesota, USA
www.capsule.us
104, 110, 136–137

| cheng design |
Seattle, Washington, USA
138–141

| ci studio |
Dublin, Ireland
www.cistudio.ie
15, 142–145

| brad clary |
Cincinnati, Ohio, USA
26

| concrete [the office of jilly simons] |
Chicago, Illinois, USA
www.concrete-us.com
50, 102–103, 146–149

| cook design |
London, England, UK
www.cookdesign.co.uk
150–153

| patrick crawford |
San Francisco, California, USA
54

| crush |
Brighton, England, UK
www.crushed.co.uk
19

| densitydesign |
Milan, Italy
www.densitydesign.org
30, 81

| d-fuse |
London, England, UK
www.dfuse.com
20–21

| meghan eplett |
New York, New York, USA
www.meghaneplettdesign.com
106

| evelock design |
New York, New York, USA
www.evelockdesign.com
114, 154–157

| founded design |
Newcastle, England, UK
www.wearefounded.com
115

| maggie gibbens |
Mason, Ohio, USA
www.maggiegibbensdesign.com
125

| renate gokl |
Chicago, Illinois, USA
64–65, 158–161

| gravica design/ talisman interactive |
Philadelphia, Pennsylvania, USA
www.gravicadesign.com
59

| hammerpress studio |
Kansas City, Missouri, USA
www.hammerpress.net
162–163

| hat-trick design |
Hampton, England, UK
www.hat-trickdesign.co.uk
105, 126, 164–167

| hoet & hoet |
Rixensart, Belgium
www.hoet-hoet.eu
174–175

| jennifer hoverman |
Cincinnati, Ohio, USA
73

| kangaroo press |
Nashville, Tennessee, USA
www.kangaroopress.com
178–179

| erin kennedy |
Dayton, Ohio, USA
12

| kinetic singapore |
Singapore
www.kinetic.com.sg
113, 184–185

| kontour design |
Houston, Texas, USA
www.kontour.com
109, 190–193

| **christopher lefke** |
Cincinnati, Ohio, USA
26

| **rebekah leiva** |
Cincinnati, Ohio, USA
26

| **heather mcfadden** |
Cincinnati, Ohio, USA
44

| **mitre agency** |
Greensboro, North Carolina, USA
www.mitreagency.com
15, 22–23, 196–197

| **nb: studio** |
London, England, UK
www.nbstudio.co.uk
84, 92, 108, 120–121, 198–201

| **nielinger & rohsiepe** |
Bochum, Germany
www.graphische-formgebung.de
www.nielinger.de
124

| **no.parking** |
Vicenza, Italy
www.noparking.it
14, 58, 77, 96–97, 202–205

| **noon** |
San Francisco, California, USA
www.noonsf.com
206–207

| **petrick design** |
Chicago, Illinois, USA
www.petrickdesign.com
208–209

| **sara piccolomini** |
Milan, Italy
www.sarapiccolomini.com
82–83

| **rick rawlins/work** |
Boston, Massachusetts, USA
210–211

| **bailey m. reinhart** |
Tiffin, Ohio, USA
70

| **hans schellhas** |
Cincinnati, Ohio, USA
www.cargocollective.com/schellhas
45

| **shinnoske design** |
Osaka, Japan
www.shinn.co.jp
218–219

| **paige strohmaier** |
Cincinnati, Ohio, USA
44

| **studio najbrt** |
Prague, Czech Republic
www.najbrt.cz
66–67, 107, 125, 220–223

| **superbüro** |
Biel/Bienne, Switzerland
www.superbuero.com
14, 35, 107, 224–227

| **katherine varrati** |
Chicago, Illinois, USA
44

| **visocky o'grady** |
Cleveland, Ohio, USA
www.visockyogrady.com
65, 82, 228–231

| **visual dialogue** |
Boston, Massachusetts, USA
www.visualdialogue.com
13, 83, 210–211

| **vrontikis design office** |
Los Angeles, California, USA
www.35k.com
38–41

Note: Contributor names found elsewhere in this book but not listed here were interviewed for the first edition of *Layout Workbook* in 2005. Since the original publication, these groups have dissolved or are no longer active in the design field, but their comments about the design process are still relevant.

BIBLIOGRAPHY

Baines, Phil and Andrew Halsam. *Type and Typography*. New York: Watson-Guptill Publications, 2002.

Bringhurst, Robert. *The Elements of Typographic Style*. Canada: Hartley & Marks, 1997.

Carter, Rob, Ben Day, and Philip Meggs. *Typographic Design: Form and Communication*. New York: Van Nostrand Reinhold, 1985.

Craig, James and William Bevington. *Designing with Type: A Basic Course in Typography*. New York: Watson-Guptill Publications, Fourth Edition, 1999.

Elam, Kimberly. *Expressive Typography: The Word as Image*. New York: Van Nostrand Reinhold, 1991.

Ginger, E. M. and Erik Spiekermann. *Stop Stealing Sheep & Find Out How Type Works*. California: Adobe Press, 1993.

Hurlburt, Allen. *The Grid: A Modular System for the Design and Production of Newspapers, Magazines, and Books*. New York: Van Nostrand Reinhold Company, 1978.

Hurlburt, Allen. *Layout: The Design of the Printed Page*. New York: Watson-Guptill Publications, 1977.

McLean, Rauri, ed. Typographers on Type. New York: W. W. Norton & Company, 1995.

Müller-Brockman, Josef. *Grid Systems in Graphic Design*. Switzerland: Arthur Niggli Ltd., Switzerland, 1981.

Rand, Paul. *A Designer's Art*. New Haven: Yale University Press, 1985.

Rand, Paul. *Design, Form, and Chaos*. New Haven: Yale University Press, 1993.

Samara, Timothy. *Making and Breaking the Grid: A Graphic Design Layout Workshop*. Massachusetts: Rockport Publishers, 2003.

Process: A Tomato Project. California: Gingko Press, 1997.

ABOUT THE AUTHOR
ACKNOWLEDGMENTS

with gratitude...

everyone at rockport publishers

the contributing designers

dennis puhalla—my mentor and friend—for your time and valuable contributions to this second edition

my family and friends

Kristin Cullen is an award-winning graphic designer and educator with a master's degree in graphic design from the Rhode Island School of Design (RISD). Her design work has appeared in national and international exhibitions and been published in books and magazines such as *Print*, *Graphis*, and *HOW*. Kristin has taught at leading institutions including the School of the Art Institute of Chicago; University of Cincinnati; University of Illinois at Urbana–Champaign; and RISD. Outside design, her artistic practice explores geometric form, order, and abstraction.

Dennis Puhalla is a Professor of Design in the School of Design, College of Design, Architecture, Art, and Planning at the University of Cincinnati. He teaches undergraduate and graduate courses in visual aesthetics, color theory, and design ideation. Dr. Puhalla is the author of published works on color and form. He holds a B.S. in design and an M.F.A. from the University of Cincinnati, as well as a Ph.D. in information design from North Carolina State University.

also available

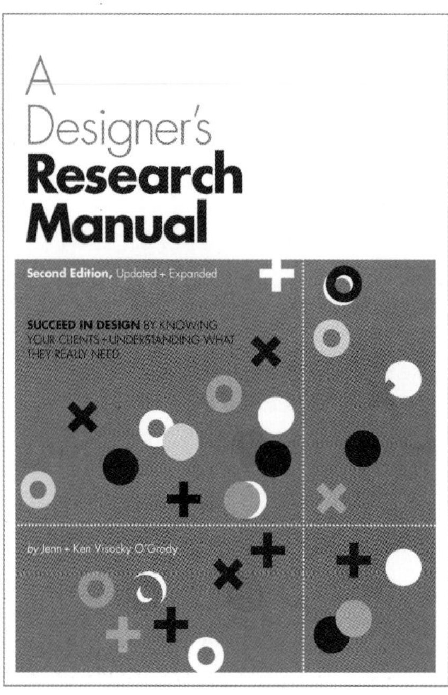

A Designer's Research Manual

978-1-63159-262-1

Making and Breaking the Grid

978-1-63159-284-3

Letterforms

978-1-63159-473-1

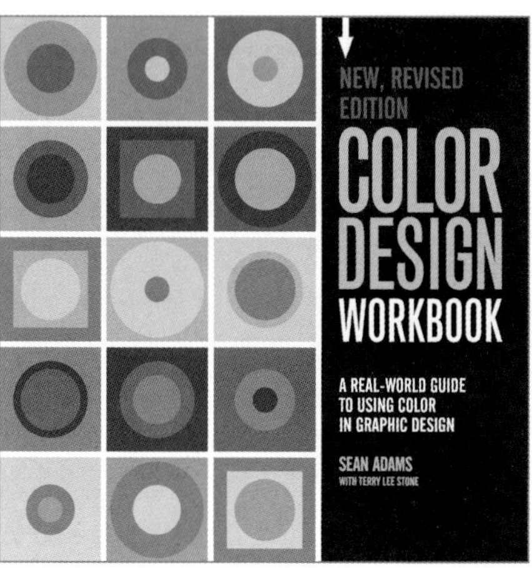

Color Design Workbook

978-1-63159-292-8